The Smithsonian Book of the First Ladies

The Smithsonian Book of the First Ladies

Their Lives, Times, and Issues

Edith P. Mayo, *General Editor*

Foreword by Hillary Rodham Clinton

Henry Holt and Company

New York

The editor would like to acknowledge with special thanks her daughters,
Melanie Mayo and Monica Mayo Condon, and John J. Costandi,
for their unfailing love and support during this project.
The publisher wishes to thank
Marc Aronson, Karen Bently, Brenda Bowen,
Doris Faber, Caroline Newman, and George Wen
for their contributions to this book.

Henry Holt and Company, Inc.
Publishers since 1866
115 West 18th Street
New York, New York 10011

Henry Holt is a registered
trademark of Henry Holt and Company, Inc.

This book was produced in cooperation with the
Book Development Division, Smithsonian Institution Press:
Heidi M. Lumberg, Editor
Anne K. DuVivier, Picture Editor
Published in Canada by Fitzhenry & Whiteside Ltd.,
195 Allstate Parkway, Markham, Ontario L3R 4T8.

Library of Congress Cataloging-in-Publication Data
The Smithsonian book of the first ladies / Edith P. Mayo,
general editor.
p.   cm.
1. Presidents' spouses—United States—Biography—Juvenile
literature.   [1. First ladies.   2. Women—Biography.]
I. Mayo, Edith.
E176.2.S66   1994   973'.099—dc20   [B]   94-6147

ISBN 0-8050-1751-8

First Edition—1996

DESIGNED BY LUCY ALBANESE

Printed in the United States of America on acid-free paper. ∞

5   7   9   10   8   6   4

pp. ii–iii: *This painting illustrates a reception given by Mary Lincoln to honor General Ulysses S. Grant.*
p. x: *Hillary Rodham Clinton.* p. xiii: *An 1867 artist's representation of a reception given by Martha Washington.*

Contents

Foreword by Hillary Rodham Clinton   *xi*

Editor's Note   *xii*

Introduction   *1*

PART I: THE NEW NATION, 1775–1830   *3*

MARTHA WASHINGTON   1731–1802   7
   Did the American Revolution Change Things
   for Women?   *13*

ABIGAIL ADAMS   1744–1818   16

MARTHA JEFFERSON   1748–1782   22
   Why Did So Many Children Have Such Short Lives?   *23*

DOLLEY MADISON   1768–1849   26
   Where Does the Term "First Lady" Come From?   *33*

ELIZABETH MONROE   1763?–1830   35

LOUISA ADAMS   1775–1852   39

PART II: GROWING PAINS, SLAVERY, AND THE CIVIL WAR, 1830–1865

45

RACHEL JACKSON	1767–1828	*50*
HANNAH VAN BUREN	1783–1819	*51*
Why Isn't There More Information About Women's Lives?		*52*
ANNA HARRISON	1775–1864	*55*
LETITIA TYLER	1790–1842	*56*
JULIA TYLER	1820–1889	*58*
How Did Women Fight Against Slavery?		*64*
SARAH POLK	1803–1891	*68*
MARGARET TAYLOR	1788–1852	*74*
ABIGAIL FILLMORE	1798–1853	*78*
JANE PIERCE	1806–1863	*81*
HARRIET LANE	1830–1903	*84*
What Does It Mean to Be a Presidential Hostess?		*88*
MARY LINCOLN	1818–1882	*90*

PART III: THE POST–CIVIL WAR ERA, THE AGE OF REFORM, AND WORLD WAR I, 1865–1920

99

ELIZA JOHNSON	1810–1876	*106*
JULIA GRANT	1826–1902	*111*
LUCY HAYES	1831–1889	*117*
What Role Did Women Play in the Temperance Movement?		*122*
LUCRETIA GARFIELD	1832–1918	*125*
ELLEN ARTHUR	1837–1880	*130*
FRANCES CLEVELAND	1864–1947	*131*
CAROLINE HARRISON	1832–1892	*137*
IDA McKINLEY	1847–1907	*142*

EDITH ROOSEVELT   1861–1948   147
    How Do Photographs Shape a Public Image?   153
HELEN TAFT   1861–1943   156
    What Was "Woman Suffrage"?   162
ELLEN WILSON   1860–1914   165
EDITH WILSON   1872–1961   169

PART IV: MODERN TIMES, 1920 TO THE PRESENT   175

FLORENCE HARDING   1860–1924   181
GRACE COOLIDGE   1879–1957   186
LOU HOOVER   1874–1944   192
    Why Was It Hard for Women to Get an Education?   198
ELEANOR ROOSEVELT   1884–1962   201
BESS TRUMAN   1885–1982   211
MAMIE EISENHOWER   1896–1979   216
JACQUELINE KENNEDY   1929–1994   221
LADY BIRD JOHNSON   1912–   230
    How Have First Ladies Contributed to Campaigning?   237
PAT NIXON   1912–1993   240
BETTY FORD   1918–   247
ROSALYNN CARTER   1927–   253
NANCY REAGAN   1921–   260
BARBARA BUSH   1925–   267
HILLARY RODHAM CLINTON   1947–   273

The Smithsonian's First Ladies Collection and the Exhibition   279
Bibliography   281
Acknowledgments   291
Index   293

Foreword

I hope you will enjoy *The Smithsonian Book of the First Ladies.* Since I have come to the White House, I have been so impressed by what I have learned about the First Ladies who came before me. Dolley Madison is one of my favorites. She cared about the welfare of children, spoke her mind about things, and in her infinite wisdom, saved priceless documents and art treasures from the onslaught of British troops who destroyed the White House during the War of 1812. Add to this her reputation as a fun-loving and magnanimous hostess and she won the hearts of the nation.

Among First Ladies in more modern times, I have become an admiring student of the life of Eleanor Roosevelt, who fought for the underprivileged and the ideals of social justice and human rights. Mrs. Roosevelt gave press conferences, lectures, and radio addresses. She even had her own daily newspaper column called "My Day." The role she chose for herself can best be described in her own words: "I am in a position where I can do the most good to help the most people."

The Smithsonian Book of the First Ladies will give you a rich glimpse of the lives of these forty-three women and their places in history. You will learn about women of great wisdom; hostesses of grace, sophistication, and style; social activists and skilled campaigners; and the many who dedicated themselves to bettering the lives of the least fortunate in our country. Some have embodied all of these characteristics. In fact, be prepared for some surprises. At times our First Ladies behaved in ways that may not fit your view of the era in which they lived. Contradicting the customs of the day, dear Mrs. Madison used tobacco snuff in public and wore extravagant turbans in which she took her naps! Each, as you will see, defined her position in a way that was right for her at the time.

Many of America's First Ladies have left important legacies to the nation and others have suffered great personal sacrifices doing so. These brief biographies will guide you through our rich social history and the great dramas of our democracy. I hope you enjoy them and will come to appreciate these personal stories as I have—with admiration, affection, and respect.

Hillary Rodham Clinton

Editor's Note

For the sake of historical continuity, short biographies of several presidential wives who did not serve as first lady have also been included in the volume.

The
Smithsonian
Book of the
First Ladies

Introduction

*A*mericans have been fascinated by the first ladies since the time we became a nation. The first family is our democratic version of royalty. Our first ladies have represented the standards of womanhood of their time, standards that have changed many times during the course of our history. Reading about their remarkable lives is like looking at a display of our changing images of men and women, homes and families, society and culture. But being a national image is not easy.

The first lady is in the spotlight because her husband holds the highest political office in the land. In the twentieth century, she has often had to work hard to help him get elected. Once in office, everything she does reflects on the president's popularity with voters. If she is well liked, has an appealing personality, and is respected by the press, it makes him a more successful president. (Ironically, until 1920 women could not vote in national elections, and during much of the nineteenth century they were discouraged from being involved in politics at all.) Having to live up to the expectations of others, having to fulfill their ideal image of the perfect woman, has been a challenging job, but a job for which the first lady does not get paid.

Every first lady has responded to these pressures in her own way. Dolley Madison, Julia Grant, and Eleanor Roosevelt flourished and achieved their own national fame, while other first ladies like Louisa Adams felt their roles to be a great burden, with an endless stream of duties and a family life that was never out of the spotlight. Some first ladies saw their role in the White House as a way to continue the supportive role they played in their marriages. Others joined with their husbands in the political issues of their times. Others took on social causes. Whatever decisions they made about their roles as first ladies, their stories are as varied and interesting as is the history of our nation.

Part I

The New Nation
1775–1830

When the British ruled the thirteen colonies that would become America, the lives women led depended a great deal on where they lived and who they were. A wealthy girl growing up in the great port cities of New York, Philadelphia, Baltimore, or Charleston led a life similar to that of girls in London. Many well-to-do families in New England encouraged their daughters to read, an opportunity few women anywhere else in the world shared. Families on farms throughout the colonies had to make, clean, and repair most of their clothing. They grew or traded for much of their food and were preoccupied with local events and relationships. Women were important economic contributors to these hardworking households. Yet the divisions in the colonies went further than rich and poor, city and country, region and religion.

There were slaves throughout British North America, and they were considered property, not people. Under slavery some women were forced to rear, often bear, their master's children, while others had to work in the kitchens or fields. Yet many enslaved women found ways to retain their own traditions. Though owners could,

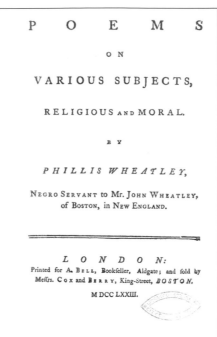

Phillis Wheatley, born in Africa, mastered the English language within eighteen months of her arrival in Boston, where she was bought as a slave. She published a book of poetry in 1773 and later enjoyed success as a writer on both sides of the Atlantic. Her brilliance and talent showed a doubtful public that enslaved Africans were capable of high intellectual achievement.

and often did, break up families, slaves used stories, songs, and messages passed from friend to friend to stay in touch. Some enslaved women even broke through racial boundaries and defied prejudice. Female slaves carried on African ways, embraced European ideas, or combined the two in their own creative blends.

By the time of the Revolution, Native Americans had been exposed to European settlers for over two hundred years. While some nations had converted to Christian faiths, learned English, and lived lives patterned after their white neighbors, others fought or fled. Still, whether as neighbors, allies, or enemies, the first Americans were a constant presence in the colonies. Both frightening and appealing, they showed that men and women, families and nations, did not have to follow European rules to thrive in North America.

Separated by great distances, kept apart by political, social, and racial boundaries, inspired by many heritages and beliefs, the women of colonial British North America still had much in common. They most commonly passed from girlhood to courtship, marriage, motherhood, and—all too often—widowhood. Most women did not have a political voice.

The tumultuous events of the Revolution disrupted many of these patterns, however, bringing women new opportunities, as well as new challenges. Now one nation asked for their allegiance, and one woman, the first lady, would stand for all of their very different aspirations.

The first great change came with the Revolution itself. White women who had never had to consider political questions were now faced with stark choices. Deciding whether to support the British or the colonists meant not only picking one side in war, but often which neighbors, friends, or family members to support. When men went into battle, women had to furnish food, supplies, and shelter for soldiers. A few women disguised themselves as men in order to fight.

Even when they stayed at home, there were women who learned to shoot to protect themselves and their families. Others, like future first ladies Martha Washington and Abigail Adams, took over the running of farms and plantations while their husbands were away at war. In colonial times, it was not unusual for a widow to manage her late husband's business and to run it successfully. Now women took on the same responsibilities while their husbands were away. But women had more to offer the Revolution than taking care of the home front: they were also active supporters of the war effort.

This cover of Harper's Weekly *magazine, published to celebrate the centenary of American independence, shows a romanticized version of a Revolutionary War soldier.*

Women formed groups such as the Daughters of Liberty, which supported the colonists' cause by refusing to buy British goods or to pay taxes on British products. They gathered together to make shirts and uniforms for soldiers and raised money for the army. All of these experiences made women feel more engaged in public life and political issues. After all, they were fighting for what they thought of as freedom and democracy and were teaching their children to be good citizens. That made some women think about what their own place could be in the new nation. The experience of being self-reliant in the Revolution served as an important source of inspiration.

Political independence from Britain was only one kind of change that came with the Revolution. Starting in 1790, when Samuel Slater opened his spinning mill in Pawtucket, Rhode Island, America's economy underwent a great transformation. In time, this would change everything about American life. This change was called the Industrial Revolution. As more and more goods that had been made in the home were mass produced in factories, women's work, homelife, and expectations took on new forms.

Now women did not have to spend their time making yarn, fabric, and other items that could as easily be bought. (In 1825, for example, the average New York State homemaker produced 8.95 yards of finished textile goods herself at home. Just ten years later she produced only 4.03 yards.) But to buy the new materials women needed money. Since the new factories were eager to hire them, many young women spent years working and earning money outside the home before getting married. This changing economy brought with it a new view of what a woman should be.

Starting early in the 1800s, and gaining greater acceptance throughout the century, many Americans came to believe that the two sexes had totally different abilities and roles in life. While the middle-class husband was expected to work hard, make money, and participate in the rough-and-tumble of public life, the middle-class wife was supposed to remain in the home, nurture the family, and set a pure moral example for others. This image of a woman's role did not include slave women, who often worked in the fields and were afforded little protection from their masters, or working-class women, who needed to work outside the home. But many free African Americans shared in the ideal of the virtuous domestic woman. Ironically, as the debates over slavery grew ever more fierce, the very fact that women were expected to be guardians of morality forced them to be vocal public advocates and activists.

Fighting for independence, working in a mill, laboring in a field, or raising a family, women sometimes embraced common ideas about who they should be and at other times challenged them. The stories of thousands of these women were embodied in the lives of the first ladies.

Martha Washington

JUNE 2, 1731–MAY 22, 1802

" . . . as if I had been a very great somebody"

This 1853 portrait of Martha Washington was painted by well-known portrait artist Rembrandt Peale a half-century after her death.

*D*uring the early days of the Revolutionary War, Martha Washington was on her way to join her husband. When her carriage entered Philadelphia, the city's leading citizens welcomed her and thirteen cannons were ceremonially fired—"as if I had been a very great somebody," she wrote a bit uneasily to one of her sisters in Virginia.

While George Washington's wife never got completely used to being singled out for special attention, she was a likable and warmhearted woman who as the nation's first first lady earned her own place in American history.

George Washington sometimes gave people the impression of being cold and distant. His wife, however, smiled easily, so her presence by his side made him seem more approachable.

Martha was a twenty-six-year-old widow with two small children when she became acquainted with George Washington. She was born on June 2, 1731, at the plantation along Virginia's Pamunkey River known as Chestnut Grove. Her parents were John Dandridge, the son of an English merchant, and Frances Jones Dandridge, whose grandfather had crossed the Atlantic to become the first rector of one of the churches in Virginia's colonial capital of Williamsburg.

Although Martha's family belonged to the top layer of Virginia's plantation-owning society, the Dandridges were only moderately well-off. The eldest of seven children, Martha was taught how to manage a large household by her mother, but she otherwise learned just the basics of reading and writing so that she could exchange letters with her mother and sisters after she moved to a home of her own.

At eighteen Martha married Daniel Parke Custis, a man in his thirties whose family owned one of the finest plantations on the Pamunkey. This marriage seemed very happy, despite the tragic loss of two infant sons. But after the birth of a healthy boy John, called Jackie, then a little girl Martha, nicknamed Patsy, Daniel Custis himself died.

Wealthy, socially prominent widows were expected to remarry, and Martha quickly had many suitors. While she, too, was eager to find a husband, marriage meant losing control of her property. Not for another hundred years or so would married women be allowed to make business decisions by themselves, even if they wanted to. Until new laws were passed, husbands had complete control over any property their wives had inherited.

Martha Custis had no difficulty in making her selection from among the suitors who appeared. Colonel George Washington was winning distinction during this period by fighting in the Indian Wars to the west, and he took an active part in Virginia politics too. They may have become acquainted at some gathering in Williamsburg even before her husband died.

Colonel Washington visited the Custis house in the spring of 1758, about eight months after Martha had become a widow. He was already regarded as a man with unusually good judgment. He seems to have proposed marriage to her within just a few days.

Records show that Martha and George each wrote separately to England after his brief visit to her home to order the new finery they wore at their wedding—elegant yellow silk for her, the best grade of blue velvet for him. She was twenty-seven and a half and he was nearing his twenty-seventh birthday by the time the ceremony took place on January 6, 1759. Martha Custis brought two important things to the marriage—wealth and social position—that helped George Washington to advance in his career as a military and political leader. Their marriage took place at the Custis home, called the White House. (The presidential mansion we know today as the White House wasn't built until after George Washington left office, and it wasn't referred to as the White House until much later.)

Washington had resigned from the army shortly before marrying. He brought his bride and her children—four-year-old Jackie and two-year-old Patsy—to his own plantation on the Potomac River, Mount Vernon. For the next sixteen years Martha Washington contentedly supervised the kind of busy household she had always been accustomed to.

Martha's adored son and daughter had been taken in by her second husband and he treated them just as if they were his own. Indeed, his devotion to them seemed to increase as it grew clear that he and his wife would have no additional children. Jackie, though, showed more interest in amusing himself than in doing well at school. Far more seriously, Patsy began collapsing with seizures when she was about twelve. Five years later she died of epilepsy, a condition for which at that time there was no medication.

The loss of her daughter plunged Mrs. Washington into deep grief. But her sense of duty made her soon resume welcoming the guests her husband kept inviting to Mount Vernon. As long as she could look forward to interludes of privacy, she liked having company herself—a house without a lot of coming and going seemed "very dull" to her.

The public phase of her life that started in 1774 provided much more activity than even she would have chosen. That year her husband journeyed all the way to Philadelphia as one of Virginia's delegates to the First Continental Congress, which met to consider how the thirteen colonies should deal with increasing tensions between American colonists and their British rulers. The following year George Washington was elected commander in chief of the colonial army. From then on Martha Washington lived her life under almost constant public scrutiny.

She was forty-four years old when her husband began serving what soon would be called the United States. Fortunately she had already "learned from experience that the greater part of our happiness depends on our dispositions and not on our circumstances," as she put it herself. She traveled many thousands of miles, at a time when travel was very difficult. Throughout the Revolutionary War she repeatedly went back and forth from Mount Vernon to her husband's various military headquarters, always doing her best to create comfortable surroundings for General (and later President) Washington.

Mrs. Washington suffered greatly during the final stage of the Revolutionary War, when her dear son, Jackie, serving as one of his stepfather's aides, died of dysentery, or "camp fever." Jackie Custis left a wife with four small children. While the two older children remained with their mother, George and Martha took the two youngest grandchildren to bring up as their own. Once more a little boy and girl, George Washington Parke Custis and Eleanor (Nelly) Parke Custis, enlivened Mount Vernon, very much raising their grandmother's spirits.

Martha Washington displayed great personal courage and support for the Revolution by regularly visiting her husband's field headquarters. This note is an account of her travel expenses for one of those visits.

For about five years after the Revolutionary War ended, Mrs. Washington and her husband stayed close to home, though they kept up their social and political contacts. However, the government of the new United States was proving far from effective, and a move toward improving it inevitably involved George Washington. A new constitution was written for the country and ratified in 1788. It called for the election of a president. By 1789 there could be no doubt that Washington would be elected the first president of the United States.

"Lady Washington," some people started calling his wife. It was difficult to know what to call the president's wife as there were few nations whose example the new country could follow. Washington would be president, but what would his wife's role be? George and Martha Washington, and members of the president's cabinet, discussed this a great deal. They realized that they were setting precedents that other presidents and their wives would follow. The Washingtons answered the question by behaving in a dignified and formal manner, but not acting like royalty.

As she had been at Mount Vernon, Martha continued to be her husband's social partner, presiding with him over receptions, dinners, state gatherings for foreign officials, and ceremonial occasions. In this way Martha Washington established the important role that every first lady has played since: that of the hostess for the nation.

As soon as Mrs. Washington joined President Washington in the nation's first capital of New York City, they began holding a regular series of gatherings in the Broadway home they had rented. Once every two weeks the president himself greeted gentlemen only at formal receptions known as "levees." Every Thursday invited guests joined the president and his wife at solemn dinner parties, where the food was very good but the conversation was rather formal.

In addition Mrs. Washington gave weekly Friday evening receptions, called "drawing rooms," where her husband greeted their company in a more relaxed manner. To make sure that no visitors overstayed their welcome, she told them, "The General always retires at nine, and I usually precede him."

Her role as first lady took its toll on Martha Washington. In a letter to her sister, she wrote:

> I lead a very dull life and know nothing of what passes in the town. I never go to any public place, indeed I think I am more like a state prisoner than anything else. There [are] certain bounds set for me which I must not depart from and as I cannot do as I like I am obstinate [and] stay at home a great deal.

Martha Washington was the first of many in her position to feel this way.

Nevertheless, Mrs. Washington dutifully continued a similar routine after the country's capital moved to Philadelphia the following year. At last, in 1797, at the conclusion of her husband's second term, she joyously looked forward to their peaceful retirement back in Virginia.

After only two years at Mount Vernon, though, Washington came home from one of his daily inspections of his property feeling ill. It had been snowing heavily. A severe sore throat developed, and the doctors of his era could not help him. With his wife constantly at his side, his health continued to fail until he died a few days later, on December 14, 1799.

Two and a half years after his death, shortly before her seventy-first birthday, on May 22, 1802, Martha Washington died at Mount Vernon. She was buried there beside her husband.

Did the American Revolution Change Things for Women?

While men were busy building a new nation and talking about their new "rights" to govern themselves, women under the new government were "civilly dead" once they married—just as they had been under the English government. English laws said that once a woman married, she and her husband were "one" under the law—and that *one* person was the husband. The Revolution did not change this.

After the Revolution women still had few rights: no rights at all to their children, no rights to buy or sell property once they were married, no rights to keep whatever wages they earned, no legal existence apart from their husbands'.

Women who owned or inherited property faced laws called "coverture" after they married. This meant that a woman's property was taken under her husband's control as long as they were married. She had no say in how the property was used and no claim to any money made from its use. Usually a married woman could not make a will, and in most states she could not sign a legal contract. If a husband died, then his widow could inherit his property, manage it, or continue to run his business or farm. If she remarried, she would lose those rights again.

On the other hand, if a woman were single or widowed, she paid taxes on her property just as men did. But she was not allowed to vote for members of state or national government. Ironically, this was "taxation without representation"—one of the basic charges against England made by men during the Revolution.

With few exceptions, women had no right to vote, take part in elections or politics, or hold positions in the government of the new nation. When the new national Constitution was written—following long-established custom—men did not even think it was necessary to put in writing that only males could vote. Few of the Founding Fathers thought that women would ever want to vote or play an active role in politics.

In the few places where women had been able to vote, the new state constitu-

This mid-nineteenth-century parlor scene of mother and children represents an idealized view of middle-class homelife. Women were reared to exert a moral influence over their husbands and children.

tions specifically took *away* that right! For instance, between 1789 and 1807, women in the state of New Jersey had the right to vote. But after New Jersey wrote a new constitution in 1807, it took women more than 110 years and many difficult campaigns to win that right again.

Courts and juries were made up only of men, and a woman bringing a case before the court was often not treated fairly because it was hard for men to understand women's experiences or points of view. This situation did not change in most of the country until after women gained the vote in 1920.

The Revolution, however, did bring some opportunities for women. When men went off to war, their wives or daughters often ran the farm or business or engaged in trade and commerce. In most places the laws and the courts recognized this activity as legal and as supportive of the marriage. Women learned many skills and were in charge of managing the money from these businesses.

The Revolution also stirred up powerful ideas about how people should govern themselves. Women struggled with the contradiction that the new nation stressed citizen involvement and "government by the people"—but not for women. Women invented a role that would gain them more power in the new nation based on the ideas of the Revolution. Even though their lives were mostly centered around the home and family, women reasoned that their role was to raise good citizens for the new nation, to give their children pride in taking part in political life. To do that well, women claimed they needed better education and should be kept informed about political matters. This idea, called "republican motherhood," allowed for the inclusion of political ideas in family life and justified a political role for women in the new nation.

Abigail Adams

NOVEMBER 11, 1744–OCTOBER 28, 1818

"I desire you would Remember the Ladies"

Abigail Adams (pictured here at age fifty-six) voiced her opinions and set a precedent for future first ladies to take an active role in public affairs.

Abigail Adams was not only the wife of one president and the mother of another—a feat no other woman in American history has matched—but extremely intelligent, strong-minded, and fascinated by politics. She was also one of the greatest letter writers of her day.

More than two thousand of the private letters she sent to members of her family during her lifetime were saved and later published. As a result, Abigail Adams ranks among the very few presidential wives more noted for their own accomplishments than for those of their husbands.

Of course, her closeness to great events gave her plenty to write about. In the spring of 1776, when her husband, John Adams, was representing Massachusetts at the Continental Congress in Philadelphia, the first major battle of the Revolutionary War erupted right near their home, and she reported to him: "From Pens Hill we have a view of the largest Fleet ever seen in America. You may count upwards of 100 [and] 70 sail. . . ."

That same month she sent him a letter filled with new ideas for the running of the nation. Playfully worded, the letter took on a subject hardly anybody of her day regarded seriously. But Abigail did. She even employed language echoing that used in the Declaration of Independence:

> By the way, in the new Code of Laws which I suppose it will be necessary for you to make I desire you would Remember the Ladies, and be more generous and favourable to them than your ancestors. Do not put such unlimited power into the hands of the Husbands. Remember all Men would be tyrants if they could. If perticular care and attention is not paid to the Laidies, we are determined to foment a Rebelion, and will not hold ourselves bound by any Laws in which we have no voice, or Representation.

This cleverly expressed, forceful statement has been a keynote for activists and historians ever since it became public.

Even though her relatives often told Mrs. Adams that she wrote wonderful letters, she always brushed aside any compliments. At a time when many people could not write at all and rules for proper spelling had not yet been firmly established, she still regretted her own lack of education and often said she wished she had received better training during her childhood.

Nevertheless, the young Abigail Smith had had many advantages that other girls of her day lacked. She was born on November 11, 1744, into the family of a respected Congregationalist minister in the town of Weymouth, about ten miles from Boston. Her father, the Reverend William Smith, had relatives who were prosperous merchants or sea captains, while her mother, Elizabeth Quincy Smith, was the daughter of the leading citizen of nearby Braintree.

Most important, her grandmother Quincy loved to read—and sensing very early that little "Nabby" might share the same passion, she borrowed her from her parents for months at a time so they could read poetry together. Although formal schooling was never available to Nabby, she was thoroughly familiar with the works of Shakespeare when she reached her teens, thanks to her grandmother. This kind of schooling—women passing down information to their daughters and grand-daughters—was common.

Nabby relished all the talk at her own home about events of the day. She and her sister Mary listened avidly as visitors discussed church business or happenings in Boston while her younger brother and sister played children's games. By the time a lawyer named John Adams first appeared at the parsonage, when she was fourteen, the topic of colonial politics had already begun to interest her.

Nabby had dark hair and keenly alert dark eyes. At first her sharply witty comments struck Adams as lacking in tenderness. Within a few years, however, she and this brilliant if rather pompous young man were writing each other love letters. "Miss Adorable," he called her privately, much to her delight.

On October 25, 1764, when Nabby was nearly twenty, they were married in the parsonage parlor, then set up housekeeping on the Braintree farm he had inherited. During the next ten years they moved back and forth between their cottage and rented quarters in Boston while John rose as a lawyer and his young wife kept having babies. Although she suffered deeply when one infant daughter died, another healthy daughter and three sons survived.

In 1774 relations between the American colonies and their British rulers reached a crisis. The very able and ambitious John Adams emerged that year as one of the leaders of the colonial cause. Throughout the next quarter of a century, while he played a major role in establishing the new United States, his wife helped him in several important ways.

During much of this period Abigail Adams stayed home in Massachusetts to manage their farm and raise the children while John Adams attended to public business elsewhere. Both Abigail and John found the separations very hard to bear because they remained deeply in love throughout their long marriage. Even when they were apart she never ceased sending him the large amounts of encouragement he always needed, again setting the pattern for first ladies of the future.

Although John Adams had an exceptionally high opinion of his own talents, he also had more than the ordinary share of doubts about whether he could accomplish his goals. His wife had no doubts at all about his greatness and never tired of reassuring him. She also did all she could to ensure a proper appreciation of his importance by other people.

For instance, while her husband was away in Europe seeking aid from foreign governments, Philadelphia newspapers reported that he and another of the new nation's diplomats had both been elected members of a select group called the American Philosophical Society. However, its announcement referred to the two men as *Mr.* John Adams and *The Honorable* John Jay. Abigail Adams immediately sent the society's secretary a four-page letter furiously noting that Mr. Adams had served in the Congress just as long as the other gentleman and had also been appointed to represent their country abroad at the same time. Since he was not present to lose his own temper over this insult to his dignity, she did it for him.

In addition, during all the years when Mr. Adams was patriotically serving the nation, Mrs. Adams took care of their property very capably. Personally supervising the planting and harvesting at their farm, she not only avoided the money problems that later plagued many other patriots but even made the Adams family richer than it might otherwise have been.

Still, Abigail Adams never seriously questioned the prevailing opinions of her day about the proper role of women. In her own mind, domestic duties were rightly the responsibility of wives, while their husbands dealt with the outside world. The idea of considering marriage a partnership appealed to her, and she felt that if both partners did their best in their own spheres, they ought to be equally respected.

She certainly worked hard at raising her four children. But the lively wit and good humor that shine through her letters to her husband often deserted her where her own sons and daughter were concerned. Instead, many of her references to them show her as a strict mother bent on correcting the slightest sign of a bad habit.

Yet for all their mother's concern, the Adams children experienced mixed fates. Although John Quincy turned out, in the 1820s, to be among the most high-minded men ever to occupy the presidential mansion, one of her other sons drank himself into an early grave and the third became an undistinguished lawyer; her only daughter married an unsuccessful businessman, but they had several children on whom their grandmother doted.

For all her commanding ways, Mrs. Adams never lost the eager interest in everything around her that had marked her girlhood. After a peace treaty finally ended the Revolutionary War, she sailed across the ocean to join her husband while he continued to represent U.S. interests there for four more years—and her letters from Paris and London to her sisters Mary and Elizabeth, back in New England, provide a matchless account of daily life in those foreign capitals, including such details as the fact that among London ladies, the color blue was "vastly the present taste."

Then a new chapter of her life started in 1789, when her husband was elected the first vice president of the United States. At any gathering including the wives of the new government's officials, Mrs. Adams took care to be seated beside President Washington's wife—not for her own sake, she insisted, but to make sure that her husband's position received proper recognition.

In 1797, when John Adams succeeded to the nation's highest office after President Washington's retirement, Abigail Adams realized that her own task of living up to the example of simple dignity set by Martha Washington would not be easy. To avoid any behavior that might make her seem too queenly, she urged both of her sisters "to watch over my conduct" and immediately tell her if they thought she was treating them any differently.

As the president's wife, Mrs. Adams directed her Philadelphia household with all the diligence that might have been expected of her. Rising daily at five o'clock, she spent the entire morning supervising servants (about whose habits of laziness she complained bitterly to her sisters). At noon she dressed more formally, then received callers for about three hours. Following a mid-afternoon dinner, she took a carriage ride to enjoy fresh air, then came home to rest until seven, when some evening entertainment was usually scheduled.

For the first three years of her husband's term of office, while government buildings were being constructed in the new Federal City on the Potomac River, Mrs. Adams followed this routine except when she went home to Massachusetts for a much-needed vacation. At times during her Philadelphia sojourns, her outspoken interest in public questions brought sarcastic comments from some of her husband's political enemies. They even claimed that he was just a puppet whose strings were pulled by "Mrs. President." Though this accusation was untrue, there is no doubt that Abigail Adams was a political partner to her husband.

Mrs. Adams's letters show that she grew increasingly fierce toward her husband's enemies as his term advanced. Indeed, she felt so disgusted by what seemed to be vicious politicking that she delayed joining him as long as possible after he moved to the new capital city of Washington to take up residence in the unfinished presidential mansion. She spent only a few unhappy months there before John Adams failed in his bid to be reelected, and early in 1801 they finally retired to Massachusetts together.

By then Mrs. Adams was fifty-six years old. Despite having suffered several bouts of poor health during her husband's presidency, she felt much better when she was back home for good. She spent the next seventeen years enjoying a mostly peaceful round of country activities with her husband and their children and grandchildren.

Surrounded by her beloved family, on October 28, 1818, less than two weeks before she would have marked her seventy-fourth birthday, Mrs. Adams died at her home. Her husband survived to see their son John Quincy elected as the nation's sixth president several years later, in 1824. Two years after that John Adams died at the age of ninety, on July 4, 1826.

Abigail Adams's impressions of the still-unfinished president's house were gloomy: "We have not the least fence, yard, or other convenience . . . and the great unfinished audience-room I make a drying-room of, to hang up the clothes in." This scene is how an artist in 1966 thought it might have looked.

Because of the eminence attained by both her husband and her oldest son, Abigail Adams was hardly likely to be forgotten. Indeed, twenty-two years after her death one of her grandsons published the first book containing a selection of her letters, and it sold so well that many others followed.

Soon anti-slavery advocates were citing some of the peppery words she had written about slave owners to prove that she had been an early supporter of their cause. Then, as the issue of women's rights began stirring controversy, feminists forcefully quoted "Remember the Ladies" and made Mrs. Adams one of their most admired heroines.

Martha Jefferson

*M*artha Wayles Jefferson, 1748–1782, died almost twenty years before Thomas Jefferson became the country's third president. Jefferson did all he could to keep his memory of her private, destroying their letters to each other and rarely referring to her after her death.

Martha Wayles was born to a prominent Virginia family in 1748. At eighteen, she married a young man from a similar background, Bathurst Skelton. He died when she was twenty-two, leaving her with an infant son.

Some two years later, Martha met Thomas Jefferson, then serving in the colony's legislature. They were married in 1772 and had six children, though only two daughters survived. The strain of childbirth took its toll on Martha; she died on September 6, 1782, at the age of thirty-three.

Jefferson did not remarry, though some historians believe that Sally Hemings, the daughter of Martha's father, John Wayles, and Betty Hemings, a slave on the Wayles plantation, was Jefferson's intimate companion for many years. Both of Jefferson's daughters, Martha and Maria, and Dolley Madison, the wife of his secretary of state, acted as Jefferson's official hostesses while he was president.

Why Did So Many Children Have Such Short Lives?

*T*he infant and maternal mortality rate, or the death rate of babies and their mothers, is an important factor in the overall health of the nation. Childbirth, without the benefits of modern medicine and drugs, was often dangerous and difficult in colonial times and during the early years of our nation's history. Many women feared becoming pregnant because so many died during childbirth. Frequent pregnancies were debilitating for mothers, even when there were no complications.

Mothers, sisters, and other female relatives gathered to encourage and assist women at childbirth, and babies were often delivered by midwives, skilled women trained to deliver babies. Some parents tried to withhold their emotional attachment to their infant because they feared the baby might die. Women's letters and diaries mention the deaths of mothers and babies as a common occurrence, so we know that repeated pregnancies and births were the rule. Having numerous children ensured that some would live to become adults. In 1800 the average number of children in a family was five or six.

By the middle of the 1800s, society strongly emphasized the importance of becoming a mother as "the fulfillment of a woman's destiny." Women were told that it was their moral duty to have children. This emphasis was meant to counter a declining birthrate among white families during the nineteenth century. By the beginning of the twentieth century, however, the average family size had dropped from five or six children to 3.4 children.

During the nineteenth century children came to be regarded as sacred, and motherhood was elevated to special status. Still, infants and young children died frequently during epidemics of disease or from childhood illnesses. In our own times we think of death as happening primarily to those who are old. In the nineteenth century death was equally common among the very young. In New York City in 1853, for example, 50 percent of those who died were children under the age of five.

During the nineteenth century the percentage of mothers who died before the age of fifty-five continued to be high. It began to decline only after 1920, as medical knowledge advanced. The generation of women born in 1920 was the first in our history in which a majority (57 percent) lived until their children had grown up.

During the 1800s elaborate rituals evolved around the death and mourning of children, and it was not uncommon to have a dead baby painted or photographed in its coffin as a way for the parents to remember the child. No doubt these keepsakes were comforting in a society where infant mortality rates were so high. Children who died were thought to have gone to "our better home" in heaven.

In the period between 1890 and 1925, millions of immigrants came to the United States from southern and eastern Europe. Most settled in cities and could not afford decent housing. They often lived in crowded and dirty slums and tenement houses where epidemics of disease were frequent, and the infant death rate soared. Public health became a crisis of national proportions. Reformers, many of them women, considered this one of their most important causes and were determined to bring down the death rate by creating the Visiting Nurse Association in major cities. This medical care of immigrants and the poor by visiting nurses reduced the death rate significantly. The Frontier Nursing Service brought similar health care to rural areas in Kentucky and Tennessee, reducing the infant mortality rate there as well.

During the nineteenth and early twentieth centuries the infant death rate remained high. Memorials to dead children were common. This gravestone from 1884, in the form of a baby's cradle, marks the grave of the Wigglesworth baby in Mount Auburn Cemetery, Cambridge, Massachusetts. Mrs. Wigglesworth lost five children.

In 1893 Lillian Wald moved to an immigrant section of New York City to bring health care to the poor by starting the Visiting Nurse Association. This photograph shows a Visiting Nurse climbing over tenement rooftops to reach sick families. Women like Wald and the Visiting Nurses created the profession of public-health nursing in the United States.

In the early 1920s, just after women gained the vote, women's groups successfully lobbied Congress to pass the Sheppard-Towner Act, which set up a series of clinics across the nation and provided money to the states to offer maternal and infant health care. Unfortunately, by the end of the 1920s, Congress stopped funding this program, and the clinics were forced to close.

After World War II progress in developing vaccines against childhood diseases and modern health-care practices greatly reduced the infant and maternal death rates. Between 1940 and 1970 infant death rates dropped to about twenty in every thousand. In the past ten years, however, the situation has changed. Greatly increased drug abuse has resulted in higher numbers of infants born addicted to drugs and a higher number of infant deaths. Despite the advances in medical technology and lifesaving procedures, infant and maternal death rates, particularly in large cities, have soared once again.

Dolley Madison

May 20, 1768–July 12, 1849

"There is something fascinating about her"

Dolley Madison sat for this portrait by Gilbert Stuart when her husband, James, was the secretary of state. She already showed a strong enthusiasm for combining entertaining with politics.

Dolley Madison became one of this country's great heroines during the War of 1812. When word reached the President's House that the British were approaching the capital city of the young United States, she personally saved a priceless painting—the portrait of George Washington by the famous artist Gilbert Stuart. Removing the picture from its frame, she rolled it up and brought it with her in the carriage that drove her to Virginia only shortly before her official residence went up in flames.

Heroic as this was, the wife of the nation's fourth president would probably have been remembered almost as fondly even if no such dramatic incident had ever occurred. Dolley was such a personable hostess that she spread sociable warmth throughout her husband's two terms in the nation's highest office. Indeed, she held a special place in the hearts of Washingtonians over a period of almost fifty years.

Born Dolley Payne, on May 20, 1768, she was the daughter of high-minded Quakers who wore only the plainest clothing and whose religious beliefs barred them from amusements such as playing cards or dancing. Yet her parents showed their pleasure at the birth of their first little girl, after having had several sons, by formally giving her a name ordinarily considered an affectionate nickname. "Dolley," they spelled it in their family Bible, and that was how she would always spell it herself.

Her father, John Payne, had come from England to Virginia in his youth; her mother, Mary Coles Payne, belonged to a family already established there. But after their marriage the couple joined a group of Quakers aiming to start a new community in Guilford County, North Carolina, which became Dolley's birthplace. Then the Paynes moved back to Virginia during her infancy.

Because Quakers were among the first to open schools that welcomed girls along with their brothers, she received a good basic education instead of learning just a few essentials at home as girls in her day usually did. In addition, although the Paynes had acquired slaves as well as land on taking over their plantation, their religion held that slavery was an evil that should be abolished.

Because of this belief, Dolley's life changed drastically soon after she turned fifteen. Following the American victory in the Revolutionary War, the state of Virginia passed a law allowing slave owners to free their slaves. Her father immediately took advantage of this opportunity, which also led to selling his plantation. With the money it brought, he took his large family—by then Dolley had eight brothers and sisters—all the way to Philadelphia.

The leading city of the new United States, Philadelphia had a population of around forty thousand when the Paynes arrived there in 1783. Along its tree-lined streets were rows of redbrick houses that reflected the orderly habits of its Quaker founders. Its thriving waterfront promised many opportunities for Dolley's father to prosper as a businessman. Unfortunately, John Payne lacked any money-making talent.

The shop that he opened failed after only a few years. Then came an even worse blow. When he could not pay his debts, the Quaker meeting he attended held him unfit to remain a member and voted to expel him. Dolley's father felt this disgrace so deeply that he refused from then on to leave his bedroom. Of necessity, Dolley's mother began taking in boarders, whose rent provided the family's only income.

By this time Dolley herself had grown into a young woman. Taller than was common then, measuring about five feet six inches, she also had such a striking figure that even wearing her plain gray garb she often caused heads to turn when she walked down a street. Other Quaker girls wondered if she might not be tempted to marry outside of the faith—but a young Quaker lawyer soon put an end to such gossip.

At the age of twenty-one, on January 7, 1790, Dolley Payne married John Todd. In a fine brick home only a five-minute walk from the rest of her family, she began housekeeping on her own with the assistance of one of her unmarried sisters. Three and a half years later she had a young son named John Payne Todd and was expecting another baby.

Then a terrible epidemic of yellow fever struck Philadelphia during the summer of 1793. That October, Dolley lost both her husband and their infant son; she herself, and her two-year-old Johnny, almost died too.

After she recovered, the twenty-five-year-old widow urgently needed advice about legal matters involving property her husband had left to her. As it happened, Dolley Todd lived hardly more than a block away from the building occupied by the U.S. Congress during the period when Philadelphia was temporarily the nation's capital. Congressmen often stayed at her mother's boardinghouse—and Dolley soon had many offers of assistance.

Then, about six months after becoming a widow, she received a note from the senator who had done the most to help her solve her complicated legal problems. On reading it, Dolley Todd quickly dashed off a few lines urging a close friend to come at once because she had something amazing to talk over.

"Aaron Burr says that the great little Madison has asked to be brought to see me this evening," Dolley told her friend.

Practically anybody in America then would have been able to read a wealth of meaning into that brief sentence. "The great little Madison," of course, was the brilliant congressman from Virginia who had done more than any other man to bring about the adoption of the U.S. Constitution. (James Madison, in person, looked smaller than his actual height of five and a half feet because of his slenderness and awkwardness among strangers.) At forty-three, Madison appeared to be a lifelong bachelor. His sending word through Burr, a well-known ladies' man, indicated that he was ready to change his status as a single man.

Less than six months later, on September 15, 1794, at the Virginia home of one of her sisters, the marriage of Dolley Todd and her "great little Madison" was celebrated; the bride was twenty-six then, and her new husband seventeen years her senior.

Dolley Madison saved this portrait of George Washington by Gilbert Stuart, as well as copies of important state documents, before the President's House was set on fire in 1814.

Their marriage turned out to be extraordinarily happy, despite the differences in their ages and their personalities. His wife's gift of making friends wherever she went always delighted the shy Madison, while she marveled at the soundness of his judgment. Although he may have been disappointed because she had no more children, Dolley's son, Johnny, brightened their lives, along with her many nieces and nephews.

The couple lived in Philadelphia at first, but in 1797 Madison felt that he had served long enough in Congress and they "retired" to Montpelier, his Virginia plantation. However, right after Thomas Jefferson was elected president a few years later, he appointed his most trusted political colleague as his secretary of state. In 1801 James Madison took up this important post in the new city of Washington— and Dolley Madison found herself embarking on a grand new career of her own.

Both President Jefferson and Vice President Aaron Burr were widowers, so the rules of protocol made Mrs. Madison the highest-ranking wife at governmental gatherings. Although Thomas Jefferson purposely tried to steer clear of undemocratic formality, even welcoming foreign ambassadors while he was wearing carpet slippers, he realized that a certain amount of official entertaining was unavoidable. Whenever his daughters were not visiting him, he assigned the role of presidential hostess to the charming woman his closest friend had married.

As a result Dolley Madison already was regarded as the leader of Washington society by the time her husband was elected to the presidency in 1809. Right after his inauguration, though, she blossomed forth so impressively that residents of the young capital city—still hardly more than a few clusters of buildings amid a sea of mud—rubbed their eyes with awe.

At the Inaugural Ball in Long's Hotel, Mrs. Madison "looked a queen," wearing "a pale buff-colored velvet dress," one writer reported. Her head was adorned by an elaborate sort of bonnet of purple velvet, trimmed with white satin and towering plumes of white feathers.

Mrs. Madison was no longer accepted as a Quaker since she had married out of the faith, and, perhaps because she had wished as a girl that she could have worn colorful finery, now she appeared in some spectacular costumes.

Even so, her unfailing kindness and good humor disarmed other ladies who felt tempted to ridicule her taste in clothing. "There is something fascinating about her," the stern sister-in-law of one congressman admitted in a letter home to Pennsylvania. And the famous author Washington Irving wrote that although Mrs. Madison could not be described as a great beauty, she was "a fine, buxom dame who has a smile and a pleasant word for everybody."

As a gesture of great admiration and respect, Congress voted in 1844 to grant Dolley Madison the privilege of a seat in the House of Representatives "whenever it shall be her pleasure to visit the House" and to attend its sessions (which she is shown doing here, seated in the top row, in a turban). This honor had never before been granted to an American woman.

At the highly successful Wednesday evening receptions she instituted, anyone who wished to meet the president and his wife received such a warm welcome from her that Mrs. Madison was often credited with much increasing her husband's popularity. Indeed, the friendly way she greeted all arrivals made one congressman marvel that nobody could tell from her manner whether the person she was conversing with was a political friend or an enemy. Nevertheless, as the tensions that led to the War of 1812 kept mounting, the political climate of the capital grew more and more stormy throughout Madison's presidency.

On the completion of Madison's second term in office, early in 1817, he and his wife returned to Virginia, more than ready to enjoy a peaceful retirement together. But Mrs. Madison's days as a hostess were far from over—every year hundreds of visitors, invited or otherwise, flocked to Montpelier. Often there was so much company for dinner that long tables had to be set up on the lawn in front of the large brick plantation house.

These were very happy years, apart from two recurring causes of pain. Mrs. Madison's son, John Todd, had turned into a likable but weak young man who gambled away large sums of money. Although he repeatedly promised to mend his ways each time his stepfather paid his debts, he kept getting into further troubles, even landing in jail a few times.

Worse, the former president grew frail. His wife proved to be a tireless nurse, and he survived several alarming illnesses. Finally, though, on June 28, 1836, he died at the advanced age of eighty-five.

By then Dolley Madison was sixty-eight herself. Yet she was not ready to remain quietly in Virginia. Instead she used money Congress paid her for her husband's papers and moved into a small house on Lafayette Square in Washington, right near the White House.

The capital welcomed her back enthusiastically. She was invited everywhere, she went everywhere, and, although the gowns and hats that she appeared in sometimes made her look outlandish, her admirers cherished her all the more for wearing whatever pleased her. Gracious and sociable, she continued to hold open-house receptions attended by scores of Washingtonians every New Year's Day and Fourth of July.

Year after year, she seemed indestructible. In 1845, when President James Polk took office, he took time away from his duties to pay only three visits—and one of them was to Mrs. Madison. Then, the month before he left office four years later, at his last formal reception he made a point of walking through the gathering with Mrs. Madison on his arm.

That turned out to be her last public appearance. After several months of declining health, Dolley Madison died in her Washington home on July 12, 1849, at the age of eighty-one. The capital bade her farewell at a crowded funeral service; then her body was brought to Montpelier to be buried beside her husband.

Where Does the Term "First Lady" Come From?

When the new country of the United States was founded, a debate began over what to call the chief executive and his wife. People felt strongly that they should not be called "Your Highness" or "Your Majesty," like the kings and queens of Europe. They also did not want them to have titles like the nobles of royal courts. The House of Representatives decided on a simple "Mr. President" for the chief executive. The question of what to call his wife was more difficult. Many called Martha Washington "Lady Washington," but the term "lady" was quickly dropped after Washington was no longer president because people thought it sounded too much like a title for nobility. Some presidents' wives were called "Mrs. President" or simply "Mrs." with their husband's last name.

The debate over what to call the president's wife mirrored the new nation's struggle to combine respect for its leaders with a democratic spirit. This painting, an 1867 artist's representation of a reception given by "Lady Washington," suggests an atmosphere more like the royal courts of Europe than that of a populist leader greeting visitors.

By the 1850s the meaning of the term "lady" had changed from a title for nobility to a term of address for a respected and well-mannered woman. The use of "first lady" as a term for the president's wife or hostess came into popular use at about the time of the Civil War.

The earliest public use of "first lady" occurred after Dolley Madison's death in 1849. Her longtime popularity and influence prompted President Zachary Taylor to say, "She will never be forgotten, because she was truly our First Lady for a half-century."

On May 8, 1858, a popular magazine, *Harper's Weekly,* carried a likeness of Harriet Lane, the niece and hostess for then-president James Buchanan. The magazine captioned her picture, "Our Lady of the White House." On March 31, 1860, *Frank Leslie's Illustrated Magazine* called Harriet Lane "First Lady."

By 1861, when the Lincolns lived in the White House, the *New York Herald* and the *Sacramento Union* newspapers referred to Mrs. Lincoln as "First Lady." This term for the wife or official hostess of the president has remained popular ever since.

Elizabeth Monroe

1763?–SEPTEMBER 23, 1830

A very private person

Elizabeth Monroe was an extremely elegant and fashionable first lady.

Although Elizabeth Monroe played a leading part in one of the most dramatic episodes of her husband's long political career, not a word of her own has ever turned up to give us any clues about her own thoughts and feelings. Other people spoke of her as a beautiful woman who had learned to appreciate elegant clothing and furniture during the years when James Monroe was the U.S. minister to France.

Elizabeth Monroe kept out of the public eye as much as possible after her husband became the nation's fifth president. Because she clearly lacked the outgoing warmth of her immediate predecessor, Dolley Madison, Mrs. Monroe was often labeled haughty. Perhaps, though, it was shyness, rather than a strong sense of her own importance, that made her seem standoffish. Whatever the cause, she remained in the background to such an extent that even the date of her birth has never been definitively established.

It is believed she was born in 1763 as Elizabeth Kortright, the daughter of a well-off New York City merchant named Laurence Kortright and his wife, Hannah Aspinall Kortright. Apart from the fact that she was the second of five children, nothing else is known of her until 1785.

That year the Congress of the United States met in New York, and among the men attending its sessions was a twenty-seven-year-old Virginia bachelor. Exactly when and where James Monroe became acquainted with Elizabeth Kortright did not get recorded. We do know that they were married at New York's fashionable Trinity Church on February 16, 1786.

While Monroe's keen mind had already marked him as a most promising young leader, his family owned only a small farm and had barely managed to send him to the College of William and Mary. He was obliged to earn a living, and right after marrying he started practicing law—as well as trying to expand his landholdings in order to operate a prosperous plantation back in Virginia.

Monroe's bent for public service kept him, and his wife, on the move. She gave birth to two daughters, Eliza and Maria, along with a son who died in infancy, during the next several years while he alternated between practicing law and holding various governmental positions in Richmond or Philadelphia. Then, in 1794, President George Washington appointed him U.S. minister to France.

That was a very tense period in Paris, because the French, who had overthrown a hated king five years earlier, had now begun a horrifying round of political executions. The Committee of Public Safety had started imprisoning and executing any person suspected of loyalty to the old regime. Among those thrown into jail was Madame de Lafayette, the wife of the young French nobleman who had joined General Washington in fighting the British during the American Revolution.

Minister Monroe wished he could do something to secure her freedom but dared not take any step in his official capacity. Instead he asked his wife to drive in an elaborate hired carriage to the gate of the prison. In his own words:

> At the prison gate a crowd gathered round it. Inquiry was made, whose carriage was it? The answer given was, that of the American Minister. Who is in it? His wife. What brought her here? To see Madame Lafayette. The concierge brought her to the iron railing in which the gate was fixed.

A short time before, her mother and grandmother had been taken from the same prison and beheaded, and she expected from the first summons of her to experience the same fate. On hearing that the wife of the American Minister had called with the most friendly motives to see her, she became frantic, and in that state they met. The scene was most affecting. . . . The report of the interview spread through Paris and had the happiest effect.

Informal communications took place between Mr. Monroe and the members of the Committee, and the liberation of Madame de Lafayette soon followed.

Elizabeth Monroe's role in securing the release of Madame de Lafayette (depicted here with her husband and daughters) from a French prison revealed a strong interest in participating in diplomatic affairs.

But how did Mrs. Monroe herself feel when she drove out to visit that prison? Unfortunately we do not know. Despite spending many more years as the wife of a man occupying increasingly high positions, she preserved an almost total personal privacy.

Besides holding other diplomatic posts in Europe, Monroe also was twice elected governor of Virginia before President James Madison asked him to become secretary of state. Then six years later, in 1817, Monroe and his wife moved into the President's House themselves.

The mansion became known as the White House because of the bright new coat of paint it received after it was rebuilt, following its burning by the British in 1814. Mrs. Monroe's European-trained taste gave the building an elegance it had until then lacked.

Indeed, White House dinners were notably formal during the eight years the Monroes lived there. Because Mrs. Monroe preferred not to attend many of these functions, the etiquette of the day forbade inviting any other women. Although President Monroe's two terms became known as "the era of good feelings" because of its political calm, socially the situation was quite different.

Deprived of the opportunity to accompany their husbands to White House gatherings, many wives of congressmen and other officials complained about Mrs. Monroe's policy. Yet if her unpopularity distressed her at all, she gave no sign of it— she even restricted the guest list to barely thirty relatives and close friends when, in 1820, her younger daughter Maria became the first child of a president to get married in the White House.

Possibly part of the reason Mrs. Monroe avoided social events was that her health had already begun to fail. After they retired in 1825 to Oak Hill, their Virginia home, she seemed to enjoy the comfortable routine of plantation life. But comments about her growing frailty became increasingly common in her husband's letters to members of his family and old friends.

On September 23, 1830, Elizabeth Monroe died at Oak Hill around the age of sixty-seven. Her husband for the past forty-four years was so shaken by her death that his daughters decided he could not stay at Oak Hill any longer. At the New York home of one of their daughters, James Monroe died the following year.

Louisa Adams

FEBRUARY 12, 1775–MAY 15, 1852

Ahead of her time

Before coming to the White House, Louisa Adams often entertained at social gatherings by playing her harp. So strong was her love of music that this portrait depicts her as a musician.

During the four years Louisa Adams lived in the White House, she spent many hours alone—"scribbling, scribbling, scribbling," as she put it. She wrote so much about her own feelings and opinions that today we can get to know her a lot better than other early presidential wives.

It is easy to like Louisa because her outlook would make her right at home in our world. Unfortunately, the same cannot be said of her husband.

Anybody who delves into American history will soon discover that John Quincy Adams had one of the prickliest personalities of all the men ever elected to the nation's highest office. With a strong mind and high moral standards, he regarded life as a continuous series of tests he had to pass. Even in his younger days, he thought that doing something purely for enjoyment showed weakness of character.

Still, Louisa Catherine Johnson consented to marry him.

She was the daughter of a Maryland merchant, Joshua Johnson, who had moved to England early in the 1770s to be the London agent for several well-off relatives. There he met and married an Englishwoman named Catherine Nuff. Louisa, their second daughter, was born at their home on February 12, 1775.

Due to the increasing difficulties between England and its American colonies, which brought the outbreak of the Revolutionary War the following year, Joshua Johnson took his wife and children to France during Louisa's infancy. Her first memories were of a large house where her family lived in the seaport of Nantes. At a school there, she learned to speak French fluently.

Louisa was eight years old in 1783, when the end of the war made it possible for the Johnsons to return to London. Then the government of the victorious former colonies appointed her father as the first American consul in the British capital. Spending his own money lavishly, he employed eleven servants to relieve his wife of all housekeeping chores.

By that time Louisa had several more sisters—eventually her family included eight girls and one boy. Her parents considered her the most promising of all their children. Having a perfect ear for music, she became an accomplished singer and harp player, besides reading widely and developing a lively interest in everything around her.

Nevertheless, the idea of her embarking on a musical career never arose because the only acceptable goal for a young woman then was to marry and bring up a family of her own. Late in 1795, when Louisa was twenty, a twenty-eight-year-old American diplomat visited the Johnsons. Although John Quincy Adams had a manner as sober as an elderly man's, he was quite impressive.

This was at least partly because his father, John Adams, held the post of vice president of the new United States and seemed likely to become its president as soon as George Washington retired. However, John Quincy had already demonstrated his own superior intelligence while representing his country abroad. He was also, in his own solemn way, quite a handsome young man.

Louisa Johnson married John Quincy Adams at a church near her London home on July 26, 1797. By then, after having been engaged for more than a year, she realized that she had chosen a life bound to be unusually interesting—as well as unusually irritating.

There was one unhappy prospect that Louisa did not have to face right away because John Quincy's duties took the newlyweds to the German city of Berlin immediately after their marriage. Although her husband's father had written to her that he was fully prepared to love her, no similar welcome had arrived from her husband's mother. Indeed, the awesomely strong-minded Abigail Adams made no secret in the letters she sent across the ocean that she doubted if "a fine lady" who had never even seen New England could make a fit wife for her son.

Perhaps the senior Mrs. Adams felt too that her son had been tricked by the Johnsons—from having spent too freely, Louisa's father owed large sums of money—and soon after his daughter's wedding, he hurried the rest of his family onto a ship bound for America to escape being sent to prison. Now poor, he was not greeted very warmly by his Maryland relatives.

Louisa Adams worried a great deal about her mother and sisters during the four years she spent with John Quincy in Berlin. She also tried hard to accustom herself to her husband's way of giving her orders instead of considering her as his valued partner—nothing in her own upbringing had prepared her for such treatment. She kept hoping that by giving her mother-in-law a grandson she could win her affection.

Louisa finally gave birth to a healthy boy named George Washington Adams in the spring of 1801, shortly before her husband's overseas mission ended. But when she arrived in America at last, even three-month-old baby George failed to melt the heart of Abigail Adams more than briefly.

In Boston, Louisa showed her talent as a hostess by giving a series of successful dinner parties for the city's leaders. She felt lonely there, though. Most of the women she met seemed to devote themselves entirely to caring for their husbands and children, and had few other interests.

Even so, she was elated to give birth to another son in Boston, and she made sure this boy received the name John Adams II. Still, he didn't solve her problem. "Do what I would," Louisa wrote later, "there was a conviction on the part of others that I could not *suit*."

After John Quincy's election to the U.S. Senate, however, Louisa's spirits rose. In Washington she was happily reunited with her mother and sisters. She gradually won over her mother-in-law back in Massachusetts by writing her long letters about John Quincy's daily activities—as well as about the latest gossip in the capital. What is more, she provided a third grandson: Charles Francis Adams, born in 1807.

Louisa's simmering unhappiness at her husband's lack of appreciation for her burst into virtual rebellion two years later when he suddenly announced a plan that horrified her. To advance his own career, without any regard for her, he had accepted an appointment to be U.S. minister to Russia—and he expected her to accompany him, bringing two-year-old Charlie with her but leaving their two older sons with their grandparents in Massachusetts.

Louisa Adams begged to be spared the "agony" of traveling thousands of miles to the Russian capital for an indefinite period, without any possibility of even receiving letters from two of her boys during the six months of every year when ice prevented American ships from docking at St. Petersburg. But John Quincy Adams selfishly brushed aside her objections. Unless she was willing to take the nearly unthinkable step of separating from him—in which case, in those days, she would have no legal right ever to see any of her children again—she could do only as her husband wished.

"I do not like the place or the people," Louisa wrote to her mother-in-law in one of her first letters from St. Petersburg. Despite her continuing anger, and her terrible suffering when a beautiful little daughter she gave birth to in Russia died a year later, her six years there were not entirely miserable.

Never having lost her ease in speaking French, the language often used by Russia's ruling class, she charmed the czar and his wife, who often paid her informal visits. Then, after John Quincy went to Paris by himself to help negotiate a peace treaty following the War of 1812, Louisa had the most exciting adventure of her life.

From Paris her husband sent her instructions to sell all their belongings and bring eight-year-old Charlie to join him there. On February 12, 1815—her fortieth birthday—Louisa set forth to travel across most of Europe during the frightful winter weather. In a Russian-style carriage mounted on a sleigh, drawn by two teams of horses, and accompanied only by her young son, a maid, and two menservants, she braved ice, snow, and war.

Such a trip would have been considered remarkably daring for a woman to undertake in that era even in peacetime. Louisa was traveling during the dreadful final days of the Napoleonic Wars, when the remnants of the French emperor's defeated army were burning and killing all across the map. Miraculously she and her party reached Paris safely after forty days filled with danger and narrow escapes.

So many people marveled at the amazing bravery of Mrs. Adams that even her husband seemed to regard himself a lucky man. The next few years, during which he served as American minister in London, were by far the happiest of their long marriage.

But as soon as President Madison summoned him back to Washington in 1817 to become his secretary of state, John Quincy Adams relapsed into preoccupation with his own career. Above all, Adams yearned to become president himself, and now he bent every effort toward this goal. Even when he finally achieved his aim eight years later, however, his difficult personality made him one of the least popular men ever to occupy the White House.

His wife hated living there. "That dull and stately prison in which the sounds of mirth are seldom heard," Louisa described it as she sat by herself writing down her thoughts on many subjects—especially about the position of women.

In 1824 Louisa Adams threw a brilliant ball in honor of General Andrew Jackson. She successfully used the occasion to "campaign" for her husband among the congressmen and their wives who attended.

Pondering over her own experiences, she advanced far ahead of her own time and foresaw a new era when "timid females" would no longer allow men to treat them as inferiors. Then, she wrote, the world would discover that the mind of woman "is as capable of solid attainment as that of man."

Yet having passed the age of fifty, she felt too old to do more herself than merely write about her unhappiness. The depth of her private misery was shown by the title she gave one of her manuscripts: *The Adventures of a Nobody.* Locked away amid all the Adams family papers in various special libraries, hundreds of pages in her own handwriting have given historians a matchless picture of the way the customs of the past crushed the spirit of a gifted woman.

Further adding to Louisa's woes, the two sons she had been forced to leave behind more than a decade earlier when she went to Russia both died during this period. One committed suicide, the other drank himself to death. In anguish, she kept blaming herself for the tragic turn their lives had taken.

With the end of her husband's single term as president, Louisa wanted nothing more than the peace of quiet life at the Adams family home near Boston, far from the bitter political battles of Washington that disgusted her. But after less than a year in Massachusetts, her husband astounded her—and the entire nation—by returning to the nation's capital in a much-diminished role.

During the next seventeen years John Quincy Adams served as a member of the House of Representatives, repeatedly reelected to Congress by his home district in Massachusetts. No longer motivated by personal ambition, he emerged as something like the conscience of the nation, winning wide respect for his outspoken opposition to slavery.

During those seventeen years Louisa Adams also achieved a serenity that had eluded her before. As admiration for her husband grew, so did Washington's admiration of his wife. Instead of being regarded as standoffish because she refused to spend most of her time paying calls on other officials' wives, she was admired as a font of information about the capital's social history practically since its founding.

In her later life Louisa Adams herself awed some very perceptive observers, particularly her grandson Henry Adams (son of the diplomat Charles Francis Adams), who turned out to be one of America's most noted historians.

Finally on February 23, 1848, John Quincy Adams collapsed while making an anti-slavery speech in the House of Representatives and died there at the age of eighty. Louisa Adams lived quietly in Washington another three years, cared for by a widowed daughter-in-law. She died on May 15, 1852, when she was seventy-seven.

Part II

Growing Pains, Slavery, and the Civil War
1830–1865

*T*he Civil War was America's most divisive conflict, but in a sense it was also a product of the forces that were linking more and more of the nation together. The construction first of canals and then railroads brought goods, people, and ideas from one region to another—principally from northeast to northwest. Along the lines, cities grew. In 1840 the nation had twelve towns with populations over 25,000 people. Twenty years later, on the eve of the War, there were 36 such towns, and they held 37 percent of the total population. The North developed great industries, and factories produced the majority of goods and wealth in that section of the country. Yet in the South, life continued to center on small farms and the great plantations, based on the labor of slaves. As more territory outside the original Republic was developed by new settlers, the central political question was whether that territory would be slave or free. Thus the very expansion of the nation brought on its division. Naturally, women's lives were shaped by these large-scale changes in American society.

By the 1840s, the young middle-class women who left their homes to work in

As the United States expanded westward, bustling scenes like this one at the Union Pacific railroad depot in Omaha City, Nebraska, became commonplace. This mingling of many different types of Americans was recorded in Frank Leslie's Illustrated Newspaper *in 1868.*

---

the mills were losing their places in the workforce to people who would accept lower wages: immigrants, the poor, widows, and African Americans. At the same time, the belief that woman's "sphere" was the home grew in power and strength. Along with the restrictions this imposed came new opportunities. In the 1830s public schools began to require education of girls as well as boys. By mid-century, literacy rates in New England neared 100 percent, and throughout the nation 50 percent of women could read. Education brought opportunity. Increasingly women found work as teachers. Books and magazines needed authors and editors, and they had to appeal to this rapidly growing female readership.

On the eve of the Civil War, *Godey's Lady's Book,* a magazine edited and often written by Sarah Josepha Hale, was read by over 160,000 women. While it preached that women should confine themselves to their domestic sphere, it gave women a chance to appear in print and to communicate with their sisters around the country. Not only did women write the majority of novels published in the 1850s, they were the most popular and successful novelists. Harriet Beecher Stowe's *Uncle Tom's Cabin,* with its vivid descriptions of the evils of slavery, kept eight presses running day and night when it sold 300,000 copies in 1852 alone. But this very success again pointed out the divisions in the nation: the novel could not be sold—or even be sent through the mails—in the South.

Uncle Tom's Cabin was an example of the kind of public moral views women were allowed to express. Despite being taught to limit their roles to "influencing" men, who were to take full charge of the world outside of the home, women increasingly formed societies to encourage peace, temperance (the prohibition of alcohol), the abolition of slavery, and other moral reforms. Women took leading roles in establishing charity schools, schools for infants, orphanages, and refuges for abandoned women. All of these activities not only gave women an opportunity to be heard, but also to form bonds with other women with whom they could share ideas and experiences. Yet these activities were mainly available to Eastern and then Western white women, and at times to free black women. They emphasized the differences between segments of society and the great divide of slavery.

This stereograph shows five generations of an African-American family. It was made during the Civil War in 1862 at J. J. Smith's plantation, in Beaufort District, South Carolina. As so often happened, the plantation owner's name was recorded, but the names and identities of the enslaved people remain forever unknown.

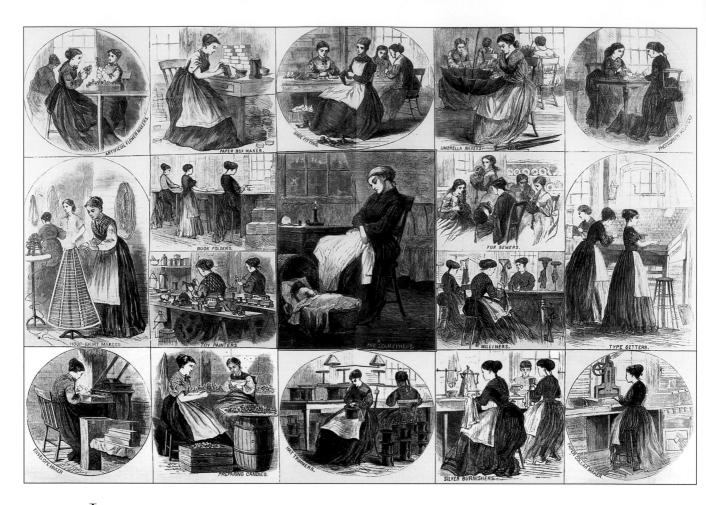

In spite of the popular idea that "woman's place was in the home," many nineteenth-century women worked for wages outside the home to support themselves and their families. This illustration from Harper's Weekly *shows the many types of jobs women held in factories, shops, and industry.*

The expansion of the nation to the west was another important feature of this time. More first ladies began to come from "the frontier," where their husbands gained fame in clashes with the Indians or in the war with Mexico over territory. This expansion had mixed meanings for women. Often the actual trek from an established home to a frontier settlement brought great difficulties. In a sense it was a trip backward through history. On the new farms, women's days were filled with the kind of never-ending household work they had done in the colonial period. They had neither the time nor the opportunity for the reform campaigns of the East. Yet with western expansion also came new political pressures that ultimately made it possible for women to be participants in the political life of the nation.

As Americans moved away from the eastern seaboard, and came to believe that a man's worth had more to do with what he did than who he was born to be, voting rules changed. Increasingly, any adult white man could vote and have a say in how the country was run. Some women began to question why they, too, should not be judged the same way and have the same opportunities. In the 1830s, the idea of women having the vote seemed absurd to most Americans, women as well as men. But women's work with the anti-slavery societies, and most men's refusal to let them take part in the political process, made some realize they must work for their own rights as well as to free the slaves. As activist Abby Kelley put it, "In striving to strike his irons off, we found most surely, that we were manacled ourselves." Women held their first political convention in 1848 in Seneca Falls, New York, and began to demand the right to vote.

The Civil War affected every woman in America. The war brought death and destruction to countless homes and families, and women were often left alone to maintain their families as best they could while their husbands served in armies. During the four years of terrible fighting, wives and daughters, in both the North and the South, found ways to support the troops. Clara Barton, Dorothea Dix, and writer Louisa May Alcott set up hospitals in Washington and nursed the sick and wounded. Thousands of other women formed committees and raised money to help care for wounded soldiers or made bandages for use in hospitals. Enslaved women, as they were freed or escaped to Union lines, had their first opportunities to have their marriages recognized by white courts and to learn to read and write.

When the war ended, many women felt confident of their ability to deal with issues outside of their homes. By becoming involved in many new reforms, women had set the stage to expand their activities into the larger communities of the state and the nation.

Rachel Jackson

Rachel Donelson Jackson, 1767–1828, was born in Pittsylvania County, Virginia, in June 1767. At twelve, she and her family took a thousand-mile journey through territory that was not part of the United States at all, but belonged to the Cherokee Nation. The Donelson family reached their destination four months after they set out, settling near what is now Nashville, Tennessee.

Because of floods and raids by the Cherokee, Colonel John Donelson and his family moved to the village of Harrodsburg, Kentucky. At eighteen, Rachel married Louis Robards. Robards's jealousy led him to seek a divorce from his wife, three years after ordering her out of his house.

In that era divorces were rarely granted, and they brought a cloud of scandal over any woman whose husband had secured one. Mistakenly thinking that she was free to marry again, Rachel was wed in August 1791 to Andrew Jackson, a twenty-four-year-old lawyer.

However, the divorce was not yet final, and Rachel was technically a bigamist until 1794, when the divorce became final and she and Jackson were rewed.

Jackson became a general in the army and entered Tennessee politics, where he was enormously successful. In 1828, he became a candidate for the presidency, and old rumors concerning his wife suddenly burst into print. Newspapers sympathetic to his political enemies viciously smeared Rachel Jackson.

Just over a month after Jackson won the presidency, Rachel Jackson suffered a severe heart attack and died five days later, on December 22, 1828. The vicious attacks on her character probably hastened her death.

During Jackson's eight years in the White House, Emily Donelson, one of his wife's nieces, and Sarah Yorke Jackson, wife of the president's adopted son, served as his official hostesses.

Hannah Van Buren

annah Hoes Van Buren was born in Kinderhook, New York, on March 8, 1783. She married her cousin, Martin Van Buren, in 1807, and together they had four children. Hannah died of tuberculosis in 1819 at the age of thirty-six; Martin Van Buren never remarried. During his four years in the White House, Angelica Singleton Van Buren, the wife of their eldest son, served as official hostess.

Why Isn't There More Information About Women's Lives?

*I*n reading about the first ladies, we discover that very little is known about some of them. It is not unusual for there to be no written records of a woman's life prior to the late nineteenth century. Several factors have made women much less visible than men in our nation's history. For most of this nation's past, "history" was defined as the lives and deeds of great men whose activities took place in the world of military, economic, or public life. Presidents, politicians, and generals; wars, battles, or major economic changes were what historians (mostly men) wrote about. The details of women's lives—their homes and families, their work in helping their husbands succeed in farming, business, or a career—often were not kept or considered important enough to record.

Historians tend to rely on written records, which many women did not leave. In the early days of the nation it was generally thought unimportant to educate women, and some never learned to read or write. At a time when the nation was more agricultural and rural, and most women married and raised families, education for daughters was not as important as it was for sons, who conducted the family's business.

When women did leave information about themselves in writing, they kept records in an informal way, through letters, diaries, and recipe and medical treatment books. While such documents were often considered important sources of information about men—because men most frequently wrote about public life— they were not considered valid in the same way for women. Stories of the family passed on by descendants, called oral or spoken history, were another form of recording events used by women (and by both men and women in other cultures). Until recently most historians didn't consider oral histories worth recording either. And if the lives of most white, middle-class women were thought not significant for history, the lives of African-American and Native American women, as well as immigrant women, were pushed even more to the side.

Because first ladies were married to presidents, who were powerful and influential men, we would expect these women's letters and papers to have been preserved as part of the family's history. But it is even hard to find information about some of the early first ladies—either because they didn't write many letters or keep a diary, or because their descendants didn't save them. Martha Washington, who had little formal education, was always embarrassed by her writing and spelling. She often told George what she wanted to say in a letter; he would write it for her, and she would copy it over in her own handwriting. After her husband died, Martha Washington burned their personal letters to each other, perhaps to protect her privacy. As a result we know very little about their personal life together.

In the twentieth century, when first ladies became more active and visible in their own right, almost all letters and papers written by or about first ladies have been saved. These papers are kept in presidential libraries, or in archives and libraries to which the president gave his own papers for safekeeping. In the days before each

Historians find Abigail Adams's letters a gold mine of information.

president had his own library, presidents kept their papers in their homes, many of which have been preserved as historic sites. Others gave their papers to the Library of Congress in Washington or to the library of the university they attended. The papers and records of first ladies are now available to authors and historians writing biographies of these women, studying their contributions in the White House, or researching the history of the president's term in office.

In the past twenty-five years the new field of women's history has emerged and grown in importance. Less formal sources for recording history, such as diaries, letters, and oral history, have become significant in learning about women's lives. Work in the home, family history, changes in the birthrate, and women's activities in informal politics have caught the interest of historians of both genders. Women historians in particular have helped people understand the role women have played in the building of our nation, and women's contributions are being recognized and given the value they deserve. Today women are becoming more and more visible in history and are entering government, politics, business, and the professions as never before.

Anna Harrison

Anna Symmes Harrison, 1775–1864, was the wife of one president and the grandmother of another. Her parents were John Cleves Symmes and Anna Tuthill Symmes, and Anna was born in Sussex County, New Jersey, on July 25, 1775. She received a more solid general education than most girls of her era—at a noted local academy, then a boarding school in New York City.

Anna married William Henry Harrison, an officer in the Revolutionary War, on November 22, 1795. Together they had ten children. Her husband not only rose to the rank of general and became a national hero after defeating Chief Tecumseh at the Battle of Tippecanoe, but also held a variety of public offices over the years, culminating with his election as president of the United States in 1840.

The sudden death of one of the Harrisons' sons kept Anna at home during the election and inauguration; in fact, she never made her home in Washington. As a result of a severe chill he caught at the inauguration ceremony, Harrison himself became seriously ill and died a month after taking office.

Anna lived at the family home in Virginia for the next eighteen years until, in 1860, she moved in with her son, John. Four years after moving to the house where her grandson, the future President Benjamin Harrison, was brought up, she died on February 25, 1864, at the age of eighty-eight.

Letitia Tyler

NOVEMBER 12, 1790–SEPTEMBER 10, 1842

"Sweet, devoted, selfless"

Having suffered from a stroke two years before her husband became president, Letitia Tyler did not often participate in social life in the capital.

Born on a Virginia plantation called Cedar Grove, on November 12, 1790, Letitia was the third of Robert and Mary Christian's eight daughters; in addition, they had four sons. Like many women of her time, nothing about her early life would ever be recorded.

But at the age of eighteen, Letitia attracted the notice of a law student from a similar background. Six months older than she was, John Tyler already had political ambitions. By the time they got married on March 29, 1813—his twenty-third birthday—he had already been elected to Virginia's state legislature.

Yet throughout the nearly thirty years their marriage lasted, his wife only rarely appeared in public with him. While his career advanced, she remained at home, caring for their nine children and occupied with housekeeping responsibilities.

According to those who knew her, Letitia Tyler was a lovely woman much admired as a model wife and mother. "Sweet, devoted, selfless," one of her husband's biographers would describe her. However, not a single letter of hers has ever turned up to cast a clearer light on her own personality.

Only a few sad details were recorded. In 1839, when Letitia was forty-nine, she suffered a severe stroke that left her partly paralyzed. Even so, when her husband became vice president of the United States two years later, she accompanied him to Washington.

Then, just a month after President William Henry Harrison took office, he died—and John Tyler became the first vice president elevated to the nation's highest post by the death of the president. In April 1841 Tyler's invalid wife moved into the White House with him. Because of her inability to assume any social duties, the role of official hostess was assigned to Patricia Cooper Tyler, a young actress who had married the Tylers' eldest son.

Letitia Tyler made only one public appearance at the White House: Early in 1842, she attended the wedding of her daughter Elizabeth. Soon afterward, though, she had a second stroke. On September 10, 1842, after seventeen secluded months as the nation's first lady, she died at the age of fifty-one.

During her lifetime, Letitia Tyler had been among the least visible of presidential wives. In 1844, less than two years after her death, John Tyler remarried—and he chose a remarkably attention-loving young woman as his second wife.

Julia Tyler

MAY 4, 1820–JULY 10, 1889

A high and daring spirit

*J*ulia Gardiner Tyler was the first incumbent
president's wife to pose for a daguerreotype,
the earliest form of photography.

*S*oon after moving into the White House, Julia Tyler wrote to her mother: "This
winter I intend to do something in the way of entertaining that shall be the admiration and talk of the Washington world."

She certainly accomplished her purpose. Although she was the nation's first lady
for less than a year, Julia scored a great social success during her short "reign," as she
herself called it. Only twenty-four then, she would never cease relishing the special
status she had acquired—throughout the rest of her long life, she often wrote letters
that she signed "Mrs. ex-President Tyler."

Julia's high opinion of her own importance was at least partly due to her upbringing. Back in the 1600s, one of her father's ancestors had purchased a small island off the eastern tip of New York's Long Island, and ever since then the family had considered this breeze-swept domain as something of a private kingdom. Born there on May 4, 1820, Julia could hardly help imagining herself a princess.

Her parents were David Gardiner and Juliana McLachlan Gardiner, who taught her to value wealth and social position more than anything else. Nobody informed her that her father had been a proud but almost penniless lawyer before marrying the daughter of a rich New York City brewer. To Julia, he was an important state senator and the lord of Gardiner's Island.

Life on an isolated little island could be boring, so she and her two older brothers and younger sister spent much of their early years in the nearest town of any size. Yet even East Hampton, an old established community about a hundred miles from New York City, seemed rather sedate to Julia. Not until she was sent to a fashionable boarding school for young ladies in the metropolis itself did she feel truly alive.

Julia greatly enjoyed the three years she spent at Madame Chagaray's school, with its regular tea parties and frequent outings to the opera or other stylish entertainments. She was so pretty and flirtatious that she enchanted practically every male she encountered. She even called herself "the Rose of Long Island." After all the excitement of the city, when she returned to East Hampton she found it terribly dull.

As a result, Julia got involved in a mischievous scheme. She let an artist draw an advertisement of her dressed up in a gaudy, fur-trimmed costume and carrying a sign that proclaimed: "I'll Purchase at Bogert & Mecamly's, No. 86 Ninth Avenue. Their Goods Are Beautiful and Astonishingly Cheap." Her signature rose appeared at the bottom of the ad.

This picture appeared on posters all over the city. It not only struck Julia's parents as disgraceful but also led, at least indirectly, toward her achieving a much more permanent sort of fame.

The Gardiners decided that their daughter's lively nature required more diversion than East Hampton could provide, and they took her on a grand tour of Europe. Then, after she had tasted the pleasures of social life abroad, it struck them that she should also be exposed to the increasingly sophisticated society in their own country's capital. Early in December 1842, twenty-two-year-old Julia arrived in Washington with her parents for a stay of several months.

By February, Julia had turned down proposals of marriage from two congressmen and a Supreme Court justice. When she went to the White House to attend a Washington's Birthday ball, she received another proposal—from the president of

THE ...... OF *"Long Island."*

the United States. John Tyler was thirty years older than she was, and he had been a widower for only five months. But he told her as they strolled together that he had fallen deeply in love with her.

If Julia hesitated, she didn't hesitate long. By the time she and her family returned to East Hampton late in March, she and the president had reached an "understanding" that they would marry after he finished observing a formal period of mourning for his first wife. While no announcement of their plans was made, the

60

president's obvious interest in a woman younger than three of his own daughters stirred a rising tide of gossip.

The following winter, when the Gardiners returned to Washington, those in the know expected to hear of an impending wedding. Instead a terrible tragedy—and a great political upheaval—occurred. On February 28, 1844, practically all the government's leaders went for a cruise down the Potomac River aboard a new U.S. Navy ship, with Julia and her father among the invited guests. The firing of the world's largest naval gun, the "Peacemaker," was to be demonstrated during the excursion.

When the gun went off, however, part of it exploded and showered the deck with chunks of red-hot metal. Although most of the ship's four hundred passengers were only badly shaken, the accident killed seven men—including the secretary of state, the secretary of the navy, and Senator Gardiner, Julia's father. Even after recovering from the first shock of her loss, she had such awful nightmares for the next few months that she decided there was only one way to ease her suffering. Despite the accepted idea that at least a year should elapse before a bereaved daughter married, she urged the president to set their wedding date as soon as his busy schedule permitted.

Without any advance notice, twenty-four-year-old Julia Gardiner became Julia Tyler on June 26, 1844, in one of New York City's most fashionable churches. Only relatives and close friends were present at the ceremony, marking the first time a president had married while in office. Newspaper accounts about the marriage were less than favorable, though, because of the thirty-year age difference involved.

The second Mrs. Tyler bubbled over with happiness as she took steps to make sure that word of the gala parties she intended to give would be widely circulated. Unofficially she arranged with the Washington correspondent of the *New York Herald* to provide him with full information about these gatherings: In effect, she hired the first press secretary ever to publicize any White House activity.

Then Julia spent Gardiner family money freely to refurbish the White House itself, which had become very shabby. (John Tyler's pro-slavery policies had prompted his enemies in Congress to cut off funds for its maintenance.) She also recruited a dozen attractive young women to wear elegant white gowns and serve as her ladies-in-waiting, following the practice of the royal courts she had seen in Europe.

Spectacularly dressed herself, with the ladies of her "court" standing beside her, Julia stirred just the sort of excitement she had hoped for when she began holding Saturday night receptions, along with frequent dinner parties, that winter. Her own high spirits as she greeted her guests created an infectious good humor. But there were some in Washington who did not find Mrs. Tyler so charming and were appalled by her pretensions to aristocracy.

Some government officials were also irritated by her interference in governmental business. Besides making determined efforts to secure jobs for her brothers and other relatives, she even tried blatantly to exert pressure in favor of some of her husband's most controversial policies, such as the annexation of Texas. John Tyler had already made so many political enemies that there was no chance of his winning a second term—and this "lobbying" by his second wife did not increase his popularity.

Yet Tyler himself was immensely fond of Julia, and he never ceased doting on her. During the next seventeen years at his large Virginia plantation, called Sherwood Forest, she provided him with a whole new family of seven children while also preserving her fame as a hostess. Despite her summer trips to fashionable Northern resorts such as Saratoga Springs and Newport, she became passionately Southern in her outlook as the Civil War approached.

The war had started by the time her husband died, early in 1862. At the age of forty-one Julia Tyler began to run Sherwood Forest on her own—under increasingly difficult wartime conditions. Somehow she managed to grow food crops even though she had never had to perform physical labor before.

When the fighting came close to her home, Julia decided she must take her children to safety under their grandmother's wing in New York. With the iron will she had developed, she demanded safe passage into Union territory. She even wrote repeatedly to a man she detested, telling Abraham Lincoln to order his army not to destroy Sherwood Forest, and signed her letters "Mrs. ex-President Tyler."

Returning to Virginia after the war ended, Julia found her plantation almost unharmed—and yet how could she run it without any slave labor? The collapse of the South's economic system, followed by a sharp decline in the value of property she had inherited up north, brought her to the brink of outright poverty during the 1870s.

Again Julia Tyler took up lobbying in Washington. By that time Congress had voted a pension of $3,000 a year to Abraham Lincoln's widow, and she saw no reason why she shouldn't receive a similar payment, even if she and her husband had actively supported the Southern cause after leaving the White House. Finally in 1881 she won at least a partial victory when Congress approved an annual pension of $1,500 for her.

Later that year, though, public outrage over the assassination of President James Garfield resulted in the adoption of a more generous policy. A new bill was passed granting $5,000 a year—in those days, enough to live on very comfortably—to all four widows who had formerly resided at the White House, Julia Tyler as well as Sarah Polk, Mary Lincoln, and Lucretia Garfield.

Julia Tyler keenly enjoyed her prominence as first lady and social hostess of the White House.

With her money worries over, Julia took up residence in Virginia's capital of Richmond, where her status as a strong defender of the South's lost cause assured her the attention she craved. After several years of failing health, she died there on July 10, 1889, at the age of sixty-nine.

How Did Women Fight Against Slavery?

*E*ven though women couldn't vote, they often took part in political and reform causes. Taught by family, church, and society to help the less fortunate and to act morally, many women joined groups that worked to end, or abolish, the slavery of African Americans. Those who joined this movement were called abolitionists. In working for abolition, women discovered that they too lacked many basic rights of citizens and that theories of personal and political freedom applied to women as well as slaves. Many women who first worked for the abolition of slavery later formed groups to work for women's rights.

Women joined abolition groups with men and also formed their own separate societies. The American Anti-Slavery Society was founded in Philadelphia in 1833. Four women attended the first meeting. They met again later that year to organize their own group, the Philadelphia Female Anti-Slavery Society, following the lead of free black women in Salem, Massachusetts, who had formed a group in 1832. By the end of the 1830s, there were over forty women's anti-slavery groups in New England; some had both black and white women as members.

Women were involved in every kind of anti-slavery work. They held fund-raising events; organized others to join abolition societies; wrote pamphlets, newspaper articles, and books; made stirring speeches; and circulated petitions to send to Congress demanding an end to slavery.

Women's anti-slavery groups were strong enough to hold their own conventions. In New York City in May 1837, the first Anti-Slavery Convention of American Women was held, attended by more than two hundred women. This convention met again in Philadelphia in 1838 and 1839.

Both black and white women were active in abolition work. Lydia Maria Child (*Appeal in Favor of That Class of Americans Called Africans*) and Harriet Beecher Stowe (*Uncle Tom's Cabin*) wrote powerful books about the evils of slavery. Maria Weston Chapman helped organize the American Anti-Slavery Society and edited two major anti-slavery newspapers, *The Liberator* and *The National Anti-Slavery Standard*. African American Sojourner Truth was a powerful speaker against slavery at many conventions. Harriet Tubman, a fearless black woman, led hundreds of slaves to freedom by planning secret escape routes. Charlotte Forten Grimké taught freed slaves in the South. White women such as Lucretia Mott and Lucy Stone, later powerful leaders in gaining women the right to vote, began their life's work organizing and lecturing against slavery.

Many people thought that women's actions in the anti-slavery campaign went beyond the bounds of proper behavior for women. Women speaking out against the political system, making friends across racial boundaries, and giving speeches on

Sojourner Truth (c. 1797–1883) was originally named Isabella Van Wagener when she was born a slave to a Dutch family in New York. She claimed to have mystical experiences; during one of them, she was commanded by voices to take the name Sojourner (meaning "traveler") Truth. Her subsequent preaching and lectures across the country on abolition and women's rights earned her great respect and a reputation as a powerful speaker and reformer.

African American Harriet Tubman (c. 1820–1913) was a runaway slave, Civil War scout, and nurse, who led more than 300 slaves to freedom in daring escapes to the North. Well known as a "conductor" on the Underground Railroad (a series of safe hiding places on the escape routes), she was called the "Moses" of her people because she led them out of bondage. Slave owners offered the staggering sum of $40,000 for her capture, but she was never caught. A famous abolitionist whose courage and cleverness were legendary, she is shown here, at far left, with some of the slaves she helped to escape.

lecture platforms angered many and created a storm of public controversy. The debate raged in homes, churches, and newspapers. Angry mobs attacked and burned the halls where abolitionists met and spoke. Preachers gave sermons about women "meddling in men's affairs" and closed their churches to abolition meetings.

These determined women dared to continue their efforts, finding that the question of whether *women* had the right to speak out on public issues was central to their rights as citizens. This prompted Sarah Grimké to write a powerful defense of women's right to take part in political activity called "Letters on the Equality of the Sexes." In 1838 her sister, Angelina Grimké, was invited to speak to the Massachusetts legislature—the first time a woman spoke before a group of lawmakers.

In 1840 the World's Anti-Slavery Convention met in London. Some American abolition groups elected women as delegates, but the convention refused to allow them to participate. They made them sit apart from the convention and listen in silence. A few American men, such as abolitionist leaders Wendell Phillips and William Lloyd Garrison, left to join the women in protest. The convention's insult made two of the women, Lucretia Mott and Elizabeth Cady Stanton, determined to form a women's rights movement when they returned to the United States.

Women's work for abolition was crucial in influencing public opinion and in pressuring Congress to pass the Thirteenth Amendment to the Constitution, abolishing slavery after the Civil War. It also inspired women to work for their own rights. The organizing, writing, fund-raising, and administrative skills that women learned took them beyond their homes, communities, and churches into the world of politics.

From the 1830s until the Civil War, opponents of slavery circulated anti-slavery tokens to popularize their cause. Josiah Wedgwood, the maker of the famous Wedgwood china, was an Englishman who opposed slavery. Wedgwood first produced ceramic images showing a kneeling male slave with the motto "Am I Not a Man & a Brother" and a kneeling female slave asking "Am I Not a Woman & a Sister." These were reproduced as tokens and widely circulated, becoming powerful tools of propaganda against slavery.

Sarah Polk

SEPTEMBER 4, 1803–AUGUST 14, 1891

"Equal partner with her President-husband"

When she entered the White House in 1845, Sarah Polk was already experienced in Washington politics, having lived in the city for thirteen years during her husband's terms in Congress.

No dancing was allowed in the White House during the four years that Sarah Polk lived there, and no visitors were received on Sundays. To most Americans of her day—those who scoffed at her strict rules, along with those who very much approved of them—she stood out because she exerted such a strongly religious influence on the capital's social life.

But to Washington residents aware of what went on behind the scenes, her impact seemed even more significant. Like Abigail Adams before her, Sarah was a presidential wife who could fairly be called her husband's political partner. Although she shared the prevailing opinion that women ought to remain in the background, she privately helped her husband in many ways throughout his career.

Sarah was well prepared to assume the role of chief aide to the nation's chief executive. Coming from a wealthy and upstanding Presbyterian family in the young state of Tennessee, she had been born near its original capital of Murfreesboro on September 4, 1803. Her parents were Elizabeth Whitsitt Childress and Joel Childress, a merchant who also served as a militia officer, thereby becoming a close friend of General Andrew Jackson.

The third of their four children, Sarah received lessons at home from the teacher at a local academy where only boys could enroll. Even as a young girl she was fond of reading newspapers, and she liked nothing better than listening to the talk about politics when General Jackson stopped in to see her father.

Showing such signs of having an exceptionally keen mind, she was sent when she was thirteen to the South's finest boarding school for girls—operated by members of the Moravian religious group in Salem, North Carolina. There she grew into a young lady who had a gracious manner and easily conversed on topics of interest to both men and women.

Before completing her studies, however, Sarah was summoned home because her father had become very ill. Not long after his death she encountered a shy young man whom she had met during her childhood when he attended school with one of her brothers. Now James K. Polk was back in Murfreesboro, serving as clerk of Tennessee's state senate.

Serious, hardworking, but unsure of whether he could ever achieve the political success he dreamed of, Polk soon decided that Sarah Childress would be the perfect wife for him. When he asked her to marry him, he later confided to a friend, she said that she would if he won a seat in the Tennessee legislature. He managed to accomplish this, and—on New Year's Day of 1824—they began their life together; Sarah was twenty, and her husband twenty-eight.

Their marriage proved to be a great success. Too restrained to write each other effusive love letters or display their personal feelings in public, they clearly were very fond of each other. The similarity of their interests in politics created the basis for a very close companionship.

In effect Sarah Polk set the pattern for a new sort of political wife. She had said that if she and James ever lived in the White House, she would "neither keep house nor make butter." When Polk advanced into the national Congress, Sarah accompanied him on every trip to Washington—and diligently cultivated political friendships there.

In addition to becoming an expert on the social side of governmental business, Sarah also talked over every issue of the day with her husband, gave him advice, and even wrote letters for him. He relied on her assistance more than ever after his loyal support of President Andrew Jackson won him the powerful post of Speaker of the House of Representatives. Unofficially, his wife served as his personal adviser.

Still, Sarah shared the outlook of her era to the extent that she always tried to make her own role seem minor. "Mr. Polk thinks that . . ." or "Mr. Polk believes that . . ." she would say whenever she expressed any opinion about a matter under discussion. Despite her firm conviction of his greatness, however, Mr. Polk lacked the sort of personal magnetism required to make him a popular figure among the general public.

Sarah Polk brought new independence to the role of first lady. On this writing desk, she edited her husband's speeches.

Even so, the Democratic party chose him as its presidential candidate in 1844, and that autumn he narrowly defeated the more colorful but less reliable Henry Clay. With her long experience in Washington, Sarah Polk felt no qualms about moving into the White House the following March. Quickly she put her own stamp on the executive mansion's official entertaining.

As soon as her Presbyterian policy against dancing became known, it stirred dismay among some capital officials and their wives. "To dance in these rooms would be undignified," she once explained gently. "How indecorous it would seem for dancing to be going on in one apartment, while in another we were conversing with dignitaries of the republic or ministers of the gospel."

When protests against his wife's decision were relayed to the president, he replied that all domestic arrangements properly fell within her province. Similarly he abided by her religiously based bans on cardplaying or holding even private business meetings on Sundays. Despite her strictness about such matters, though, Sarah liked to wear elegant gowns, and she enjoyed giving glittering dinner parties.

Indeed, she took pains about her appearance, arranging her jet-black hair in a cascade of stylish curls, so that the wife of the British minister described her as "a very handsome woman." At White House receptions Sarah's ability to find the right words for making all the guests feel welcome charmed even her husband's most outspoken political enemies.

On one occasion the man her husband had defeated in the presidential election gallantly told her that he could not help approving of *her* administration as mistress of the White House. Henry Clay mischievously added, though, that there was some difference of opinion about her husband's administration.

Sarah Polk instantly thanked Clay for the compliment he had paid her, then she smiled and went on: "If a political opponent of my husband is to succeed him I have always said I prefer you, Mr. Clay, and in that event I shall be most happy to surrender the White House to you." Her clever political response to his teasing brought a hearty laugh from Clay himself as well as from everyone else who heard it.

Even Senator Charles Sumner of Massachusetts fell under her spell. One of the severest critics of President Polk's efforts to fulfill the country's "Manifest Destiny" by expanding the United States westward—efforts that in 1846 had involved the nation in a war with Mexico—Senator Sumner said after dining at the White House that Mrs. Polk's "sweetness of manner won me entirely."

Still, it was Sarah's behind-the-scenes participation in important political decision making that most notably distinguished her from previous presidential wives. Although it would have aroused a storm of disapproval then—as it would even now—if she had ever attended meetings of her husband's cabinet, day after day, when officials came calling on him individually, "she was always present," one of them later recalled.

Furthermore, Sarah still relished reading newspapers while her husband did not. So every morning she spent several hours going through a stack of leading journals, marking articles that she thought he should see, and then she piled her selections neatly on his desk in his office. "Equal partner with her President-husband," one of Polk's biographers would call her.

Sarah also tried hard to prevent her husband from overworking and risking serious harm to his always frail health—as did many first ladies who preceded and followed her. He had a tendency toward sinking into low spirits, and though she

This extraordinary early photograph captures three first ladies in the same group: Sarah (with President Polk, center); Harriet Lane (far left); and Dolley Madison (second from right).

constantly strove to encourage him, even Sarah couldn't find a way to make the majority of Americans appreciate her husband.

Her husband's expansionist policies antagonized many of his fellow citizens, and his aloofness and inability to see the light side of any topic made him personally unpopular. He would have had no easy time winning a second term—but he had promised not to run again for various political reasons, so there was no possibility of his gaining another four years in the White House.

Leaving Washington in March 1849, both Polks aimed to put politics behind them and enjoy the first vacation they had ever taken. Traveling by train, boat, and even stagecoach, they embarked on a four-week tour of the South on their way back to Tennessee, where they had built a grand new home for their retirement.

At every stop along their route Sarah and her husband were greeted warmly by groups of well-wishers. Ceremonial banquets were hastily arranged. At first the enthusiasm of these welcomes was wonderfully exciting, but James Polk had always been subject to digestive upsets, and soon he felt so ill that his sufferings prevented any further festivities.

On arriving in Nashville, Polk's health seemed much improved. However, his symptoms soon returned. Only three months after departing from the White House, he died on June 15, 1849, at the age of fifty-three.

Widowed at the age of forty-five, Sarah Polk survived her husband for more than forty years. Living in the fine home they had planned together, with one or another of her nieces to keep her company, she became Nashville's most respected citizen. During the Civil War, when opposing armies repeatedly fought for control of the area, generals on both sides of the conflict paid her visits as soon as they entered the city to assure her of her safety.

Over the years every person of any importance who came to Nashville made a point of visiting Mrs. Polk. She had become a national monument, some Tennesseans joked fondly. As she grew increasingly frail, she never left her home except to go to church, but she still welcomed callers because she felt it was her duty to keep alive the country's memory of her husband. She died at her home on August 14, 1891, two weeks before she would have marked her eighty-eighth birthday.

Margaret Taylor

SEPTEMBER 21, 1788–AUGUST 14, 1852

A lady who did not smoke a pipe

For reasons she kept to herself, Margaret Taylor made the decision never to sit for her portrait or even for a photograph. She assigned most of the duties of official hostess to her youngest daughter, Mary Elizabeth ("Betty") Bliss.

In his long career as a soldier, General Zachary Taylor won an affectionate nickname from the men under his command. Old Rough and Ready, they called him. When he became a candidate for the presidency, some of his political opponents wanted to cast doubt on his fitness to hold the nation's highest office—without directly attacking such a popular hero.

So they made fun of his wife.

During the summer of 1848, the rumor spread that Old Rough and Ready was married to a crude frontier woman who always kept a small sack of tobacco in a pocket of her skirt. Cartoonists had a fine time picturing "Mrs. President" presiding at the White House while puffing away on her corncob pipe.

The truth was very different, though. Actually, Margaret had such a strong aversion to tobacco that, for her sake, the soldier she married gave up cigars. What's more, everybody who knew her used words such as "gentle" or "refined" to describe her. While she did spend much of her life at primitive army forts to which her husband was assigned, she never forgot the lessons about proper ladylike behavior that she had received during her girlhood on a prosperous Maryland plantation.

She was born Margaret Smith on September 21, 1788, to parents Ann Mackall Smith and Walter Smith. Major Smith, who had led a battalion of militia during the Revolutionary War, possessed the further distinction of being descended from one of Maryland's first settlers back in the 1600s. So the future Mrs. Taylor—her family always called her Peggy—grew up comfortably amid the plantation-owning aristocracy along the Chesapeake Bay near the Virginia border.

At the age of twenty-one Peggy paid a visit to a married sister who had moved to Kentucky. There she met Zachary Taylor, a twenty-five-year-old Virginian serving as an army lieutenant, and the following year, on June 21, 1810, she married him. The wedding took place in a far-from-elegant log house: It was a fitting start to the adventurous new life on which she was embarking.

Peggy Taylor proved surprisingly able to make the best of whatever conditions her soldier-husband's career brought her way. During the next fifteen years she gave birth to five daughters and then a son at remote army posts all over the map, from Minnesota to Florida to Arkansas.

In this period these areas were frontier territories beyond the borders of "the States," with only a scattering of settlers. At one point Captain Taylor wrote to one of his brothers: "Peggy says she is very lonesome. If you come, she says you must bring her some cotton for nitting [*sic*]. . . ."

Still, she managed to create a homey environment wherever she went, having her fine mahogany dining-room furniture sent to each successive post so that she could entertain other officers and their wives with at least a semblance of the civilized surroundings she had left behind. Yet the rigors of the wilderness caused a terrible series of losses in the Taylor family.

Over a three-year period, three of the Taylors' young daughters died of the dreaded "bilious fever" that often afflicted pioneers in swampy areas during hot summer weather. Then Peggy herself got so sick that word of her impending death was sent to her husband, away on official business.

"This information has nearly unmanned me," he wrote to a friend, "for my loss will be an irreparable one. I am confident the feminine virtues never did concentrate in a higher degree in the bosom of any woman than in hers."

Fortunately, however, Peggy Taylor recovered from her severe illness, and after a few months she was able to resume her usual household duties. But never afterward would her family cease worrying about her health: As the years passed, other, lesser ailments aroused such concern that she was treated like a semi-invalid.

By the time her husband became a great hero, during the Mexican War of 1846–1848, the Taylors had acquired a small plantation in Louisiana as their permanent home. Near Baton Rouge, where General Taylor had recently been stationed, his wife spent the war years improving the small house on their property to make it a pleasant place for their retirement—and praying for her husband's safety.

Surrounded by members of her family, Margaret Taylor only briefly enjoyed the peaceful retirement she had been planning. Soon after her husband returned to Louisiana, she heard that some leaders of the Whig party were planning to make him their candidate in the 1848 presidential election because he was now a famous general in the war. She was approaching the age of sixty then—and this idea provoked a sharp comment from her.

It was "a plot to deprive her of his society, and to shorten his life by unnecessary care and responsibility," she told several relatives. As scarcely any other words of hers have come down to us, these can only suggest that Margaret Taylor had a clear idea of how difficult the work of being the president's wife was. Nevertheless, a few days after her husband's inauguration she arrived at the White House without any public notice and quietly took up residence in the family quarters there.

She picked a bright and cheerful sitting room on the second floor as her private domain. There she welcomed a steady stream of relatives and longtime friends, who in the Southern style paid her extended visits. While the president's wife impressed one of her young nephews as a "stately" old lady, she took no part at all in any governmental gatherings downstairs.

Instead her youngest daughter, recently married to a lieutenant colonel on General Taylor's staff, served as the executive mansion's official hostess. Although Betty Bliss was only twenty-three, she carried out the social duties she had been assigned with a poise and charm that some in the family said reminded them of her mother many years earlier.

But even if Margaret Taylor's frail health had long ago made those close to her expect that they might lose her soon, it was her seemingly robust husband who suddenly grew seriously ill during the summer of 1850. After only sixteen months in office, Zachary Taylor suffered a mysterious digestive upset and died at the White House within just a few days.

Far too grief-stricken to attend Washington's elaborate funeral ceremonies for her husband, Margaret remained in seclusion upstairs at the White House until eight days after his death. Privately, then, she was taken to her daughter's Baltimore home. Betty brought her mother back to Louisiana three months later.

At another family property in nearby Mississippi, Margaret Taylor died two years after losing her husband—on August 14, 1852, a month before she would have reached her sixty-fourth birthday.

Abigail Fillmore

MARCH 17, 1798–MARCH 30, 1853

"A lady of great strength of mind"

An avid reader and a well-educated woman, Abigail Fillmore had a thorough knowledge of current affairs and the issues affecting her husband's presidency.

*A*bigail Fillmore stands out as the first first lady who had ever held a job outside her own home. While she was in her twenties, she worked as a schoolteacher for almost seven years.

Although she came from a family that could trace its ancestry back to early New England settlers and put a high value on books and learning, Abigail had needed to earn money. She grew up on the edge of poverty, her father having died in her infancy.

He was a Baptist minister named Lemuel Powers in the village of Stillwater, New York, about thirty miles north of Albany. Abigail, the youngest of seven children, was born there on March 17, 1798. Her mother, Abigail Newland Powers, just a few months later found herself a widow left to care for five sons and two daughters, and she soon decided to join a group of relatives moving west.

As a result young Abigail's first memories were of an isolated farming community called Sempronius, in New York's Finger Lakes region. This was still a frontier area with few schools, but the Powers children received whatever education was available. Abigail was nearly twenty when a fine academy opened in Moravia, the nearest town, and even though she was well beyond the age of most of its students, she managed to enroll there.

At the academy Abigail rapidly qualified to become a teacher—and she also fell in love with a young man from a similar background. Millard Fillmore, eighteen then, had already worked for several years at a textile mill that had just closed down. Ambitiously he hoped to prepare for studying law. Her warm encouragement led very soon to their getting engaged, but both of them realized that they would not have enough money to marry for several years.

Nearly eight years elapsed before the couple felt that they could afford to wed. During this long engagement Abigail earned her own keep by teaching in Moravia while Millard studied in the office of a lawyer in the town of East Aurora, near Buffalo, then started practicing law on his own. Finally on February 5, 1826, when she was twenty-eight and he was twenty-six, they were married.

Still far from prosperous, the new Mrs. Fillmore found a teaching job in East Aurora after her wedding. She kept it only a few months, though: Within a year, she gave birth to a son named after his father. In those days it was practically unheard of for a white married woman who was also a mother to continue any sort of work outside the home.

From then on Abigail Fillmore devoted herself to domestic duties. Meanwhile, Millard Fillmore began cultivating important political friends in the city of Buffalo. In 1830, four years after their marriage, he had already advanced politically to the extent that moving to Buffalo seemed a wise step.

Besides watching over her son—and her cherished daughter, Mary Abigail, born in 1832—Abigail Fillmore's main pleasure as the years passed was in reading books. Her husband held increasingly important public offices, and she carefully followed the political issues of the day and discussed them with her husband.

In 1848, when Mrs. Fillmore was fifty, her husband was elected vice president of the United States on the Whig party's ticket headed by General Zachary Taylor, a hero of the Mexican War. Then, in 1850, President Taylor's death elevated Millard Fillmore to the nation's highest office.

His wife by that time was having health problems. She served as White House hostess for required official receptions and formal dinners, but preferred small, intimate family gatherings. In the White House, her main contribution was in urging her husband to remedy a lack she quickly discovered: The Executive Mansion had no collection of books for the use of its official families. Thanks to her, a library was established in one of its upstairs rooms, which endures to the present day.

Due to Abigail's declining health, many of the social obligations ordinarily fulfilled by a president's wife were instead carried out by the Fillmores' young daughter. Despite being only eighteen when her father took over the nation's highest post, Mary Abigail had the poise and the outgoing nature to enjoy greeting White House visitors.

Her mother did rally to make one final appearance as first lady—at the inauguration of her husband's successor, Franklin Pierce, on March 4, 1853. Unfortunately the ceremony took place on a bitterly cold day with snow in the air and wet slush underfoot. Seated outdoors with other dignitaries, Abigail Fillmore caught a severe chill.

At the nearby Willard Hotel, where the Fillmores had expected to stay only briefly before returning to Buffalo, the wife of the ex-president became alarmingly ill. Her cold had developed into pneumonia, doctors said, and she could not be moved. In this Washington hotel, less than a month after her husband's term of office had ended, Abigail Fillmore died on March 30, 1853, at the age of fifty-five.

Perhaps her work as a teacher gave her the deep, enduring love for books that led her to found the White House library. Although she had been one of the White House's least visible first ladies, compared with the traditional presidential wife from a rich, well-connected family, her efforts to establish the library had not gone unnoticed. In its account of her death a Washington newspaper called her "a lady of great strength of mind."

Jane Pierce

MARCH 12, 1806–DECEMBER 2, 1863

"Oh, how I wish he was
out of political life!"

A photograph from about 1850 shows the shared affection of Jane Pierce and Benny, the last of her three sons.

There were only a few brief periods of happiness in the life of Jane Pierce. Sadly, a terrible tragedy that she could not forget made her last eleven years utterly miserable.

Many girls growing up in New England in the same era might have envied Jane during her youth. Her father, Jesse Appleton, was a leading Congregationalist minister and her mother, Elizabeth Means Appleton, came from a rich family that owned a textile mill. The third of her parents' six children, Jane was born in the pleasant village of Hampton, New Hampshire, on March 12, 1806.

A year later her father became president of Bowdoin College in Brunswick,

Maine. On its tree-lined campus Jane's childhood was spent comfortably amid the professors and their families.

Holding to the stern beliefs of the early Puritans, her father instilled a deep fear of sin in this sensitive daughter. Although he died when Jane was thirteen and she moved back to Hampton with her mother, these religious teachings shaped her whole personality. Intensely shy, she was also subject to frequent illnesses—even in a period when well-brought-up young women were supposed to be delicate creatures, her extreme frailty made her family worry that she might develop the then-common disease of tuberculosis.

Jane proved to be a good student with a special interest in literature. When she was twenty, she met Franklin Pierce. A recent graduate of Bowdoin, he could hardly have been more different from her. Friendly, and fond of parties, he was planning to study law as a means of entering politics, which had fascinated him ever since his boyhood. He courted her, and she agreed to marry him.

Jane Appleton's relatives did all they could to prevent the marriage. Besides his belonging to a family that ranked lower than theirs socially, during his college days he had taken part in drinking sprees they could not excuse. And his political opinions—he was a great admirer of the decidedly unintellectual General Andrew Jackson—struck them as entirely unsound.

Following a long engagement, Jane married Frank on November 19, 1834, at the home of one of her wealthy uncles; she was twenty-eight, and her husband twenty-nine. Having already served four terms in New Hampshire's legislature, he had recently won election to the House of Representatives in Washington. Immediately after their wedding the couple departed for the nation's capital.

From the first, Jane Pierce was distressed by Washington's constant talk of political deals. When she discovered how much her husband relished after-hours gatherings with other congressmen—rowdy gatherings at which he could not seem to help drinking too much wine—she was horrified. "Oh, how I wish he was out of political life!" she wrote home to New Hampshire. "How much better it would be for him on every account!"

Finally, after eight increasingly unhappy years, Jane prevailed on Frank to quit politics and take up practicing law back in New Hampshire. Its capital, Concord, was a town with only about five thousand residents, most of them regular churchgoers. Could there be any doubt that this would be a safer place than sinful Washington to bring up their sons?

After many pregnancies that did not come to term, Jane now had two little boys—the elder, named after his father, was two years old when the family moved to Concord in 1842, and Benjamin, always called Benny, had just passed his first birthday.

But Frank Junior died of typhoid fever just two years later, plunging his mother into such extreme grief that only the thought that she still had Benny preserved her sanity. From then on she devoted herself so entirely to watching over Benny that she seemed hardly to notice her husband's absence during the Mexican War, when his bravery won him the rank of brigadier general.

By 1852 Benny was a bright eleven-year-old boy who seemed not a bit spoiled by his mother's absorption in him. That summer something amazing happened: For complicated political reasons, delegates to the convention of the Democratic party nominated the practically unknown Franklin Pierce as their candidate for president of the United States. When Jane Pierce heard the news, she fainted. On reviving, she said that only the prospect of having Benny with her in the White House made the possibility of her husband's victory bearable.

Fewer than two months after Pierce won the election, the family was returning by train to New Hampshire from a Christmas visit to Boston. Suddenly a freak accident occurred. The car in which they were riding left the tracks and tumbled down an embankment. Neither parent was hurt, but somehow Benny toppled out onto the tracks—and was killed.

Her son's death devastated Mrs. Pierce. She lived another eleven years, wearing black as a sign of mourning for her son and sometimes behaving very peculiarly. She spent most of her husband's four years as president upstairs in her own White House sitting room, often scribbling notes to her dead son. She thought God must have caused Benny's death to punish the boy's parents for their sins, and she kept trying to explain this to Benny.

Franklin Pierce, whose own sorrow over the loss of his son as well as his weakness as a leader made his presidency far from successful, did his best to ease his wife's misery. Just before moving into the White House, he hired a New Hampshire hotel keeper to free the first lady from any responsibility for housekeeping details. In addition he arranged for Mrs. Pierce's most trusted relative, Mrs. Abby Means, the widow of one of her uncles, to live upstairs and look after her. Mrs. Means also filled the role of hostess whenever official gatherings were held during the troubled Pierce administration.

After leaving office in March 1857, ex-President Pierce made every possible effort to help his wife recover, even taking her on a tour of Europe with the hope that new scenery might stir new interests. Each time she returned to Concord, memories of Benny brought back her painful fantasies. She died at their New Hampshire home on December 2, 1863, at the age of fifty-seven.

Harriet Lane

"Our Democratic Queen"

Fun-loving and spirited, twenty-six-year-old Harriet Lane became White House hostess for her bachelor uncle, who called her his "mischievous romp of a niece."

In 1856 some of James Buchanan's political opponents tried to sway voters against him by singing a song that started:

> *Whoever heard in all his life*
> *Of a candidate without a wife?*

But Buchanan won the presidency anyway and became the first bachelor to hold the nation's highest office. White House social gatherings were remarkably lively during his four years there because a flirtatious young woman with golden blond hair and violet eyes served as his official hostess.

Harriet Lane was Buchanan's niece and had been under his care since the age of eleven, after the death of both her parents. Her mother had been Jane Buchanan Lane, one of the future president's sisters, and her father, Elliott Tole Lane, a Virginia merchant whose business dealings had brought him to the Pennsylvania town of Mercersburg, where the Buchanan family operated a prosperous store.

The youngest of six children, Harriet had been born in Mercersburg on May 9, 1830. Besides being a beautiful little girl, she was also blessed with a cheerful outlook. Instead of being crushed by losing her mother when she was nine and her father two years later, she herself settled the question of who should look after her from then on.

A clergyman uncle had immediately taken over and sent her to a boarding school near his Pennsylvania home. But Harriet wished that another of her relatives—her uncle James, then serving as a U.S. senator—could be her guardian, and she told various relatives that she had always been particularly fond of him. As soon as this message was relayed to him James Buchanan said he would be very pleased to assume responsibility for bringing up "this mischievous romp of a niece."

Although Harriet continued to attend boarding school for the next several years, her vacations were spent in Washington with "Nunc," as she took to calling her uncle James. No doubt part of the reason she enjoyed these interludes so much was that Nunc let her do almost anything she wanted to, without setting a lot of rules she had to obey.

As a result, when Harriet was fifteen the director of her school wrote to Secretary of State Buchanan urging him not to let her stay with him during school vacations. "You must know," she told him, "that indulgence is subversive of all discipline where she is concerned."

Instead, Buchanan took her out of that school and enrolled Harriet at a highly regarded academy on the outskirts of Washington. There girls from the capital's leading families were given a classical education and a firm training in proper behavior. Although she resisted learning to play the harp and failed to heed warnings about the dangers of flirting with young men, Harriet emerged from this school well prepared for helping her uncle socially as his career advanced.

The first major test of Harriet's ability to win friends came when at the age of twenty-three, she sailed across the Atlantic to join him in London. Although it was her uncle James who had been appointed American minister to England, it was his niece who enchanted Queen Victoria as well as her philandering son, the Prince of

Wales. Such encounters made Harriet turn down numerous suitors who wanted to marry her.

Practically ever since she had come under Nunc's wing, he had been talked of as a possible candidate for the presidency, even making several unsuccessful attempts to win the Democratic party's nomination. Although he had reached the age of sixty-five by 1856 and had begun planning for his retirement at his Pennsylvania home, how could his twenty-six-year-old niece help hoping that instead they would move into the White House?

By 1856 the country was so deeply split over the issue of slavery that many people believed a war between the North and the South was inevitable. Since James Buchanan came from the North, yet sympathized at least to a certain extent with the Southern viewpoint, he won the election. He seemed the man most likely to achieve some sort of compromise acceptable to both sides. Unfortunately this proved impossible.

Yet during the four increasingly tense years of Buchanan's administration, Harriet Lane gave the White House a gaiety and a glitter it had not known since the days of Dolley Madison. From the start, when she appeared at the inaugural ball wearing a gorgeous white satin gown and many strands of pearls, observers of the Washington social scene were awed by her. "Our Democratic Queen," they called her.

Despite the growing bitterness between Northern and Southern supporters, Harriet somehow managed to enforce her own policy forbidding political talk at the White House "frolics." Her greatest coup was to secure the presence of England's Prince of Wales at a three-day series of receptions and less formal White House parties (she even beat the prince at a bowling match before he regretfully left Washington to continue his tour of the United States).

But Harriet's years of glory were already being succeeded by years of pain by the time she and Nunc moved out of the White House on March 3, 1861. During the five months since the Republican party's candidate, Abraham Lincoln, had been elected as the next president, it had become clear that a civil war was bound to break out after he took office. Even if the failure to find any acceptable compromise could not fairly be blamed on James Buchanan alone, he—and his niece—suddenly found themselves very unpopular.

Living quietly in Pennsylvania throughout the Civil War, Harriet watched over Nunc as his health declined. For the first time she began to think seriously about finding a suitable husband. She was thirty-five, when on January 11, 1866, she married a Baltimore banker named Henry Elliott Johnston.

As Mrs. Johnston, Harriet had two sons she cherished; however, they both died when they were approaching adulthood, and their father died not long afterward. Becoming a widow in 1884, at the age of fifty-four, she moved back to Washington, then proceeded to show that her character had a more serious side than she had displayed during her younger White House years.

Having inherited substantial amounts of money from both her uncle and her husband, Harriet Johnston spent the next two decades supporting worthy causes in the capital. Her main aims were providing hospital care for needy children and expanding Washington's opportunities for appreciating works of art. Most notably her gifts of money as well as artworks that she herself had collected led toward the establishment of the Smithsonian Institution's National Collection of Fine Arts (now the National Museum of American Art).

Harriet Lane Johnston died of cancer on July 3, 1903, at the age of seventy-three, during a summer trip to Rhode Island. After her death her will left all that remained of her fortune to various charitable agencies and museums.

What Does It Mean to Be a Presidential Hostess?

*H*istorically it has been an important part of a woman's role to help advance the business or career of her husband by planning social events. These events made guests feel welcome, encouraged pleasant conversation, and built friendships. The woman who planned the event or gave the party was known as the hostess. This role was particularly important for the hostess of the president because in the nation's capital of Washington, dinners, parties, and receptions set the stage for political and diplomatic events. At these elegant social occasions politicians often had important conversations, planned political strategies, soothed the hurt feelings of their opponents, or made political deals and alliances. A politically smart wife could structure a social event to benefit her husband's political goals.

In the twentieth century, the term "first lady" has evolved into the name we use for the president's wife, but not every first lady has been the wife of the president. The term also refers to other women who served as the official hostess in the White House. In the nineteenth century it was thought improper for women to attend social gatherings with men without a hostess present. Therefore, if a president's wife died, or was ill or an invalid, or for any reason could not act as the White House hostess, the president chose another woman, usually someone from his family, to act as first lady and preside over the social life of the White House.

In the twentieth century every president's wife has lived to move into the White House with him, so all the first ladies in this century have been the wives of the presidents.

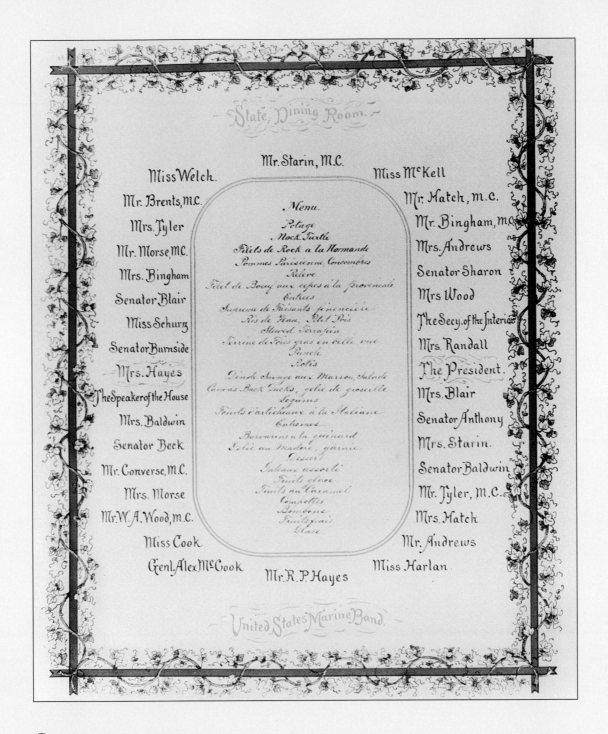

In her role as the nation's hostess, the first lady oversees the planning, preparation, and entertainment of state dinners at the White House. This beautifully elaborate seating arrangement was prepared for a state dinner during the administration of President Hayes and his wife, Lucy.

Mary Lincoln

DECEMBER 13, 1818–JULY 16, 1882

"She wishes to loom largely"

This photo of Mary Lincoln was taken by the well-known photographer Mathew Brady during Mary's White House years.

Mary Lincoln's behavior was often erratic and unstable. At times she showed a sharp temper. But those who knew her well were far more likely to pity her than to blame her, for it seemed to them that her outbursts were brought on by an ailment the medical science of their day could not cure. Over the years this opinion has come to be widely shared, with one or another illness, from diabetes to some kind of brain damage, being suggested as the underlying cause of Mrs. Lincoln's unpredictable behavior. Today, Mrs. Lincoln would probably be diagnosed as having an emotional disorder. Both she and her future husband, Abraham Lincoln, suffered deep periods of depression during their lives. It appears clear that her health must also have been affected by the exceptional series of losses she endured from the age of six onward.

She had started out seemingly blessed with good fortune. As a little girl Mary Ann Todd was bright, lively, and pretty, and belonged to one of Kentucky's leading families. Born in the young state's capital of Lexington, she was the third daughter of Robert Smith Todd, a prosperous businessman with a strong interest in politics, and Eliza Parker Todd, whose relatives were equally prominent.

At the age of six Mary suffered her first great loss. Her mother, who had borne three sons as well as four daughters, died at the age of thirty-one, shortly after giving birth to her seventh child. Being deprived of maternal love hurt such a sensitive youngster, and the stepmother who soon took over running the Todd household had neither the time nor the disposition to give Mary the special attention she craved.

Indeed, her father's second wife, Betsy Humphreys Todd, quickly began producing a second large family—eventually she had nine children. Mary's feelings as she found herself less and less noticed can be surmised from two stories her older sisters often told about her girlhood.

When Mary was only around nine, it struck her that she would surely be treated as a more important member of the family if she wore a stylish grown-up hoopskirt instead of just a child's simple muslin gown. So she secretly made wide hoops from willow branches and stretched one of her dresses over them. Then, before church one Sunday morning, she swooped downstairs in her new creation, proudly expecting to be praised for her ingenuity.

"Take those awful things off," her stepmother ordered her. So Mary had to hurriedly put on proper childish attire and pretend to join the general laughter when the tale of her homemade hoopskirt was repeatedly told from then onward.

The other story involved a visit to Senator Henry Clay, one of her father's close friends. "Mr. Clay," Mary boldly told him, "my father says you will be the next president of the United States. I wish I could go to Washington and live in the White House." Laughing, Clay assured her that if he were ever elected president, he would certainly invite her to be one of his first White House guests. Although Clay's several presidential campaigns all failed, Mary's family never forgot her remarkable early ambition.

During her growing-up years Mary seemed more absorbed by poetry and drama than by politics. She was a good student at the local academy, with such a talent for imitating the way other people talked that she often won a leading role when plays were performed. Classmates remembered her as popular and witty—except that now and then she indulged in sarcastic remarks that could cut deeply.

After six years at the academy and then another four years at a renowned boarding school nearby, Mary Todd, who had a fine mind, acquired an exceptional education for a woman of her time. (In fact, the French she learned there would later be used to charm Napoleon III at a White House dinner.) It seems that she gave some thought to becoming a teacher. However, at the age of twenty-one she went to live with a married sister in Springfield, Illinois—where she met a thirty-year-old lawyer named Abraham Lincoln.

Mary Todd and Abe Lincoln could hardly have been more different. He had begun life in a backwoods log cabin, his manners were unrefined, and he did not care a bit about many things, such as elegant clothing, that she valued very highly.

Even in their appearance they were opposites, she being short and on the plump side while he was a tall, ungainly string bean of a man. "The long and the short of it," he himself joked, but she so much disliked calling attention to the somewhat comic disparity in their size that she would never allow any photograph to be taken of the two of them standing together.

Despite their many differences, they fell in love. Mary's sister and brother-in-law, Elizabeth and Ninian Edwards (he was the son of a recent governor of Illinois), considered this country lawyer beneath their family's dignity. Maybe their disapproval had something to do with a mysterious quarrel soon after the couple decided to get married.

Whatever its cause, the dispute broke off their engagement for a year and a half. Then a month before Mary's twenty-fourth birthday, the depression that had plunged Abe into the gloomiest spell he had ever experienced was somehow lifted. On November 4, 1842, at her Springfield relatives' home, the two finally married.

The marriage undoubtedly brought them much joy. During the next decade they had four sons they both doted on: Robert, born in 1843, then Edward, William, and Thomas—fondly called Bobby, Eddie, Willie, and Tad. The Lincolns' modest but comfortable home in the Illinois state capital was the scene of many tea parties and other gatherings, with Mary earning at least local fame for being a charming hostess.

But Mary gave signs of wishing to star on a bigger stage. After her husband had served a term in the Illinois state assembly, in 1846 he was elected to the national Congress. "Mrs. L., I am told, accompanies her husband to Washington city next winter," a Springfield political figure informed his own wife. "She wishes to loom largely."

But staying at a capital boardinghouse with two little boys didn't open up any of the social opportunities Mary had hoped to enjoy, and for various political reasons her husband couldn't make much of an impression on Washington himself. Back in Springfield gossips began reporting some peculiar episodes. For instance, one morning as Lincoln emerged from his front door on his way to his law office, his wife leaned out of an upstairs window, shouting angrily—then poured a bowl of water over him.

Despite such tales of her temper, many of those who knew the couple thought that Mary was in part responsible for Abe's political rise. Referring to him always as Mr. Lincoln, she made no secret of her belief in his future fame. She constantly gave him encouragement in his political career, and prodded him to run for higher public office. When he told her that he couldn't run for higher office because nobody knew who he was, she kept assuring him: "They soon will."

In 1850 Mary had to endure the death from lung disease of her four-year-old son Eddie. She then gave birth to her two younger boys within the next few years. Despite being increasingly subject to migraine headaches, she kept urging her husband onward.

As disagreement about the issue of slavery grew more and more intense all over the country, in Illinois the new Republican party chose a practically unknown small-town lawyer as its candidate for U.S. senator in 1858. Although Abraham Lincoln lost that election, his stirring speeches during a series of debates with his Democratic opponent, Stephen A. Douglas, attracted wide attention. Two years later, amid mounting talk of outright war between the North and the South, he ran for the nation's highest post.

When word of his presidential victory reached the Springfield telegraph office, Lincoln rushed home. "Mary, Mary," he called out, "*we* are elected." Regarding his wife, a neighbor reported: "She is in fine spirits!"

At the beginning Mary Lincoln made a very favorable impression on newspaper writers, who described her as "especially gracious" and capable of "brilliant flashes of wit." Yet her powerful drive to shine in the White House prevented her from realizing that the outbreak of the Civil War meant she must modify her plans and convey an appropriate image. When Mary spent many afternoons visiting wounded soldiers at Washington hospitals, she did so without any reporters' notice. During her frequent shopping expeditions to New York, however, newspaper accounts of the expensive sets of dishes and elaborate gowns that she purchased spread the idea that she had no proper sense of wartime restraint. She was often ridiculed by the Washington social set as uncouth and unrefined because she was

Mary Lincoln (third from right) tried to dispel the idea that she was an unrefined "frontier woman" through her skill as a hostess. This painting illustrates a reception given by the Lincolns to honor General Ulysses S. Grant.

from the "frontier." In fact, she was neither, though she did flaunt her taste and social skills.

More troubling was Mary's great need to show her political influence by trying to secure government jobs for the husbands and brothers of her friends. Because she had been born in a state with strong Southern leanings and several of her relatives were actually fighting to defeat the Union army, the rumor that President Lincoln's wife was a traitor and a spy for the Confederacy popped up repeatedly.

Another horrible loss further diminished her ability to control her outbursts of temper. In 1862 her eleven-year-old son, Willie, died at the White House, probably of typhoid fever. Doctors of the day could not diagnose or cure his sudden illness, nor could they relieve the fearful headaches his mother suffered ever more frequently thereafter.

Probably it was under the stress of these attacks that Mary Lincoln gave several public displays of her temper. Then came the fateful evening in 1865, shortly after the war ended, when she accompanied her husband to Washington's Ford's Theater—and sat beside him holding his hand when he was fatally shot.

Lincoln's assassination left his wife totally shattered. So consumed by her grief, she would not leave her darkened room upstairs at the White House for more than a month. She refused even to consider returning to her Springfield home because she could not bear being reminded of happier days. When she finally realized that she must let new President Andrew Johnson move into the executive mansion, she miserably departed for Chicago.

By then her eldest son, Robert, had begun studying law in Chicago after having graduated from Harvard. His mother took up residence at a shabby hotel near his law school with twelve-year-old Tad, a boy with a loving nature on whom she depended as if he were a grown man. She started behaving so shockingly that she soon lost the sympathy of many people who might otherwise have felt very sorry for her.

Money was the root of her new series of troubles. She was obsessed by the irrational thought that she was now in dire poverty. Abraham Lincoln had left a reasonable sum to his widow, but while he had been so occupied with his wartime duties, her compulsive shopping had rung up thousands of dollars of debts he had not known about. Mary plunged into one bizarre scheme after another so she could pay her bills and also live in the grandiose style she believed she deserved.

She hired aides to beg for donations from rich Republicans, and she even arranged with a shady firm of auctioneers to put trunkfuls of her own expensive gowns on sale. Newspaper stories headlined OLD CLOTHES SCANDAL made most Americans shudder at the financial panic that a president's wife displayed.

The process of mourning the death of a loved one was quite elaborate in the nineteenth century, and women often wore special clothing and jewelry for the first few years of widowhood. This lapel watch was a piece of mourning jewelry belonging to Mary Lincoln.

Such a furor arose over this episode that she took Tad to Europe, hoping to escape any further painful publicity and her tormenting memories. While they were abroad, some loyal friends in Washington kept striving to convince members of Congress that the widow of a murdered president was as much entitled to a government pension as the widow of any soldier who had died in battle. In 1870 a bill granting Mrs. Lincoln $3,000 a year was finally passed.

Mary sailed home the following year in a more hopeful frame of mind. But only a month after she and Tad returned, this son on whom she depended so much became seriously ill. He died at the age of eighteen—and his mother could not cope with still another loss.

For the next four years she wandered from one town to another, distractedly going on buying sprees. Desperately convinced that she had no money, she carried thousands of dollars worth of bonds she had inherited sewn into pockets of her petticoats. At least where money was concerned, she behaved so irrationally that her remaining son finally took a drastic step.

Fearing for his mother's safety and health, in 1875 Robert asked a Chicago court to declare his mother legally insane. Then on the basis of testimony from a panel of doctors, Mary Lincoln was confined in a private hospital. After only three months there, though, she hired a woman lawyer—one of the few in the country—to represent and defend her, and thus cleverly engineered her own release. After winning this fight, her sister and brother-in-law offered her a place in their Springfield home.

The stigma of having been labeled a lunatic distressed Mary so deeply that again she tried escaping to Europe. She spent another four years there before returning because she had become nearly blind and was too weak to manage any longer on her own.

On July 16, 1882, Mary Lincoln died at her sister's home at the age of sixty-three.

Part III

The Post–Civil War Era, the Age of Reform, and World War I
1865–1920

*A*fter the Civil War, Americans began the work of rebuilding their nation. Directed by Congress, Northern soldiers occupied the defeated states of the South. A strict set of guidelines was established for Confederate states to reenter the Union. The country was still deeply divided during this period, which has come to be called the Reconstruction.

The Thirteenth, Fourteenth, and Fifteenth Amendments to the Constitution freed slaves, made all African Americans citizens, and gave black men the right to vote. At a stroke, more than 1.9 million black women were added to the paid job force. African Americans eagerly sought opportunities to farm their land, educate their families, and take control of their lives. Some blacks were elected to Congress and to the legislature in Southern states. But many of these gains proved to be temporary. After 1876, when federal troops were withdrawn, white men's control in the South was imposed with ever greater force. They passed laws strictly enforcing the separation of blacks and whites in public. This was called segregation.

The first, often bravest, and most vocal speaker against the rise of segregation was the African-American author Ida Wells-Barnett. She wrote a book about the horrors of lynching called *A Red Record*. Another forthright author, Helen Hunt Jackson, made Americans aware of how they had treated the people who had first lived on the continent. Her *Century of Dishonor* was published in 1881 and showed that a hundred years of liberty for white Americans had brought an equal period of deception and losses to Native Americans. Even as people read her work, though,

Religious persecution and poverty in their homelands, plus the lure of jobs in America, drew millions of immigrants to the United States. Between 1890 and 1924, about twenty-three million people immigrated to this country from European countries, including Russia, Poland, Italy, and Greece. The port of New York alone admitted seventeen million people. This photograph shows hundreds of immigrants tightly packed together aboard ship as they arrived to be processed at Ellis Island in New York City.

federal troops were forcing the last Native nations onto reservations. This mixture of new ideas and remarkable national growth with disturbing internal conflict continued throughout the remainder of the nineteenth century.

In the years after the Civil War, more and more of the American economy came to center on factories, on ever larger corporations, on the trains that brought goods to the cities, and on the magnificent department stores in which they were displayed. The new economy gave some women a chance to take on new kinds of jobs in offices and stores. On the other hand, strikes, labor conflicts, and angry demonstrations over workers' rights became ever more frequent.

Running the machines in the factories, doing piecework at home, laboring in the most difficult and poorest-paying jobs were immigrants. In the 1850s and 1860s, Irish immigrants arrived in especially large numbers. Irish women continued to work, often as domestic servants, while most middle-class women confined themselves to family life. The pace of immigration continued to grow exponentially in the 1880s and 1890s. Chinese men, many of whom had been brought to America to help build the great railroads, were not allowed to bring equal numbers of women to join them. The new wave of immigrants at the turn of the century came from Central and Southern Europe and included large numbers of Italians and Jews. Arriving here with little money and few skills, they had to learn a new language and a new way of life. As a result, many lived in the worst parts of cities under terrible conditions.

Established women realized that these social problems were affecting their homes and families. How could they continue to watch over the health, safety, and education of their children if they had no say in the laws that governed their lives? Many women from different races and ethnic groups, the rich, the middle class, and the workers proposed reforms to deal with these problems.

Some women started "settlement houses," community centers that brought services to the poor and to immigrants in cities and communities across the country. The settlements got their name because reformers, mostly women but also some famous reform men, "settled" or lived in the neighborhoods they served.

Settlement workers taught the English language to immigrants; provided health services and job training; trained public health nurses to care for the sick and the poor; and organized recreational dances, singing groups, plays, and crafts. They set up girls' clubs and boys' clubs and often represented the immigrants in their dealings with the city or state authorities. They started day-care centers for working mothers whose long hours in the factory took them away from home, and began kindergartens and playgrounds so children could learn and have safe places to play while their parents worked. Settlement workers gathered facts on wages and living

These young girls in a textile mill were like thousands of children who worked to support themselves or their families. Their meager earnings were a crucial part of the income of many immigrant families in farming, mining, and textile communities, yet child labor set a lifelong pattern of poverty, illiteracy, and poor health. The National Child Labor Committee worked for laws to abolish child labor, but the Supreme Court ruled the laws unconstitutional. A child-labor amendment failed. Reformers were more successful in passing compulsory attendance laws to keep children in the public schools. Finally, in the 1930s, New Deal laws ended child labor in many industries.

conditions, on illnesses, and on long work hours and low wages—presenting them to lawmakers so conditions could be improved. These activities created the new profession of social work for women.

Both immigrant and wealthy women came together to work for labor reform— forming women's unions to demand better wages, safe working conditions, and shorter hours. Wealthy women often provided money to support working women when they went out on strike; many walked with them in picket lines. Some working women rose to powerful leadership positions in the labor movement and became organizers of women's unions.

Women did not limit their reform efforts to the problems of immigrants. In the 1880s and 1890s, many joined women's clubs to improve themselves and their communities. They studied social problems, gathered statistics, lobbied the government, and petitioned for changes. Women's club members understood that because so many aspects of their homes and families were controlled by laws, if they were serious about change, they needed the right to vote.

In the 1890s women's clubs across the country joined to create powerful national groups: the General Federation of Women's Clubs, the National Association of Colored Women's Clubs, and the National Council of Jewish Women. These associations gave women great power to lobby for causes both in their states and in Congress.

Other women took up the problem of alcoholism, which was destroying many homes and families. They joined the temperance movement, led by Frances Willard, and worked for laws to end the manufacture and sale of liquor.

The number of women attending college and earning professional degrees increased in the 1870s and 1880s. Exceptional women enlarged the scope of women's achievements. Elizabeth Blackwell, the first woman doctor, opened a hospital for women in New York where they could train to be physicians. Belva Lockwood, the first woman lawyer to practice before the Supreme Court, won landmark cases and also ran for the presidency as a minority-party candidate in 1884 and 1888. Victoria Woodhull was the first woman stockbroker and the first to testify before a congressional committee. Maria Mitchell, the first woman astronomer, became a professor at Vassar College.

Many highly educated women wanted to elevate housework and the care of home and family to the level of a profession—much like the professions of men. College-educated women became professors in the new field of home economics, which created career opportunities for women as teachers, dieticians, and consultants and cooks in test kitchens. They promoted the study of science and nutrition so that women could better care for their families. They lobbied for pure food and drug laws and were the first to study the environment and to develop tests for clean water and air.

In addition, they stressed the need for wives to be educated consumers and promoted "consumers' leagues" that urged women to buy from manufacturers whose products delivered what they advertised and who didn't take advantage of women and children workers. They encouraged women to boycott products from manufacturers who didn't earn the "seal of approval." The consumer movement, with its concerns for consumer product safety and testing, had its start with the home economics movement in the 1890s.

While women were undertaking all of these reform activities, they did not neglect their own cause. Disappointed and angered that their support of freedom for the slaves during the Civil War had not been rewarded with the right to vote, many women continued to work for that goal. Four states in the West granted voting rights to women in state elections, but most Americans were still not ready for women to be active in politics. Suffrage groups continued to educate the public and gain support. In 1890 the groups merged to form the National American Woman Suffrage Association. NAWSA, as it was known, became a large and powerful group by the time of World War I, with a membership of more than two and a half million. After strong lobbying by women, the Nineteenth Amendment was finally passed by Congress, then ratified by two thirds of the states in 1920. Women had finally won the vote.

World War I created new job opportunities for women. When the United States entered the war, thousands of men left to serve as soldiers in Europe, and thousands of women filled their jobs. More than one hundred thousand women worked in defense industries. This 1919 photograph shows a young woman assembling gas masks for the armed forces at the Goodrich Rubber Company.

With the outbreak of World War I, women took a step further into public life. They joined the armed forces as nurses, supported war bond drives to raise money, worked in factories to produce goods for the war, and served on Women's War Work committees.

The first ladies of this period reflected the changing times. Lucy Hayes was the first college-educated first lady; Frances Cleveland hostessed teas for working women; Helen Taft and Edith Wilson both were political partners with their husbands. Each woman in her own way reflected the many paths women were taking toward greater participation in public life. As women took a more active role in reforming society, improving social conditions, and educating Americans, their eyes also turned to government and politics. Their collective power could not be ignored.

Eliza Johnson

OCTOBER 4, 1810–JANUARY 15, 1876

"I do not like this public life at all"

*M*arried at sixteen, Eliza Johnson taught her husband writing and arithmetic. This portrait of her was painted in 1961, from a photograph taken during her White House years.

*L*egend has it that Eliza Johnson taught her husband how to read and write soon after they got married. Otherwise, she is one of the nation's least-known first ladies. Even while she lived in the White House, she stayed out of the public eye to such an extent that a Washington writer reported: "Her very existence is a myth to almost every one."

Weak health was given as the reason the wife of President Andrew Johnson hardly ever left her own room—off and on, through much of her life, she had flare-ups of tuberculosis. This, coupled with an unwillingness to play a role she did not feel at all qualified for, had much to do with her remaining upstairs at the executive mansion.

Certainly Eliza was a quiet woman in no way prepared to become the capital's social leader. She had lived most of her life in the village of Greeneville, in the mountains of eastern Tennessee, where she had been born on October 4, 1810. The daughter of a shoemaker named John McCardle, who died during her girlhood, she grew up without any luxuries, if not in outright poverty.

Eliza spent several terms at a local school, but when she entered her teens she was obliged to stay home to help her mother, Sarah Phillips McCardle. Together they supported themselves by sewing quilts as well as a type of cloth-topped sandal her father had formerly made.

Not very long afterward, on May 17, 1827, sixteen-and-a-half-year-old Eliza married Andrew Johnson, who was just eighteen. He came from an even less prosperous background in North Carolina, and at fourteen he had been apprenticed to learn the tailoring trade. Some difficulty with the tailor he worked for spurred him to walk over the mountains into the state of Tennessee, where he couldn't be compelled by law to complete his apprenticeship.

Still, as he had to earn his living, he began plying his trade in the Greeneville area. He and Eliza started their life together in the back room of a two-room house there—the front room was his tailor shop. When he entered politics, Andy Johnson liked to tell audiences about his early hardships, and he often said that his wife had played an important role in educating him, teaching him how to write and reading to him while he sewed.

Outgoing and ambitious, Andy soon started running for local and then state and national offices. While his duties as a lawmaker took him to Nashville or Washington for months at a time, Eliza stayed in Greeneville taking care of their children—she had a daughter, Martha, the year after her marriage, followed by Charles, Mary, Robert, and finally Andrew Junior.

Only the Civil War caused Eliza to leave her familiar surroundings. Because some of the people of Tennessee felt a strong bond with the new Southern Confederacy, whereas others just as strongly favored the Union cause, controversy over the state's allegiance made it a major battleground. By this time Eliza's health had become very uncertain. Then, during the second year of the war, her husband's position required her to embark on a difficult and dangerous journey.

At the outbreak of the fighting, in 1861, Andrew Johnson had been serving as one of Tennessee's senators in Washington. His continued loyalty to the Union led President Lincoln, the following year, to appoint him military governor of

Tennessee—in charge of preserving law and order in areas of the state under Union control.

But Greeneville lay within the territory claimed by the Confederates. As the wife of a Union leader, Eliza was informed that her personal safety could not be guaranteed unless she left her home and joined her husband in Nashville. To travel across the state would not have been easy for a woman as frail as she was even in peacetime, but having to make her way through shifting battle lines turned the trip into a terrible ordeal.

Two years later, when President Lincoln ran for a second term, the war was still being fought, and for political reasons the Republican party accepted Andrew Johnson as its candidate for vice president, despite some doubts about his commitment to its aims. Then, hardly more than a month after Lincoln was reelected, on April 15, 1865, he died from an assassin's bullet.

Nobody recorded the feelings of Johnson's wife on being told that her husband, under such tragic circumstances, had suddenly become president of the United States. Since Eliza never had accompanied Andy to Washington during his sixteen years as a congressman or senator, she probably would have stayed in Tennessee throughout his vice presidency. After his unexpected elevation, though, she couldn't avoid making new plans.

While Lincoln's grief-stricken widow lingered at the White House, Eliza had time to think about the problems her own new status posed. No doubt the many critical newspaper stories about Mary Lincoln's behavior as first lady must have further strengthened Eliza's desire to avoid any such publicity herself.

She finally arrived in Washington without the least bit of ceremony, and her poor health excused her from assuming any responsibility for White House entertaining. Fortunately her daughter Martha—by then the wife of Tennessee's Senator David T. Patterson—proved a very acceptable substitute.

At the first gathering that Martha supervised, her capable and yet unassuming manner won general approval. "We are plain people from the mountains of Tennessee, called here for a short time by a calamity," she told her White House guests. "I trust too much will not be expected of us."

During the next several years Martha was sometimes assisted by her widowed sister, Mary. Meanwhile, their mother stayed upstairs sewing and reading and enjoying frequent visits from members of her family. In her corner room right above the room where her husband conducted his official business, she also seems to have kept in very close touch with him.

Although this couple had such different personalities and they had often been

separated by his public duties, it appears that they still felt extremely fond of each
other. Every morning as well as every evening, Andy made a point of sitting with
Eliza, talking over everything going on in the capital. Despite almost never leaving
her room, she too had news to impart.

Eliza regularly clipped articles from the leading newspapers and magazines to
paste into scrapbooks she kept. Her children later recalled that she had a canny way
of trying to ensure that her husband didn't lie awake nights worrying over his
mounting political troubles. When he visited her at the end of each working day,
she would show him only the favorable stories she had clipped—and reserve the
unfavorable ones for his visit the next morning, right after breakfast.

Only twice in the nearly four years that Eliza lived at the White House did she
attend any gathering downstairs. Once she broke her rule about not meeting any
strangers to greet visiting Queen Emma of Hawaii. The other occasion was a "ball"
for children arranged by Martha to celebrate her father's sixtieth birthday. It was
then that Eliza spoke a few words to President Johnson's bodyguard, W. H. Crook,
which he later included in a book he wrote.

"Crook," she said, "it's all very well for those who like it—but I do not like this
public life at all. I often wish the time would come when we could return to where
I feel we best belong."

Andrew Johnson's presidency was beset with conflict. Throughout Johnson's administration, he and the Congress quarreled bitterly over the policies of Reconstruction. Although he was a Republican and the Congress was dominated by Republicans, Johnson took a more lenient approach to readmitting the former Southern Confederate states to the Union, and he pardoned many former leaders of the rebel cause. His actions infuriated many in Congress, who wanted the army to occupy former Confederate states and govern them as if they were conquered territory. Congress also wanted to change the political and social structure of the South by granting citizenship to African Americans, establishing their right to vote and installing them in political power.

Constant clashes between the president and Congress caused the legislature to bring charges against him in an attempt to remove him from office, a course of action called impeachment. Although Johnson was charged with violating the laws that Congress had passed, his trial by the Senate failed to convict him—by just one vote! He remained president and served out his term of office.

Eliza Johnson and her family must have been very relieved that the trial was over and that her husband could continue his presidency until his term ended.

In March 1869, shortly after the inauguration of President Ulysses S. Grant, the Johnsons went back to Greeneville. As far as Eliza was concerned, her husband had more than earned a peaceful retirement, surrounded by their children and grandchildren. But his combative nature craved a more decisive victory over his political enemies, so he kept trying to win back a seat in Congress, and in 1875 he once more became a U.S. senator.

He died of a stroke only a few months later, however, while he and Eliza were visiting their daughter Mary near Greeneville. Six months afterward, sixty-five-year-old Eliza suffered a similar collapse, and she too died at Mary's house, on January 15, 1876.

Julia Grant

JANUARY 26, 1826–DECEMBER 14, 1902

"She enjoyed her presidential life"

Julia Grant called her years at the White House "quite the happiest period of my life."

Julia Grant always remembered her childhood as "one long summer of sunshine, flowers, and smiles." Picturing herself as rather like a little princess, she grew up cheerfully, expecting that someday she would become a queen.

So it happened that right after her husband, Ulysses S. Grant, was sworn in as president of the United States, he turned toward her and took her hand. "And now, my dear," he said quietly, "I hope you're satisfied."

Julia certainly was.

"She enjoyed her presidential life, and good-naturedly said so," a White House visitor reported. Her frankness disarmed even people who might otherwise have been tempted to make fun of her.

Julia's own romantic notions about herself were not quite justified—she really lacked some major qualifications for presiding over Washington society during the period following the Civil War, when the nation's capital was becoming an increasingly sophisticated city.

Yet her early years had truly been almost as perfect as she recalled. Born at a comfortable country home in Missouri, about ten miles from St. Louis, on January 26, 1826, Julia was the fifth child of Frederick Dent and Ellen Wrenshall Dent. She was their first daughter, so she grew up accustomed to being especially cherished by her parents and her four older brothers, even after she had two younger sisters as well as another brother.

Julia was born with a minor but very noticeable birth defect involving her right eye, which moved constantly up and down without her being able to control it. Perhaps partly for this reason Julia's family showered her with extra affection.

And Julia amply returned their love. "My gentle, beautiful mother and noble father, of whom I was *so* proud," she wrote about them when she told the story of her own life in her old age. However, her glowing description of her father as a rich Maryland gentleman who had chosen to operate a Southern-style plantation in Missouri was not exactly accurate, nor did she actually have an aristocratic Southern belle girlhood.

Although Frederick Dent could indeed trace his ancestry back to early Maryland settlers, his own branch of the family had moved two generations earlier to Pennsylvania. Achieving some success in various business ventures there, he had been able to buy a Missouri farm that vastly disappointed his Pennsylvania-born wife because it was so isolated. The Dents' farm was run by the dozen black slaves they had brought with them to White Haven.

Julia went to a rude log cabin school near her home until she was eleven. Then she spent six winters at a boarding school in St. Louis, where she was not a very diligent student. Outdoor pursuits interested her much more than books did—she was a fearless horseback rider and adored going fishing.

Julia was free to accompany her brothers on their outings, perhaps because she knew that she was referred to as the plainest of the Dent sisters. Sturdy rather than graceful, she also had the handicap of her eye defect. It probably came as a surprise to those who judged her by her appearance that when she was eighteen and her brother Fred invited a fellow army officer to spend his leave at White Haven, she easily won the visitor's heart.

*J*ulia Grant (fourth from left) reportedly decided to venture into the Big Bonanza Silver Mine in Nevada after hearing that her husband had bet she would be afraid to go.

Lieutenant Ulysses S. Grant, a graduate of West Point who was four years older than Julia, came from a singularly unaffectionate Ohio family. Her warmth and lively ways immediately captivated him, and she too fell in love almost at first sight. However, Julia's father opposed any talk of marriage because he believed that his daughter couldn't stand the hardships of living as a military wife at remote army posts.

Finally, four years after the couple began considering themselves engaged, this parental opposition melted. Julia married Ulys, as she always called him, on August 22, 1848, at her family's home. By that time, Lieutenant Grant had displayed exceptional courage during the Mexican War. In the peacetime army, however, promotions came only rarely and his prospects for being able to support his wife comfortably seemed far from promising.

Their marriage proved to be exceptionally happy—despite a very trying series of difficulties during its first dozen years. The Grants had four children in quick succession: Frederick, Ulysses Junior, Ellen, and Jesse. Then the army sent Ulys to Alaska, where Julia couldn't accompany him. Separated from his family, he developed a serious drinking problem. In 1854, at the age of thirty-two, he resigned from the army with the rank of captain and had to seek some other occupation that would enable him to support his family.

His attempt to become a farmer on land owned by Julia's father failed. So did a business venture in St. Louis. Then Ulys had to beg a job from his own father, a domineering man he had never been able to get along with. Jesse Grant operated a chain of harness shops, and in 1860 he hired his son as a clerk at his store in the town of Galena, Illinois.

This was the low point in the life of Ulys and Julia. Though they shared the simple tastes of the ordinary people who were now their neighbors, the Grants also shared a strong belief that they were destined to rise above their circumstances. So the following year, when the Civil War broke out, the former Captain Grant unhesitatingly put on his uniform again.

Rapidly promoted because the Union Army urgently needed experienced officers, Ulys was a general by early 1862. He showed a great gift for improvising victorious battle plans in Tennessee and Mississippi. But rumors that he was an alcoholic began to spread. These were followed by another rumor about one very effective way to keep him sober: It was said that the officers on his staff sent for his wife to join him at his camp whenever he started giving in to alcohol, and her presence immediately ended the danger.

How much truth there was to such tales has never been definitely established, but Julia did visit her husband on the battlefield more often than most other officers' wives did. She deserves at least some of the credit for his advancement to top commander of all the Union forces. Certainly nobody could have been happier than she was when the South's General Robert E. Lee surrendered to her husband on April 9, 1865.

By this time Julia had often been reminded of a fact of American history: From George Washington onward, military heroes had been elected to the office of president of the United States. Thus, wasn't it likely that at the earliest possible opportunity, the victorious General Grant—and his wife—would move into the White House?

Julia and Ulys certainly didn't discourage talk along these lines. While he supervised the disbanding of the Union Army from a desk in Washington during the next few years, she absorbed as much information as she could about the capital's social life. During the presidential election year 1868, they returned to their humble home in Galena to await being summoned back triumphantly.

When word came, Julia felt ready. Realizing that she would need constant guidance in the proper social etiquette to keep her from impulsively speaking or acting in ways not befitting a first lady, she cultivated the friendship of a New York society leader whose husband was going to be her husband's secretary of state. Mrs. Hamilton Fish willingly accepted the role of unofficial adviser to President Grant's wife.

Julia made no secret of this arrangement. "In matters pertaining to good sense and fine tact, I rely upon Mrs. Fish," she openly admitted. By not pretending to be anybody but herself, she won wide approval, even from the sort of people who might otherwise have judged her severely.

Julia's frank delight in all her new experiences struck sophisticated Washington as refreshing. Her obvious pleasure at finding herself associating with the nation's richest as well as its most famous figures also gave countless ordinary folk the feeling that she was one of them.

Although the Grants had very little money in the early years of their marriage, Julia Grant (seated at left) created a warm and lively family life that captivated the public while they were in the White House.

When Julia arranged an enormously showy White House wedding for her daughter, the whole country relished reading about it. When she gave gala dinner parties featuring as many as twenty-nine different courses, no outcry arose about such elaborate feasts. Julia's informal manner made her seem like a neighbor who had suddenly come into a fortune.

Yet during the eight-year period when Julia and her husband lived in the White House, there were numerous scandals involving the corruption of high government officials. Despite evidence that both of the Grants had shown poor judgment in their choice of unscrupulous friends, they both remained very popular. The idea of electing the general to a third term appealed to many people—including Julia herself.

Much to her disappointment, her husband refused to run again. Without any home to return to—they had sold their small house in Galena soon after leaving it—Julia broke down in tears as they were departing from the White House. "Oh, Ulys," she commented, "I feel like a waif."

Because they had never previously been able to take any vacation, they soon embarked on a glorious round-the-world tour lasting over two years. Treated like visiting royalty wherever she went, Julia chatted companionably with England's Queen Victoria, rode sidesaddle on a donkey to see ancient Egyptian temples, sailed up the Yangtze River in China—and, back in the American West, even descended into a deep silver mine before they finally concluded their trip.

There were those who surmised that the much-publicized journey had really been a clever ploy to keep General Grant's name before the public so that he would be drafted in 1872 to serve a third term in the White House after all. But that did not happen.

When it became clear that his political career had really ended, Julia and Ulys took up residence in New York amid the rich friends they had made while in the White House. There Ulysses Grant lent his name to an investment scheme, and for a time they had all the money they could wish. Then the unsound scheme collapsed; they lost all their money. In failing health, Ulys doggedly began writing his own account of his Civil War campaigns to earn enough for his wife to live on after his death.

He barely finished his memoirs before succumbing to cancer in 1885. Julia lived as a wealthy woman for another seventeen years, supported by the $450,000 income from her husband's book—a surprise best-seller. She was consoled by her children and grandchildren and later wrote her own romanticized memories, which were published in 1975 as *The Personal Memoirs of Julia Dent Grant*. At the comfortable home she had bought herself in Washington, she died on December 14, 1902, when she was seventy-six.

Lucy Hayes

"Everything looks bright and cheerful"

Lucy Hayes became a symbol for women reformers, and the Woman's Christian Temperance Union honored her with this portrait.

Lucy Hayes is remembered as "Lemonade Lucy" because no wine or other liquor was served at the White House while she lived there. The first first lady to have graduated from college, the wife of Rutherford B. Hayes was a staunch supporter of her husband's political and moral convictions. As the question of whether alcoholic beverages should be banned was becoming a major political issue during

117

this period, it was her dear "Ruddy" who actually set the controversial policy forbidding them in the executive mansion.

Lucy's upbringing and her religious convictions made her a supporter of temperance, the anti-drinking movement. Born in Chillicothe, Ohio, the young state's original capital, on August 28, 1831, she was the daughter of two early temperance advocates.

Lucy's father, James Webb, had been a Kentucky rifleman during the War of 1812; then he studied medicine and began practicing his profession in Chillicothe. There he met and married Maria Cook, from one of the town's most prominent families. Her father, Judge Isaac Cook, was a leader in the new temperance movement whose enthusiasm for the cause made him sign up even his infant grandchildren.

James and Maria had two sons, then their little girl. But when Lucy was only two years old, her father went back to Kentucky to free the slaves he had inherited. He fell ill and died during a cholera epidemic. Isaac Cook took over James's role as Lucy's father; her very religious and very loving grandfather Cook had a great influence over her childhood.

She would always recall being taken to temperance lectures while she was still a little girl. She also learned early that it would be unseemly for a woman ever to speak up in favor of any type of reform. In her world, girls were valued more for the sweetness of their tempers than the strength of their minds.

While attending the Chillicothe Female School, though, Lucy showed that she wouldn't be stopped from protesting injustice. One day when her young cousin Joe came along with her, the strict teacher, Miss Baskerville, imagined that he had misbehaved behind her back. She began hitting him with the stick she kept for punishing such wrongdoing.

Lucy jumped up, another student would recall many years later, and defended Joe with such vigor that Miss Baskerville stopped, then with a sarcastic remark, but no further corporal punishment, sent both Lucy and her visiting cousin home for the rest of the day.

At the age of thirteen, she wasn't sorry to see the last of Miss Baskerville. Because Lucy's mother wanted her sons to have the advantage of a higher education, in 1844 she moved north with her three children to the town of Delaware, where Ohio Wesleyan University, a Methodist school, had recently been established. A preparatory department was operated under the same Methodist sponsorship, and Lucy enrolled there, also sitting in on a few of the college classes, to which young women were not officially admitted at the time.

At church, Lucy's mother had become very friendly with a like-minded widow whose only son was an upstanding student at Harvard Law School—and the two women soon decided that their offspring would make a fine match. Lucy heard a lot about Rutherford B. Hayes before she ever saw him.

She was fifteen and he was twenty-four when they finally were introduced. In his diary Ruddy noted at last encountering the young lady his mother had picked out for him: "A bright sunny hearted little girl not quite old enough to fall in love with—and so I didn't." However, just a few years later, while Lucy was attending Cincinnati's Wesleyan Female College and he was starting to make his mark as a lawyer in the same city, he wrote about her in another diary entry:

> Her low sweet voice is very winning, her soft rich eyes not often equalled, a heart as true as steel, I know. . . . Intellect she has too, a quick, sprightly one. . . . It is no use doubting or rolling it over in my thoughts. By George! I am in love with her!

As to Lucy herself, she vastly enjoyed her three years at the college, from which she graduated in June 1850 when she was almost twenty. She became a symbol of the college-educated "new woman" at the latter part of the nineteenth century. Yet few options were open to her beyond becoming a wife and mother. Although she had numerous other suitors, she felt that none could compare—and, much to the satisfaction of all concerned, she and Ruddy were married at her mother's Cincinnati home on December 30, 1852.

A more successful marriage would be hard to find. Despite the sorrow of losing three babies in their infancies, over the years Lucy had five other children she and her husband both cherished: Birchard, Webb, Rutherford, Fanny, and Scott. Even the Civil War didn't bring this very happy family any severe troubles, although Ruddy's strong anti-slavery views made him enlist as an officer in a regiment of Ohio volunteers early in the fighting.

Lucy visited his camps several times during lulls between battles, bringing their young sons with her. As her husband rose to become a major general, his wife's many kindnesses to the men he commanded won her the title of "Mother Hayes." She sewed their torn shirts, wrote letters for those who had never had much schooling, and spent many hours comforting wounded soldiers.

By the time the war ended, General Hayes decided to run for one of Ohio's seats in the national House of Representatives. Having already held some lesser offices while practicing law in Cincinnati, he easily won election. Then a few years later he became his state's governor.

Lucy very much enjoyed being "the governor's lady." Besides carrying out the traditional social duties connected with her position, she played a leading part in some of the public-spirited activities women of her background were beginning to sponsor. As her husband put it in a letter to one of their sons away at college, Lucy was employing herself "about the soldiers' orphans . . . about the decoration of soldiers' graves and about the deaf and dumb pupils at the reform school for boys."

Forty-five years old in 1877, when she moved into the White House, Lucy still had her two youngest children under her wing—Fanny was nine then, and Scott six. Without any grown daughters of her own to help her greet guests, she invited a constant stream of nieces and daughters of friends to serve as her unofficial assistants.

Following their longtime pattern, President Hayes and his wife expected all these young people to assemble daily for morning and evening prayers, as well as hymn singing every Sunday night. Many Americans had been distressed by the showiness of White House entertaining during the eight years the Grants had lived there— a time that was known as "the Gilded Age." They were still more distressed by numerous disclosures of corruption among high governmental aides and felt relieved that the first family was now setting a wholesome example for the rest of the country.

Because of her widespread popularity, some of Lucy's college classmates, and even her own relatives, urged Lucy to join them in demanding new rights for women, especially the right to vote. "You are the representative of the *women* of our country," one old friend wrote to her. She was appealing to Lucy to try to influence her husband in favor of woman suffrage, the movement to give women the right to vote.

But even if Lucy personally approved of some of the goals of the women's rights movement, she was firm in her belief that wives should not influence their husbands on any matter involving politics. Although she graciously showed a group of suffrage leaders through the White House, she refused to say a single word publicly about her own stand on the issue.

Instead of brooding about the severe political storms afflicting Washington in the aftermath of the Civil War, Lucy remained optimistic. After one of her husband's rare victories over a rebellious Congress, she gave a good example of her ability to emphasize the positive. "Everything looks bright and cheerful," she wrote to one of her sons.

Nevertheless, Lucy was more than glad to leave the pressures of Washington behind her. As her husband had pledged for political reasons that he would serve only one term, in 1881 the Hayes family happily retired to their handsome home on the outskirts of the northern Ohio town of Fremont.

When Lucy Hayes ordered a new state dinner service for the White House, she requested that the china makers create something distinctly American by using native plants and animals as decoration. The result was a service unlike any that had been seen before.

Lucy busied herself with many charitable and church activities, and she even broke one of her own rules about accepting any office that would require her to speak at a public meeting. As president of the Methodist Woman's Home Missionary Society, she very capably addressed delegates attending the group's annual convention, and year after year they insisted on reelecting her.

Eight years after moving out of the White House, Lucy suffered a slight stroke while attending church. As she was only fifty-seven years old, doctors hoped she would recover completely. However, just a few weeks later, while she was seated by a bay window sewing and watching her children playing tennis on the lawn outside, she had a much more severe attack. She died a few days later, on June 25, 1889, two months before she would have marked her fifty-eighth birthday.

Lucy's devoted husband mourned her deeply until his own death three and a half years afterward.

What Role Did Women Play in the Temperance Movement?

Alcoholism was a major social problem in America in the nineteenth century. Most women depended on a husband's wages for economic support because they did not work outside the home as they do today. If a woman was married to an alcoholic husband, it threatened the very heart of her home and family.

After hearing a series of stirring sermons against the evils of alcohol by a preacher in Hillsboro, Ohio, in 1873, many women left their homes, took to the streets, and began direct actions against saloons. Praying in protest and singing hymns, women became a familiar sight at liquor establishments throughout the Midwest as they went about what they called "the work of the Lord." Some women took more daring action, dragging barrels of whiskey into the streets and breaking them apart with axes. The protest spread to other parts of the country.

Women banded together at first to persuade people to renounce the use of alcohol voluntarily, a movement called temperance. While giving up alcohol on one's own sometimes worked, women soon realized that effective laws were needed to control the sale and manufacture of alcohol. The Woman's Christian Temperance Union (WCTU), founded in 1874, organized thousands of women across the country in its crusade against alcohol, which it linked with poverty, corruption, and the ruin of family life.

Frances Willard, the leader of the WCTU for twenty years, had superb political skills even though she was never elected to a public office. Willard and the WCTU worked through Protestant churches, raising funds and collecting signatures on petitions to state lawmakers and to Congress.

Women felt they had a special mission to bring moral family values into public life, but ending the sale of liquor would take more than persuasion and preaching. Frances Willard gradually led the women of the WCTU to work for what she called the "Home Protection Ballot," a nonthreatening name for gaining women the right to vote. Miss Willard talked about reform in the language of the Bible and

advocated that her temperance workers "do everything" in their crusade to reform society. In carrying out this program, temperance women supported prison reforms, set up kindergartens and child care for mothers who worked, founded groups to care for abandoned and neglected children, gave women job training so they could find work in industries, supported labor unions and the eight-hour working day, tried to end prostitution, and joined groups that worked for world peace.

Frances Willard and the WCTU built a major grassroots network that gave women a national political voice. The WCTU succeeded in having laws passed against the manufacture and sale of alcohol in many states. In addition, the WCTU and other temperance groups demanded an amendment to the Constitution that would prohibit the manufacture and sale of alcohol, a political movement called Prohibition. Such an amendment to the Constitution, the eighteenth, was ratified in 1919. (After much resistance, it was repealed with the passage of the Twenty-third Amendment in 1933.)

When the temperance movement began to decline, other kinds of groups, such as women's clubs and suffrage organizations, became more popular. But the temperance movement was a pioneering effort in organizing women and bringing them into politics, giving women a sense of effectiveness and power that they took

Carry Nation, a controversial temperance supporter, helped found a chapter of the Woman's Christian Temperance Union in Kansas in 1892. Following a practice of early temperance women in the 1870s, who smashed barrels of liquor in saloons with hatchets, Nation set out on a career of "smashing" and "hatchetation" of saloons. She soon became known nationally and successfully sold her autobiography and thousands of miniature hatchet-shaped pins engraved "Carry A. Nation." She pub-lished temperance magazines called The Home Defender, The Smasher's Mail, and The Hatchet. *Her notorious approach to the liquor question was applauded by some, but embarrassed mainstream temper-ance women.*

with them into other organizations. Frances Willard herself said, "Perhaps the most significant outcome of this movement [for women] was the knowledge of their own power."

Lucretia Garfield

APRIL 19, 1832–MARCH 13, 1918

"The bravest woman in the universe"

Lucretia Garfield's diaries show that she was an intelligent, independent-minded woman.

Only two months after moving into the White House, Lucretia Garfield fell ill with a severe case of malaria. It was a common ailment in the Washington of her era, which still had many swampy areas where disease-carrying mosquitoes bred freely. Crete, as her family and friends always called her, had just started to recover when a crushing heat wave descended on the capital.

Her husband brought her to a breezy cottage along the New Jersey shore and left her there to finish recuperating while he went back to work. On the very day Crete was expecting him to join her again, she received a horrifying telegram.

Her husband had been shot. Striding through a Washington railroad station, accompanied only by one of his secretaries, the president had been wounded by a mentally disturbed man wielding a gun. Crete completely forgot her own weakness as she hurried to board a southbound train.

During the next eighty days the whole country focused on James Garfield's fight for life. The bullet that a disappointed office seeker named Charles Guiteau had fired at him caused an infection that the doctors of the 1880s could not cure, but Crete wouldn't give up hope. Before her husband died, she impressed people everywhere as a great heroine—"The wife of the President is the bravest woman in the universe," one newspaper said.

Forty-nine years old in 1881, when even England's Queen Victoria sent her a personal note of sympathy, Crete had appeared to be only unassuming and to possess common sense. Yet those who knew her had been well aware that she had unusual strength of character.

Born on a farm in northeast Ohio near the village of Garretsville on April 19, 1832, she was the eldest of the four children of Zeb Rudolph and Arabella Mason Rudolph. Although they gave her the classical name of Lucretia, from her earliest years they had shortened it to sound less formal. Both her parents were hard workers who never showed any affection—they kept their feelings locked up to the extent that Crete later told her own children she could not remember ever having been kissed or hugged by her mother or her father.

Besides operating a small farm, Zeb Rudolph was a skilled carpenter who also did part-time preaching for the Disciples of Christ religious group that he and his wife both strongly supported. Despite their outer coldness, they treated Crete with special care because her health seemed very fragile. Small and delicate during her childhood, she was subject to painful winter coughing spells that aroused fears of her developing a serious lung disease.

Crete did so well at the local one-room school that when she was seventeen, she was sent to a seminary in the next county offering more advanced classes. Among the students there was an outgoing young man from a similar background—but she and James Garfield, six months older than she was, were not initially attracted to each other.

Within a year they were transferred to a new college, called the Western Reserve Eclectic Institute, established by the Disciples of Christ in the nearby town of Hiram. When James took over teaching Crete's Greek class, she found herself increasingly fascinated by his wide-ranging mind—his "genius," as she put in her diary. He began during a summer of traveling to address long, serious letters to "Lucretia, My Sister."

Yet it would take several more years of disappointments and misunderstandings before Crete and James committed to each other. During this period she finished her own schooling and taught in a few different towns, enjoying the sense of achievement the work brought her as well as the independence that came with earning her own money. Even though she didn't fully agree with the aims of the growing women's rights movement—in particular, its demand for the right to vote—her leaning toward "radical" ideas of female equality worried James.

He firmly believed in the old ways of family life. Also, he doubted whether Crete had "that warmth of feeling" he needed to make him happy, and he kept seeking such warmth elsewhere. But the forces drawing these two together proved stronger than the differences keeping them apart. At the home of Crete's parents, at last they were married on November 11, 1858, when she was twenty-six.

At first the marriage was far from happy. James gave up teaching to enter politics soon after their wedding, leaving Crete at their little house in Hiram while he went to Columbus as a member of Ohio's state senate. Then following the outbreak of the Civil War, he became a lieutenant colonel in an infantry regiment that fought in several major battles. The strains caused by their living almost separate lives were further aggravated when their first child—a beautiful girl they had named Eliza—died of diphtheria at the age of three. But the experience of having come through the war together also drew them closer.

When James was elected to the national Congress while the fighting was still going on, Crete found a compelling way to convince him that she wanted to join him in Washington. She presented him with a written account showing that during their four and three-quarter years of married life, they had actually spent only twenty months together. He quickly agreed that such a record was most unsatisfactory.

So Crete and their expanding family were always with James while he served one term after another as a congressman. First in rented quarters, then in a comfortable house they built not far from the Capitol, Crete raised four sons and a daughter: Harry, James, Mary, Irvin, and Abram. A son, Edward, died at the age of two.

Although Crete found the drudgery of housework to be somewhat stifling, she managed to find a creative way of dealing with it. One day while mixing a batch of bread dough, the notion flashed into her mind that if she tried to make the best bread in the world, she might like baking better. As she later wrote in her diary:

> It seemed like an inspiration, and the whole of my life grew brighter. The very sunshine seemed flowing down through my spirit into the white

loaves, and I now believe my table is furnished with better bread than ever before; and this truth, old as creation, seems just now to have become fully mine—that I need not be the shrinking slave of toil, but its regal master, making whatever I do yield its best fruits.

So as James rose to a top leadership post in Congress, becoming Speaker of the House of Representatives, Crete creatively met her own daily routine and looked forward to discussing her husband's political news with him every evening. Instead of making appearances around the capital attending formal dinners or receptions, they much preferred staying home with each other and their lively children.

Although James showed no ambition to advance any further politically, the Republican party's convention in 1880 had a difficult time choosing its candidate for the presidency. One ballot after another was taken, but none of the men striving to win the nomination could muster sufficient votes. Finally, on the thirty-sixth ballot, a majority of the delegates stunned Speaker of the House Garfield by picking him to be their candidate.

Crete felt enormously proud of James when she listened to him deliver his inaugural address on March 4, 1881—in her diary she wrote that he seemed "a majes-

The Garfield family was extremely popular with the American public. Pictured here (left to right) are Mary, Harry, James, Irvin, and Abram Garfield.

tic figure" as he stood on the Capitol steps facing a huge throng, "with the inspiration of the time and the occasion lifting him up into his fullest grandeur."

Yet Crete had only a brief two months of pleasure from their new position. On a very warm May evening, while dressing for a White House reception after having attended a ceremony in one of Washington's parks, she felt a strange chill. By the next morning she had such alarming symptoms of malaria that nearly seven weeks elapsed before she was pronounced out of danger—and departed for a reviving stay near the ocean in New Jersey.

She had just started to enjoy taking healthful walks by the sea when that terrible telegram arrived. Then, from early July until James died on September 17, she remained almost constantly at his bedside. Overcome by grief when he finally lost his long struggle, she still summoned up the strength to attend the grandly solemn funeral rites marking Washington's farewell to the slain president.

At least Crete had no money worries. Even before her husband's death, one of the country's most successful businessmen—Cyrus Field, the promoter of the first undersea cable between the United States and Europe—had begun a campaign based on his belief that Congress had treated the widow of Abraham Lincoln very shabbily.

Calling it a national disgrace that another president had been assassinated hardly more than fifteen years later, he urged his fellow citizens to make sure that Mrs. Garfield would be able to provide a good home for her five children. More than $385,000, a large sum for the era, was contributed to this drive. In addition Congress itself voted to give Mrs. Garfield $50,000, along with an annual pension of $5,000. So she could well afford to live comfortably throughout the thirty-six years she survived her husband.

Back in 1876 the Garfields had bought a run-down farm on the outskirts of the Ohio town of Mentor and improved it into a fine country home they named Lawnfield. Crete lived there after leaving Washington, surrounded by her family. Although she took pride in her sons' successful careers, as well as the grandchildren they and her daughter gave her, she never ceased using the black-bordered stationery of mourning whenever she wrote a letter.

She devoted much of her time to searching out all of her husband's papers and having them carefully arranged. Then she donated her collection to the Library of Congress, where it became a valuable resource for writers of history books.

As Crete advanced into old age, she began spending her winters in the warmth of southern California. At her home there in South Pasadena, she died of pneumonia on March 13, 1918, a month before she would have celebrated her eighty-sixth birthday.

Ellen Arthur

Ellen Herndon Arthur, 1837–1880, was the daughter of Frances Hansbrough Herndon and William Lewis Herndon, a venerated officer in the U.S. Navy. Ellen spent much of her childhood in and around Washington, D.C., but moved to New York City with her widowed mother in 1858. The following year, she met and married Chester Alan Arthur, a twenty-eight-year-old lawyer. During the Civil War, Chester Arthur gained rapid advancement and had reached the rank of general at the war's end. Chester and Ellen Arthur had two children, a boy and a girl.

Just as her husband's political career was burgeoning, Ellen Herndon Arthur died suddenly of pneumonia on January 12, 1880.

Later that same year, the vagaries of politics made Chester Arthur of New York the Republican candidate for vice president of the United States, even though his name was hardly known elsewhere. Then the assassination of President Garfield elevated him to the nation's highest office. President Arthur's sister, Mary Arthur McElroy, served as his official hostess.

The president arranged for a stained-glass window to be installed in Ellen's memory upstairs at the Washington church she had attended during her girlhood. It was placed on the south side of St. John's Episcopal Church, so he could see it from the White House windows.

Frances Cleveland

JULY 21, 1864–OCTOBER 29, 1947

"The most popular woman in the country"

This photograph of Frances Cleveland captures her youthful beauty and fashionable elegance. She became a campaign symbol in her own right for her husband's later campaigns.

The year after she graduated from college, at the age of twenty-one, Frances Folsom married the president of the United States—and became the youngest first lady in the nation's history. Two years after Frances Cleveland's White House wedding, one of the capital's most widely read newspaper columnists called her "the most popular woman in the country." He reported that generals and admirals who had made their bows before the court ladies of Europe went wild over her virtues, as did statesmen and statesmen's wives.

Only a few of Democratic president Grover Cleveland's political enemies refused to join the nearly universal chorus of praise. "I detest him so much," one leading Republican said, "that I don't even think his wife is beautiful."

The object of all this attention serenely posed for photographs—and pictures of her adorned tens of thousands of American homes. But she believed that it wasn't proper for women to speak up in public, so she was never interviewed nor did she ever give her own personal version of the 1880s-style fairy tale in which she played the starring role.

An only child, Frances Folsom had been born into a fairly prosperous household in the western New York city of Buffalo on July 21, 1864. She was the daughter of Emma Harmon Folsom and Oscar Folsom, a lawyer whose closest friend was his politically ambitious law partner named Grover Cleveland.

Frankie, her parents affectionately called her. Always tall for her age, with lustrous brown hair and violet eyes, she was a notably pretty little girl. When she was eleven, however, the peaceful course of her life was suddenly shattered by a horse-drawn buggy accident that killed her father.

Although Oscar Folsom left enough money to care for his wife and daughter, he had died without ever taking the formal step of making a will. As a result quite a tangle of business affairs remained to be settled. His partner and close friend naturally did all he could to solve Emma Folsom's financial problems—and "Uncle Cleve" also became, at least unofficially, Frankie's guardian.

Cleveland, having long ago assumed responsibility for supporting his own widowed mother, had never felt he could afford to support a wife, too. Teased about his bachelor status after he entered his forties, he sometimes jokingly told the young lady he now called Frank that he was waiting for her to grow up.

Then in 1882, while she was a sophomore at Wells College in the central New York town of Aurora, he was elected mayor of Buffalo. The following year he won the post of governor of New York State, and talk of his advancement into the White House began to be heard.

As none of Frank's private correspondence has ever been found, it is impossible to say when the couple's feelings for each other made them begin thinking of marriage, despite the nearly twenty-seven-year difference in their ages. Without any doubt, though, they did fall in love. Yet it appears that Cleveland purposely delayed proposing to his unofficial ward until after she graduated from college early in the summer of 1885.

By then he was President Cleveland, and his unmarried sister Rose had taken a year off from her schoolteaching to serve as his White House hostess. Among the guests she welcomed, Washington gossips noted, were a widow from Buffalo around the right age to marry a forty-eight-year-old suitor, accompanied by her young daughter; they stayed at the mansion ten days during a college vacation period. So it was widely assumed that Frank's mother might soon become Mrs. Cleveland.

But rumors about the true state of affairs started popping into print after the Folsoms sailed off to Europe for several months following Frank's graduation. Somehow word that *Miss* Folsom was purchasing a wardrobe of elegant gowns in Paris reached American newspapers—and dozens of cameramen prepared to meet the ship on which she and her mother were returning when it docked in New York.

To thwart this crowd of photographers, the president had his secretary arrange for the two women to disembark secretly onto a small boat the night before their expected arrival. Cleveland hoped he could restrict publicity about his impending

Wanting to project a serious side to her image, Frances Cleveland had pioneering woman photographer Frances Benjamin Johnston photograph her at her writing desk in the White House.

marriage. He felt very strongly that even holders of high office deserved to have their personal privacy respected. His special sensitivity on this subject resulted from the airing of scandalous charges against him during the recent presidential campaign.

The claim that Cleveland had long ago fathered an illegitimate son, and admitted his responsibility by paying for the child's support, had started a national orgy of gossip about the seemingly upright candidate. The truth of the matter, Cleveland told his leading supporters, was that he had indeed made the payments—on behalf of a married friend whose family would have suffered grievously if the friend had been exposed. However, many historians believe the child was Cleveland's own.

Although this extremely unpleasant scandal blew over, without depriving Cleveland of a narrow election victory, his reputation had been badly damaged. He remained very disturbed by the increasing tendency of the press to pry into matters he considered none of its business. So he personally planned a simple wedding no cameras could record. It took place on June 2, 1886, in the flower-bedecked Blue Room of the White House, with only about thirty relatives and close friends present. No other president had been married within the mansion (John Tyler, the only previous president to wed while he held the office, had done so at a New York City church), and as soon as the Blue Room ceremony ended, a twenty-one-gun salute was fired from the nearby Navy Yard. Then church bells all over the capital started ringing.

The presidential honeymoon at a cottage in the mountains of western Maryland did not escape the scrutiny of reporters. The morning after arriving there, Cleveland was infuriated to find a large contingent of the press, armed with spyglasses, stationed on a road only a few hundred yards away. Some writers even lifted the covers on dishes of the elaborate meals delivered to the cottage so they could tell their readers what the newlyweds were eating.

As a result Cleveland sent some irate letters about "newspaper nuisances"—and to ensure weekend interludes of privacy, he bought a farm near the capital from which journalistic trespassers could be barred. Still, all the publicity surrounding this president's marriage proved very helpful to him politically.

At the first White House reception his young bride presided over, he stood watching proudly as she gave guest after guest a winning smile and a warm handshake. He tapped Frank's mother on the arm and exclaimed: "She'll do! She'll do!" Indeed, she did so well in the traditional role of White House hostess that she worried a Republican strategist looking toward the next election. "It will be so much harder to win against both Mr. and Mrs. Cleveland," he said glumly.

To make it possible for women who worked during the week to visit the White

*F*irst Lady Frances Cleveland (front row, third from left) is pictured here in 1894 with the wives of members of her husband's cabinet.

House, Frank held weekly receptions for them. The White House was open every Saturday to women who supported themselves, regardless of their social standing. Cleveland did not share his wife's enthusiasm for working women. His old-fashioned views about the proper female sphere made him write to one of his sisters that he would feel very afflicted if Frank took up such notions herself.

Mr. and Mrs. Cleveland had to vacate the White House on March 4, 1889, after a very close election was won by his Republican opponent, Benjamin Harrison. Leaving the mansion, she smilingly urged one of its staff who voiced sorrow at her departure to take good care of the building. "We are coming back just four years from today," she assured him.

The Clevelands did return. After four years in New York City, where Frank's husband practiced law and she joyfully welcomed a baby daughter they named Ruth, they moved back into the White House on March 4, 1893. They both marveled at the improved living conditions they found as a result of extensive remodeling initiated by Caroline Harrison.

Frances Cleveland was expecting another baby—her second and third daughters, Esther and Marion, were born during her second term as first lady. She devoted less of her time and energy to official entertaining than she had previously, yet her motherhood made her even more popular than she had been before.

Nevertheless, she and her husband both felt immensely relieved to be finally out of the spotlight on his retirement from politics early in 1897. They took up residence in a secluded colonial-style mansion near Princeton University in Princeton, New Jersey. There, during the next few years, Frank gave birth to two sons, Richard and Francis.

Grover Cleveland died in 1908 at the age of seventy-one, leaving his forty-four-year-old wife with no financial worries. She continued to live in their Princeton home, devoting herself to their children. Five years after being widowed she married again. Her second husband was Thomas Jex Preston, a professor of archaeology around her own age, and the match proved very happy.

Even after becoming Frances Cleveland Preston, she didn't cease being admired as a presidential widow. During her old age she served on the board of several charitable agencies and became national president of a group called the Needlework Guild. During World War I, she headed the National Security League's speakers' bureau. When she was eighty-three, while she was visiting one of her sons in Baltimore, she died in her sleep on October 29, 1947.

Caroline Harrison

"An air of genteel gaiety"

Caroline Harrison initiated a renovation and modernization plan in the White House, including the installation of electricity in 1891.

Carrie Harrison was a gifted artist skilled at painting china; she herself designed the official presidential china service that was used for White House dinner parties while she lived there. She also started the collection of presidential china used by previous administrations that today is a valuable record of American decorative arts.

However, nothing came of her grand plans to rebuild and expand the official residence of the nation's first family, somewhat in the style of a European palace. Even so, by focusing attention on how badly run-down the existing White House had become, she spurred the most extensive renovations since the building had first been constructed nearly a hundred years earlier.

Along with her artistic interests, the comfort and convenience of her own family were her main concerns. Despite a conservative Midwestern background, she reflected an important change in the United States: During the second half of the 1800s the acceptable role for married women was slowly but surely broadening.

Born in the southern Ohio town of Oxford on October 1, 1832, Carrie—formally named Caroline Lavinia—was the third daughter of Mary Neal Scott and John Witherspoon Scott. Although her father had been ordained a Presbyterian minister, he spent most of his career as a professor of mathematics.

In 1845, when Carrie was thirteen, Dr. Scott took up teaching at an institution known as Farmers' College, on the outskirts of the growing city of Cincinnati. With three girls in his family, he held somewhat advanced views on the importance of expanding women's educational opportunities, and he founded a female department that his daughters attended.

At the age of sixteen Carrie attracted the attention of a freshman in the college itself—a rather serious-minded young man who was aware that a lot was expected of him because his grandfather, William Henry Harrison, had been the nation's ninth president. Solemn as he usually seemed, fifteen-year-old Benjamin Harrison soon declared himself in love. Although they were both quite young, they began to talk of eventually marrying.

The following year Carrie's family moved back to the town of her birth when her father rejoined the faculty of Miami University. In addition he established the Oxford Female Institute—and Carrie, besides being one of its students, was listed among its teachers as "Assistant in Piano Music." Meanwhile Ben attended classes at the university.

During Ben's final year before graduating, Carrie took a job teaching music at a girls' school in Carrollton, Kentucky. Ben figured out a way to finish his law studies while he and Carrie lived with his father. On October 20, 1853, when he was only twenty and Carric was twenty-one, they were married at a ceremony conducted by her father.

After qualifying to practice law, Ben chose Indiana's thriving young capital city of Indianapolis as a promising place to open his office. At first very few clients sought his help, but his own painstaking hard work, plus the political eminence of his grandfather, gradually brought him prosperity. As for Carrie, she occupied herself with caring for their son, Russell, born the year after their marriage, and then their daughter, Mary, always called Mamie. A second daughter died at birth, in 1861.

During the Civil War, lawyer Ben Harrison rose to be a general in command of Indiana volunteers, despite having no previous military experience. But his intense concentration on mastering a new profession also taught him another lesson. Toward the end of the war he wrote his wife an emotional letter, in which he pledged never again to give her grounds for feeling that he put anything ahead of his devotion to her and their children.

After the war, Ben's legal as well as political activities made him a leading figure in Indianapolis. When he built his family a large new house in one of the city's finest neighborhoods, Ben made sure that it contained a studio where Carrie could do as much painting with her watercolors as she wished. She even gave free lessons to schoolgirls, who envied her talent at designing dishes.

Carrie also sewed, designed clothes, and embroidered cushions and purses. She was an accomplished pianist. She grew strawberries and grapes outdoors; while indoors she made a hobby of raising exotic flowers, such as orchids. She also made time for numerous public-spirited projects sponsored by her church or other groups.

Like many American women, she had gotten her first taste of volunteer work on behalf of worthy causes during the Civil War. New hospitals had to be set up to care for thousands of wounded soldiers, and money had to be raised to equip them. As a result, thousands of women with no previous experience at managing any enterprise outside of their own homes proved that they were perfectly capable of organizing or directing whatever needed doing. The sense of accomplishment they gained was very satisfying.

Carrie Harrison served year after year on the board in charge of the Indianapolis Orphans' Asylum. During the 1880s, when her husband was elected to the U.S. Senate and they began spending months at a time in Washington, she took only a limited interest in the capital's social life. Instead she did volunteer work for a hospital and an orphans' home there.

One January, however, while crossing a street, Carrie slipped on a patch of ice and fell, hitting her head against the pavement. Although her injuries soon mended, from then on she seemed less energetic and her family treated her as if her health had become quite fragile.

Still, Carrie certainly sounded decisive when she talked to newspaper reporters soon after her husband became the nation's second President Harrison on March 4, 1889. "I am very anxious to see the family of the President provided for properly," she said, "and while I am here I hope to get the present building put into good condition."

Her concern over rotting floorboards, along with her feeling that the presidential residence ought to be beautiful as well as comfortable, led the government's Office of Public Buildings and Grounds to prepare several sets of elaborate plans. Making use of the entire White House grounds, these called for not just repairing the existing building but also adding various new wings around a central courtyard with splendid gardens and fountains. Congress refused even to consider authorizing money for any such grandeur.

Nevertheless, it did vote to spend the then-substantial sum of $35,000 for modernizing the old mansion. Besides correcting unsafe conditions and providing more privacy for the first family's living quarters, the improvements included modernizing the kitchens and such up-to-date features as a telephone switchboard and electric lights. The Harrisons still didn't trust electricity, so they insisted on keeping— and using—gas lamps.

What Carrie appreciated most about the large-scale remodeling was the increased space it made available in the upstairs family quarters. She needed bedrooms to accommodate quite an extended family: her ninety-year-old father, a widowed niece she and her husband were very fond of, and their married daughter with her husband and two-year-old son all lived at the White House. Their son and his wife and children, as well as numerous other relatives, were regular visitors.

It was their daughter's perky youngster, named Benjamin Harrison McKee after his grandfather, who drew the most attention around the country. Photography had advanced to the point where newspapers covered Washington with pictures as well as words, but the child's grandfather by now had such a sober manner that people joked about him, "If you pricked him, he would bleed ice water." Of course, the press much preferred aiming their cameras at "Baby McKee," and the first lady realized that any effort to ban picture taking was bound to fail.

She set up a weekly appointment at which photographers could snap away uninterruptedly, in exchange for their promise to leave her grandson alone the rest of the week. This arrangement of Carrie Harrison's is said to be the first example of a major feature of modern presidential public relations—the White House "photo op," as such sessions are called today.

Carrie also did much to humanize the newly refurbished White House while she lived there. Her lively yet ladylike personality gave it "an air of genteel gaiety," one visitor reported. Her fondness for flowers turned the mansion into a floral wonderland whenever formal receptions were held.

Nevertheless, Carrie continued to show her conviction that wives should pursue their own interests by accepting the post of the first president general of the newly formed patriotic organization called the Daughters of the American Revolution. Also, she headed a Washington committee working to raise money for the Women's

Caroline Harrison (front row, seated fifth from right) founded and served as the first President-General of the National Society of the Daughters of the American Revolution (DAR), which she envisioned would become "a powerful political force for women." She is pictured here with the first members.

Medical Fund of the Johns Hopkins University Medical School in nearby Baltimore after it promised to start accepting women students. By supporting these causes she lent them the visibility and prestige of the first lady, understanding that her support "had political implications" to advance their goals.

Although worries about her delicate health kept increasing, Carrie often accompanied her husband when he took official trips around the country. During a ceremonial journey to California in the spring of 1891, she caught a cold that lingered months after she returned to Washington. A year later doctors finally determined that she had fallen victim to tuberculosis.

For six months Carrie was an invalid upstairs at the White House, growing increasingly weak during her husband's campaign to win a second term. Shortly after her sixtieth birthday she died there on October 25, 1892, two weeks before Republican Benjamin Harrison was defeated in his bid for reelection by Democrat Grover Cleveland.

Ida McKinley

JUNE 8, 1847–MAY 26, 1907

"She is beautiful to me now"

Because of her invalidism, Ida McKinley was rarely photographed standing. Despite her illness she tried to carry on her White House social duties as first lady.

*I*n the 1890s, very little was known about epilepsy. As no treatment existed to control its symptoms, the mere word frightened most people. Ida McKinley suffered from epilepsy, and she often had brief seizures while residing at the White House, but her illness was never identified during her own lifetime.

Newspapers told their readers only that this first lady was unusually frail. Even so, she didn't stay behind the scenes. Unlike several previous presidential wives with health problems, she wouldn't let anyone else take over as her husband's official hostess. Indeed, she acted as if she hated having him out of her sight—and his devotion to such a demanding invalid struck Washingtonians as nothing short of saintly.

Nobody could doubt that William McKinley deeply loved his wife, despite her irritable temper and frail appearance. After one of his associates had met her for the first time, the president came closer to speaking about his feelings than he ordinarily did. "Ida was the most beautiful girl you ever saw," he recalled. "She is beautiful to me now," he added.

High-spirited and proud of belonging to two of her hometown's leading families, Ida Saxton had been born in Canton, Ohio, on June 8, 1847. One of her grandfathers published a newspaper called the *Canton Repository,* which had made him a powerful figure in the area's politics, while the other operated the most elegant local hotel.

Her parents were Kate Dewalt Saxton and James Asbury Saxton; he owned a prosperous bank and much valuable real estate. Ida was their first child, and she still craved her special status after acquiring a younger sister and brother. Years later, Canton old-timers would say that she had been an energetic and willful young lady who grew up accustomed to having her own way, but no evidence of any sickness appeared then.

After going to local public schools, Ida also spent a few terms at boarding schools in Delhi, New York, then in Cleveland, before attending Brooke Hall Seminary in Media, Pennsylvania. On completing her studies there, when she was twenty-two she convinced her father to let her join a tour of Europe being conducted by a Canton teacher, Miss Jeannette Alexander.

On that eight-month tour, in 1869, Ida made the most of opportunities that she was given. Repeatedly she separated from her group as it was being led through one museum or another and went exploring on her own. Miss Alexander angrily wrote to Ida's father that his daughter had even conspired with another young lady to attend a Paris theater "with some gentlemen."

Her father was not very distressed by Ida's refusing to abide by some of the accepted rules for proper female behavior. He took an unconventional step himself soon after she came back to Canton. At that time it was rare for a respectable young woman to work in a business office, but Ida's father offered her a job in his bank.

With her broad experience and college education, she jumped at this chance to spend her days doing something more interesting than attending tea parties with her mother. She learned the basic procedures for handling other people's money very quickly. Ida was the cashier in charge of receiving deposits when Major William McKinley opened an account at the bank.

Ida had already met this impressive-looking newcomer to Canton at a church picnic. Although he was only three and a half years older than she was, his Civil War service had given him an air of solid maturity.

Will McKinley was more than willing to pay attention to Ida. Brought up in a neighboring county by an extremely religious mother who hoped he would become a minister, he had always been tongue-tied around girls. But Ida's beauty and intelligence enchanted him—soon he was setting a bouquet of flowers on the counter, along with the money he wanted to deposit, every time he came to the bank.

Ida and Will were married in grand style at Canton's brand-new Presbyterian church on January 25, 1871; she was twenty-three. Within a year they both were overjoyed to become the parents of a beautiful baby girl they called Katie. Not long afterward Ida became pregnant again, but the couple's happiness lasted less than a year more.

Shortly before the birth of Ida's second baby, in 1873, the shock of her own mother's death severely affected her. Then the birth itself proved extremely difficult, leaving Ida very ill. Her frail new baby, also called Ida, lived only a few months.

All these traumatic experiences appear to have brought on a series of terrible attacks whose exact nature Ida's family never disclosed. Although doctors specializing in brain diseases were called in, and it was whispered around Canton that some sort of brain damage had caused the onset of epilepsy, to say this aloud then would have shamed Ida unbearably.

No name was given to her ailment. From then on, though, she was subject to frequent brief seizures when her body stiffened and she lost consciousness. She also suffered occasional more serious convulsive seizures that left her intensely depressed. Within a short period, a vivacious young woman had turned into a tense, quavery invalid.

Her state of mind was demonstrated most sadly by the way she alternately ignored or clung to her little daughter, Katie. One day when an uncle came upon the child swinging aimlessly on the front gate of her house, he invited her to take a walk with him. "No, I mustn't go out of the yard," Katie said, "or God'll punish mamma some more."

Then Katie fell ill with typhoid fever and died at the age of three and a half. That dreadful blow, in the summer of 1876, all but ended any possibility of her mother's being able to live anything like a normal life. Nevertheless, Ida's always-devoted husband still kept hoping for her recovery—while also pursuing his own increasingly successful political career.

It was only a few months after Katie's death that Will McKinley won what would

be the first of several terms in the national House of Representatives. Following the
same route as several previous popular Republican congressmen from Ohio, he
then became his state's governor. Finally in 1896 he was elected president of the
United States.

During these twenty years Ida McKinley made her husband's life much more
difficult than it might otherwise have been. But her affliction may also have helped
to spur his rise. Despite her self-absorption, she never ceased regarding him as a
great man—and she did whatever she felt she had to do to help him achieve the
recognition she was sure he deserved.

Ida accompanied "the Major," as she always referred to him, wherever his career
led him. Even though she took no part in Washington's social life during his congressional years, when he became Governor McKinley, she made up her mind to
assume her rightful place as his official hostess. To fit her new station, she ordered
a wardrobe of lavish satin gowns and ventured forth to welcome her guests.

Ida had difficulty walking more than a few steps, however, and was often carried
into the room where visitors gathered. She received them seated in a chair, rather
than standing as was customary, and she held a bouquet of flowers on her lap as a sig-
nal that she could not be expected to endure the strain of shaking many hands.
Because of the uncertainty of her health, her husband always stood or sat at her side.

Then if she had one of her sudden seizures, he would calmly reach into his pocket for a large handkerchief that he placed over her face, meanwhile continuing whatever conversation he might be engaged in. As soon as he sensed that she had recovered from her spell, he removed the handkerchief, still without giving any sign of being the least bit perturbed. This peculiar response to Ida's epilepsy was characteristic of how such illnesses were treated at the time.

This same procedure was followed after the McKinleys moved into the White House. However, not a word about the first lady's seizures ever appeared in print. Capital reporters abided by their era's prevailing standards of propriety, telling their readers only that Mrs. McKinley's health was "delicate," so she was obliged to limit her activities.

In fact, Ida's main activity was crocheting—upstairs at the White House, she spent many hours every day making woolen slippers, giving them as presents to practically every visitor. Her only outing most days was an afternoon carriage ride with her husband, which they both looked forward to very much because it allowed them uninterrupted time together.

Despite the extra stresses of White House life, while living there Ida seemed somewhat less troubled than she had been in many years. After her husband's reelection to a second term in 1900, she even accompanied him on a cross-country inspection trip. Unfortunately in San Francisco she developed blood poisoning from an infected finger—and became so ill that doctors expected her to die.

Ida proved stronger than anybody had expected. The whole country was caught up in the drama of the president's obvious deep concern over his wife, and when she almost miraculously recovered, the whole country rejoiced.

At the peak of his popularity, President McKinley visited the Pan American Exposition in Buffalo, New York. There, on September 6, 1901, he was shot and seriously wounded by an anarchist. Ida McKinley had made the trip with her husband but was resting at the home of Buffalo friends when the bullet was fired.

Again she proved stronger than anybody had expected. Ida stayed near her husband's bedside during the eight days he struggled for life, and after his death she walked unattended in the series of immensely touching funeral ceremonies honoring him.

Then Ida went back to Canton. In one of the few letters of hers that was saved, she wrote a few years later to an old friend: "I am more lonely every day I live." Five and a half years after her husband's assassination—during which time she had no seizures at all—she died of a stroke on May 26, 1907, less than two weeks before what would have been her sixtieth birthday.

Edith Roosevelt

AUGUST 16, 1861–SEPTEMBER 30, 1948

"Aunt Edith managed TR very cleverly"

Edith Roosevelt inscribed this photo to her social secretary, Belle Hagner, who in 1902 became the first person in White House history officially assigned to handle publicity for the first lady.

A few months before her fourth birthday, Edie was taken on a strange outing by her governess. They walked to the large house where her friend's grandfather lived, and suddenly she found herself in an upstairs room with windows looking down on a frightening scene.

Crowds dressed in black lined the street below, black banners flapped from the buildings opposite, and black-clad marchers stepped somberly along the pavement.

Not old enough to understand that she was watching New York's funeral procession honoring slain President Abraham Lincoln, she still felt so upset that she started to cry.

The six-year-old boy at the window beside her shushed her; then, as she continued sobbing, he hurried her into another room and rushed back to his vantage point. Already Edith Kermit Carow and Theodore Roosevelt were building their vast collection of shared memories. They even had similar nicknames.

Teedie, his family called him; the Roosevelts were very fond of somewhat odd nicknames. But "Teedie and Edie" certainly tripped off the tongue easily, and these two children spent a lot of time together during their growing-up years.

Of course, Teedie's sister Corinne—Conie, they all called her—was really Edie's best friend. Their friendship dated from the days their nurses had wheeled them side by side in baby carriages, for the Carows and the Roosevelts both occupied fine brownstone houses not far from New York City's then-fashionable Union Square. When the Roosevelts organized what amounted to a private school for their own four children, they naturally invited Edie to join the class.

Even though both families appeared to be solidly wealthy, Edie's was not. Her father, Charles Carow, had ancestors who had come to America from France during the 1600s, and he had inherited a prosperous shipowning business. An alcoholic, he had seriously hurt his business and ruined his health.

Edie, born at her Connecticut grandparents' home on August 16, 1861, grew up loving her father deeply. He marveled over her golden curls and read her enchanting stories from *Grimm's Fairy Tales.* Somehow she managed to forget his lapses, while her mother as well as her younger sister, Emily, became more and more upset by them.

Even when the Carows were obliged to move in with an elderly aunt, Edie still remained practically a member of the Roosevelt family. When she paid long visits to the Roosevelts' summer home at Oyster Bay on Long Island, she didn't often join the hilarious romping there, but her bright mind endeared her to everybody.

When the Roosevelts spent a few years touring Europe, Teedie frequently dashed off letters telling Edie about his latest interests. A special sympathy appeared to have developed between these two unusually intelligent young people. Although the Carows' money problems kept them from taking such journeys, Edie's mother made sure that this daughter got a good education at one of New York's best schools for girls.

By the time Teedie went off to Harvard—and by then he was called Teddy or even just Ted—it appears that he may have begun thinking of Edie as his future wife. He invited her for weekend visits while at college, and also saw to it that they took long walks along the beach together when she stayed at Oyster Bay the summers after his freshman and sophomore years.

Much later she would tell her children that their father had proposed to her repeatedly during that period and indicate she had said they were much too young to be thinking of marriage. Because she destroyed most of their letters to each other, writers of biographies of President Theodore Roosevelt could never find evidence of any such early romance. Indeed, some thought that the rather queenly woman Edie became was purposely trying to have the record show that she had not been her husband's second choice.

When Theodore—as she had taken to calling him—fell madly in love with the lighthearted Alice Lee during his junior year at Harvard, Edith never gave any sign of feeling hurt or disappointed. She even attended his wedding in Brookline, where, as one of her friends put it, she "danced the soles off her shoes."

After Alice Lee Roosevelt's tragic death in childbirth in 1884, Edith realized the torment Theodore was enduring. She also understood his belief that resuming their previous friendship might seem disloyal to his beloved young wife, so she carefully avoided encountering him. By chance, though, nineteen months after his loss, when he had just returned from a long interlude at the Dakota ranch where he had gone to build up his health and spirits, he arrived at his sister's house as Edith was leaving it.

Nobody knows what they said to each other, but soon they were seeing each other often, and it became clear that some private plans were being made. Since Edith's father had recently died, leaving only a small amount of money, her mother had already decided on settling with her daughters in Europe, where they could live more cheaply. The quiet ceremony in which twenty-five-year-old Edith Carow became Mrs. Theodore Roosevelt took place in London, England, on December 2, 1886.

This marriage proved to be extraordinarily happy. Edith and Theodore both took enormous pleasure from becoming the parents of a large family—during the next ten years they welcomed Theodore Junior, Kermit, Ethel, Archibald, and Quentin. From the outset Edith insisted that Theodore and Alice Lee's daughter, also called Alice, belonged with them.

Having a father noted for bursts of exuberance that made him act like a youngster himself, these six children naturally turned out to be rambunctious and always up to some kind of mischief. Despite Edith's ladylike demeanor, she seemed not a bit fazed by the constant clamor surrounding her. However when she said that enough was enough, *nobody* dared disobey her.

Besides her very satisfying family life, Edith obviously enjoyed taking advantage of the opportunities that her husband's career opened to her. By spurring Theodore's efforts to raise the tone of Republican party politics, she achieved exactly the kind of social status she craved.

Teddy Roosevelt was hailed as a "celebrity president," and his large, rambunctious family attracted considerable public interest and media coverage.

When he was appointed to the U.S. Civil Service Commission, they began spending much of the year in the nation's capital. There Edith met many kindred souls connected with the upper governmental levels. Thanks to these sophisticated new friends, who appreciated her ability to converse cleverly about art and literature, Washington became her favorite city. Still, she didn't try to discourage Theodore's intermittent yearnings for high adventure—and when the Spanish-American War broke out in 1898, his dashing leadership of the cavalry regiment known as "Roosevelt's Rough Riders" made him a great national hero.

Only three years later Vice President Theodore Roosevelt moved up to the nation's highest office, following the horrifying assassination of President William

McKinley. Only forty-two when he was sworn in, he became the youngest chief executive in U.S. history. While his own vigorous personality no doubt did more than anything else to comfort millions of Americans mourning the loss of a much-admired leader, the new president's wife and children also played a major role.

From that ingenious four-year-old spy named Quentin to the saucy seventeen-year-old "Princess Alice," all six Roosevelt offspring gave the country a constant supply of amusing pranks to read about. At the same time their wonderfully serene and dignified mother provided plenty of reassurance that the White House was being run very capably. Indeed, Edith Roosevelt soon emerged as a truly outstanding first lady.

She herself once mused to some friends about how sad it was that only a few of her predecessors had enjoyed their position. However, she loved it, for she felt perfectly capable of coping with any challenge that might arise.

Several projects that Edith firmly supervised would have a lasting effect. In part because of her husband's tremendous popularity, she won approval for the most significant changes the White House itself had ever undergone. When previous first ladies had complained about the limited space available to presidential families, Congress had repeatedly refused to spend the money that a whole new wing would cost.

Edith was determined to separate the presidential offices, with their constant stream of politicians, from the family's living space. Now a new wing for executive offices was fully built, freeing the mansion's entire upstairs for family use. Edith received authorization to bring every room's appearance up to her own high standards—as her husband put it, she transformed the White House from the likeness of a shabby, second-rate hotel to "a simple and dignified dwelling for the head of a great republic."

In this process Edith took two steps toward confirming her conviction that presidential wives had played an important part throughout the nation's history: She hung portraits of all her predecessors in a downstairs corridor, creating an impressive picture gallery of first ladies; and she worked hard to update the collection of presidential china started by Caroline Harrison and arranged for its prominent display.

Yet her main contribution was less visible to the American public. Her husband's relative Franklin Delano Roosevelt observed: "Aunt Edith managed TR very cleverly without his being conscious of it—no slight achievement."

Edith was only forty-seven when Theodore's second term ended and they left the White House. Although she would live to be a very old lady, traveling widely and privately experiencing many joys and sorrows, including the deaths of her husband and three sons, nothing else ever matched the excitement of those White House years.

She always said she felt very relieved to be free of constant surveillance by curi-

When Edith Roosevelt approved the designs for renovating the White House in 1902, she decided that the ground-floor entryway should display portraits of the first ladies, including this one of herself.

ous onlookers, but this very private person did something quite remarkable in her old age. Almost twenty years after her husband's death she delivered several speeches herself at Republican party rallies. An early phonograph record preserved one of these talks, and despite all its scratchy background noises, her voice still can be heard.

On September 30, 1948, at the age of eighty-seven, Edith died at her Oyster Bay home. Upon her death *Life* magazine called her "one of the strongest-minded and strongest-willed presidential wives who ever lived in the White House."

How Do Photographs Shape a Public Image?

By the 1880s and 1890s, first ladies had become highly popular figures in American life. The country adored the young and beautiful Frances Cleveland, who at twenty-one married the president in the White House. She became a celebrity, and her picture appeared on all kinds of items: advertising cards, plates, glasses, posters, sheet music, and cards similar to trading cards for celebrities today. She even became a campaign symbol in her husband's later campaigns for reelection. Her popularity can be compared with that of movie or sports stars today.

After the 1850s the use of photography completely changed the way the first lady and the American people related to each other. The growing popularity of photography made first ladies even more accessible to the public. By the 1880s and

Frances Benjamin Johnston took this photograph of President Theodore and Edith Roosevelt's children Archie and Quentin, "playing photographer" at the White House. Appealing portraits of the first family's children were a Johnston specialty.

This fanciful self-portrait of Frances Benjamin Johnston shows her keen awareness of how a photographer could manipulate subjects and settings to create a desired image. Here she portrays herself as doing very improper things for a nineteenth-century lady: She is smoking, holding a beer stein, showing her legs and petticoat, and displaying photographs of many male friends on the mantelpiece.

1890s Americans expected—even demanded—a look at the "real" first lady. Stereo cards, which were popular from the 1850s through the 1930s, were printed with images that appeared three-dimensional when looked at through a stereo viewer. Stereo cards gave people in their own homes a vivid glimpse of the first lady and the White House. By the 1890s commercial photography studios sold small portrait photocards of celebrities, including presidents and first ladies.

Then as now, magazines featuring photographs of celebrities, including the first family, were widely read. Women's magazines especially featured articles on the first lady. In major cities many prominent photo studios and photographers such as Pach Brothers, Clinedinst, Charles Parker, Waldon Fawcett, and Harris and Ewing catered to the public demand for images of the first family and their lives in the White House.

A pioneer woman photographer named Frances Benjamin Johnston (1861–1952) started creating special views of first ladies and their families in the 1890s. She was first given permission to take official photographs at the White House in 1892 and continued to photograph first ladies from Caroline Harrison to Helen Taft. Johnston's pictures were first published in 1893, and many were later printed in popular magazines.

Johnston specialized in taking engaging, close-up portraits and often showed first ladies in serious poses, studying or writing at their desks. She also photographed their children and families. Her whimsical pictures of Edith and Teddy Roosevelt's children playing with their pets and of Alice Roosevelt wearing a leopard-print dress in the White House conservatory (where tropical plants were grown) made Johnston famous as a photographer. She was especially adept at arranging the people and settings in photographs to create a desired image.

As the presidents and their families grew more visible in the early 1900s, it didn't take long for first ladies to realize that they must take a hand in making and managing their public image. Later first ladies used the radio, and then television, to advance their husband's—or their own—work in the White House. Even though the first ladies of the twentieth century have felt the burden of intense media coverage, many have used the power of the media to their advantage.

Helen Taft

JUNE 2, 1861–MAY 22, 1943

"Dearest and best critic"

*H*elen Taft *was politically ambitious and the power behind the scenes in her husband's rise to the presidency.*

One evening during a private dinner at the White House, President Theodore Roosevelt played a political game with his secretary of war. Closing his eyes, he pretended to be a fortune-teller and announced in a solemn voice that he saw something hanging over Will Taft's head.

"I cannot make out what it is," TR said. "It is hanging by a slender thread. At one time it looks like the presidency—then again it looks like the chief justiceship."

Will Taft's small, alert wife leaned forward eagerly. Her name was Helen, but to her family and friends she had always been Nellie. "Make it the presidency!" she exclaimed.

Her very large husband smiled with great good humor. "Make it the chief jus-ticeship!" he said.

As it turned out, William Howard Taft held both of these high offices, one after the other, a feat nobody else has ever matched. Yet many Washington insiders thought that without Nellie's energetic prodding, he might have contentedly risen no further than being a judge back home in Ohio. He thought so himself.

By encouraging him to do his very best, she had been "worth much" to him, he once wrote to her. "You are my dearest and best critic," he told her.

Opposite as Nellie and Will seemed, they suited each other wonderfully. Despite notable differences in their temperaments as well as their size, their backgrounds and their general outlook were really very similar. In fact, their fathers had been close friends long before they met.

Nellie, born on June 2, 1861, was the fourth of the eleven children of John Williamson Herron and Harriet Collins Herron. Having such a big family obliged them to live in rather modest style, in a gray-brick row house not far from Cincin-nati's busy waterfront. Still, the Herrons were definitely part of the well-educated, public-spirited group that had turned a raw young town on the Ohio River into "the Queen City of the West."

Nellie's father was a lawyer who took an active interest in local politics, so she learned to enjoy political talk at an early age. Yet she probably owed even more to her mother, whose "stimulating personality" and "exceedingly keen wit" she recalled many years later.

Nellie herself became quite an independent young woman. Even though she did very well at Miss Nourse's School, where girls from Cincinnati's leading families were educated, by the time she was nineteen she dared to disregard at least some of the prevailing rules about proper ladylike behavior.

One Saturday morning, she noted in her diary, she and a friend had felt thirsty after doing some errands, so they had brashly entered a beer parlor opposite the music hall. Because their presence in a room where men were drinking would have marked them as truly scandalous, they were escorted to an upstairs porch. "There we sat and drank our beer and ate our cheese sandwiches," Nellie wrote, "with our feet on the railing in front."

But even if Nellie's boldness caused a certain amount of head shaking, she didn't defy the standards of Cincinnati's conservative Republican upper class in any important way. Musically inclined, she gave piano lessons at various private schools.

Nellie told her diary that she could not be satisfied just by being loved—she wanted to spend her life with a man who considered her his intellectual equal. Such a man had to be capable of pursuing a career that provided exciting new experiences for his wife as well as himself. She thought she would like to become the nation's first lady.

This idea was not as farfetched as it might seem, for President Rutherford B. Hayes had been her father's law partner years earlier, and the two families remained warmly connected. Nellie, at seventeen, had spent a thrilling week visiting upstairs in the White House.

Then when she was eighteen, she had gone to a skating party where she met the son of another of her father's political friends for the first time. Will Taft, nearly four years older than she was, had recently returned home from Yale to begin practicing law.

Nellie and Will remained casual acquaintances during the next several years, while she continued to teach. At twenty-two she decided to organize a small group of intelligent men and women who would meet Saturday evenings in her home to discuss literary or historical topics, then partake of light refreshments—and she asked Will Taft to join her "salon."

After two years of these meetings Will realized that he had fallen deeply in love with Nellie Herron. When he told her, she said she needed more time to be sure of her own feelings. At last a joyous wedding took place in her family's home on June 19, 1886, when Nellie was twenty-five and Will almost twenty-nine.

Only a few months after they returned from their honeymoon tour of Europe, a vacancy occurred on the panel of judges presiding over Cincinnati's superior court. When Will was appointed to fill this post, Nellie felt elated. Nevertheless, she couldn't help worrying a little because the other judges were all much older than her husband and expected no further advancement: What if this unambitious attitude infected their easygoing young associate?

Nellie had become thoroughly convinced by then that Will was destined for national prominence, and she took up the task of guiding his career in the direction she wanted it to go. During the next ten years Nellie had three children: Robert, Helen, and Charles. She poured much of her energy into inspiring them with her own high ideals and her enthusiasm for all sorts of new experiences. She also organized and presided over the Cincinnati Orchestra Association, and actively supported numerous other worthy causes.

Will did rise, just as Nellie had hoped. Indeed, the most important factor in his rise was a decision that she instantly made when he returned from a mysterious trip to Washington early in 1900. During the past eight years he had been serving with notable competence as a judge in the U.S. circuit court covering the Cincinnati area.

Will informed Nellie as soon as he got home, "The President wants me to go to the Philippine Islands." The tone of his voice told her that he liked the idea about as much as he would have liked being asked to jump off the courthouse roof. But he added, "Want to go?"

"Yes, of course," Nellie replied without a bit of hesitation. Years later she wrote that even though she wasn't sure what her answer might lead to, "I knew instantly that I didn't want to miss a big and novel experience."

What it led to was a terrifically exciting three years during which the entire Taft family twice traveled all the way around the world. Nellie's own triumphs ranged from learning to ride a surfboard off Hawaii's Waikiki Beach to coping unflappably with a great variety of domestic and social complications caused by moving into a grandiose former Spanish palace in Manila.

In addition, though, because Will Taft did so well at winning Philippine goodwill while serving as the islands' first American governor, Nellie's answer led within another few years to the White House. On March 4, 1909, three months before her forty-eighth birthday, her youthful dream of becoming the nation's first lady came true.

Although it was a blustery, snowy day, Nellie's elation could not be chilled.

Helen Taft broke precedent as the first wife of a president to ride beside her husband from the inaugural ceremony at the Capitol to the White House.

The United States had grown increasingly industrialized by the beginning of the twentieth century. The Tafts were the last family to keep a cow on the White House lawn.

Breaking with longtime tradition, and symbolizing the active role she had played in his political career, she insisted on riding beside her husband after the oath-taking ceremonies instead of following behind him in another carriage. Then during the next several weeks she ordered a great flurry of changes at the White House to put her own stamp on it.

But the hectic pace she set herself had a frightening result. Early in May 1909, as she was embarking on a cruise along the Potomac, Nellie fainted—and it turned out that she had suffered a stroke. Despite public announcements describing her illness as "nervous exhaustion," doctors feared at first that she might be left paralyzed and unable to speak.

Soon, though, Nellie showed reassuring signs of improvement. It took about a year for her to recover almost completely, a year during which her husband lovingly devoted part of every day to helping her learn to talk again. While she gradually resumed an active role in Washington social life, she remained careful not to overtax her strength.

During Nellie Taft's four years as first lady, she gave future compilers of presidential lore a pair of diverting facts to record: She acquired the last family cow ever to graze on the White House grounds—and also the first White House motorcar.

More importantly, Nellie's Asian travels had shown her the spectacular beauty of mass plantings of Japanese flowering cherry trees. At her request American nurseries set out a few hundred trees along the Potomac shoreline, but they soon died. Then the mayor of Tokyo heard about her project, and thousands of Japanese trees soon arrived. It was Nellie Taft who inspired Washington's glorious cherry blossom display, which quickly became one of the capital's chief beauties.

But Nellie wasn't too sorry when an intense political struggle ended with her husband's defeat in his bid for a second term. Shortly after the Tafts left Washington in 1913, Will became a law professor at Yale University. While he was busy teaching, she wrote a book that she called *Recollections of Full Years.*

Then, in 1921, Will Taft's own dream came true when President Warren Harding appointed him chief justice of the Supreme Court. Back in Washington, Nellie enjoyed living quietly, taking much pleasure from the achievements of all three of her children: Robert, serving in Ohio's legislature, would soon emerge as the Republican party's leading spokesman in the U.S. Senate; Helen became dean of Bryn Mawr College; and Charles was a very successful lawyer.

When Will died in 1930 at the age of seventy-two, Nellie stayed on in their Washington home. She died there thirteen years later on May 22, 1943, when she was nearly eighty-two.

What Was "Woman Suffrage"?

When the national Constitution was written after the Revolution, women were not given the right to vote. But in a nation that values voting and government by the people as one of the basic rights of citizenship, many women felt that they too should be able to speak out about issues that affected them and their families, and that they should be able to vote.

By the 1840s and 1850s, after gaining organizing, speaking, and political experience working in the anti-slavery and temperance movements, some women decided to work for their own rights.

The first women's rights convention was held in 1848 at Seneca Falls, New York. It was organized by two women, Lucretia Mott and Elizabeth Cady Stanton, who had not been seated at the World's Anti-Slavery Convention when it met in London in 1840. The convention did not accept women as delegates.

When the 1848 women's rights convention met, the women wrote down a list of their grievances, just as men had done when listing grievances against King George III of England during the Revolution. The document was called the Declaration of Sentiments, and one of the most controversial rights that these women wanted was the right to vote. When the Declaration was made public, the majority of Americans were astounded that women would make such an outrageous request. Many people made fun of them and said they were emotionally unstable and hated men.

Nevertheless, a small group of women began to work for "woman suffrage," a term that meant winning the right to vote. They also held conventions to discuss unfair laws toward women and how to go about changing them. The women didn't always agree about what methods to use to achieve their goal. Brave women such as Elizabeth Cady Stanton and Susan B. Anthony founded an organization to gain the vote for women, among many other reforms; in their view an amendment to the U.S. Constitution was needed. Other prominent leaders such as Lucy Stone and Julia Ward Howe thought that voting rights for women should be fought for state by state

*S*usan B. Anthony was a major leader of the woman suffrage movement from the 1850s until her death in 1906. Seated at her desk in the study of her Rochester, New York, home, Anthony is surrounded by books, papers, and photographs of suffrage friends and co-workers. The women represented are a "who's who" of leaders of the cause.

without trying to change other laws. Finally in 1890, after a generation of disagreement, the two groups came together to form the National American Woman Suffrage Association (NAWSA).

The popular perception of women's proper role had to change dramatically before the public could entertain the idea of women voting. Suffrage groups educated, organized, circulated petitions, and kept the issue visible in the states and in Congress.

By 1910 women's activities had grown to include a wide range of public works and social reforms. New women's groups and leaders came forward with innovative ideas that gave new life to the cause. They stressed that many necessary reforms could be won only if women had the vote. NAWSA developed powerful images to "sell" the organization's ideas, emphasizing women's importance in the home, bringing up children, and improving the community. They held dramatic parades

*S*ince only men served in the legislatures and Congress, women needed their votes to pass the woman suffrage amendment. Women set up headquarters all over the country, like this one in Cleveland, Ohio, to educate and persuade men to support "votes for women."

featuring banners proclaiming "Give the Ballot to the Mothers" and "Let the Mothers Make the World Safe for the Children."

A smaller, radical group of women called the National Woman's Party, led by Alice Paul, took more dramatic steps, such as picketing the White House, an action unheard-of in its day. They burned copies of President Wilson's speeches, pointing out that while he waged a war in Europe to "make the world safe for democracy," women could not vote or take part in democracy at home. Women who picketed were arrested and sent to prison, went on hunger strikes, and were force-fed in jail. Many people were outraged that women protesters were jailed for wanting to vote.

Through parades, picketing, lobbying, petitioning Congress, and civil disobedience, women gained dramatic publicity for their cause that helped them to persuade Congress to pass the constitutional amendment for women's vote. The Nineteenth Amendment was ratified by the states in 1920. After all those years of campaigns and struggle, women were now voting partners in American political life.

Ellen Wilson

MAY 15, 1860–AUGUST 6, 1914

"Small, eager, intensely alive"

ℰllen Wilson approached her marriage to Woodrow Wilson as a partnership and played an important role in his success while pursuing her own interest in art.

𝒯he eldest of the four children of the Reverend Samuel Edward Axson and Margaret Hoyt Axson, Ellie Lou Axson was born on May 15, 1860, at the Savannah home of her paternal grandfather, a leading Presbyterian preacher.

During Ellie's early years her parents had moved repeatedly from one town to another in Georgia or South Carolina, as her father kept receiving new pastoral assignments. But when she was five, they settled near Georgia's northwestern border in the pleasant little city called Rome. Hardly touched by the recent ravages of the Civil War, it preserved an unhurried Southern charm.

Ellie's voice would always retain its soft Southern accent, and yet she grew up with a broader outlook than many young women of the time. At the age of sixteen she graduated from the Rome Female College, more an advanced high school than a college but the only institute of higher learning available to her. There she gained a thorough familiarity with the classics of literature, along with a strong interest in art.

The one great sorrow of her young life was the death of her mother following the birth of a baby boy. While this infant was adopted by relatives, Ellie took over housekeeping for her father and two other brothers. Even so, she managed to continue painting pictures of her favorite landscape scenes—and she showed such skill that in the autumn of 1882, when she was twenty-two, her father let her travel all the way to New York City for a winter of classes at the Art Students League.

Soon after her return, on a Sunday morning in April 1883, an earnest young lawyer from a similar background spied her at church. "What a bright pretty face! What splendid laughing eyes!" he is said to have thought when he saw her. By September, despite his fear that such a wonderful person would surely reject him, Thomas Woodrow Wilson dared to ask Ellen Louise Axson to marry him.

Ellie instantly and joyfully said yes. In a letter to one of her brothers she wrote: "He is the greatest man in the world and the best." After her husband came to rank among the country's most influential presidents, some writers would say that she deserved much of the credit for his rise, because he was a man who was unable to act without support and reassurance from an adoring wife.

Ellie encouraged Woodrow to follow his instinct that he would be much happier as a professor of political science than as a lawyer. However, before he could hope to be hired by any college, he would have to go back to school himself to earn an advanced degree. So he entered a Ph.D. program at Johns Hopkins University in Baltimore, where his exceptional intellectual ability was first recognized.

Meanwhile, Ellie had another two winters of art training in New York. Yet the daily letters she and Woodrow wrote to each other made it clear that they both yearned above all to begin their lives together. At last, on June 24, 1885, they were married at the Savannah residence of her Axson grandparents; she was twenty-five then, and he was twenty-eight.

During the next quarter of a century Ellie seemed completely satisfied by the course of her life. Caring for her three daughters—Margaret, Jessie, and Eleanor—occupied much of her time; as the low salary of a college professor could not be

Photographer Lewis Hine shot this image of an alley dwelling near the U.S. Capitol in 1908. Ellen Wilson sought to improve the terrible living conditions in Washington, D.C.

stretched very far, she sewed all of the girls' intricate matching dresses herself, besides cooking and gardening and melodiously reading poetry aloud to her family most evenings. Sometimes she stole a few hours at her easel to paint a vista she particularly admired.

Ellie also found time to go over everything Woodrow wrote, often suggesting changes. With the help of Ellie and his daughters, Wilson became the most popular professor at Princeton University in New Jersey. Also, the books he authored displayed such an impressive mind that in 1902 he was chosen as Princeton's president.

Ellie herself wrote that she would have been perfectly happy if her husband had kept this post until it was time for him to retire. The old-fashioned small town that was the university's home suited her, and the financial pressures that had required so much scrimping during the early years of their marriage no longer prevented them from enjoying small luxuries, now that Woodrow was paid more generously.

The many reforms he instituted on the Princeton campus attracted such widespread attention that in 1910, New Jersey's Democrats drafted him as the party's candidate for governor of the state. Ellie's work was essential in helping him win the election. When liberal Democrats began hoping he would become the next president of the United States, she even eased the path to the White House for him.

William Jennings Bryan, a major figure in the Democratic party whose support would be crucial, unexpectedly came to New Jersey while Woodrow was away making a speech. Ellie not only telegraphed her husband to come home as soon as possible but also invited Bryan for dinner—and the friendly rapport the two men arrived at did much to ensure her husband's nomination for the presidency.

Right after he won the 1912 presidential election, Ellie realized what was in store for her when she took her daughters on a shopping expedition to New York City. Never before had any of them bought more than one dress at a time, so the prospect of choosing an entire wardrobe for the inauguration festivities thrilled them all. But other shoppers crowded around them to such an extent that on returning home, she wailed, "Oh, Woodrow, we felt like animals in a zoo!"

Dismayed by her new celebrity, Ellie avoided newspaper reporters and never let herself be interviewed. One of her daughters provided the best description of her: "Small, eager, intensely alive." On moving into the White House, the new first lady presided with unassuming graciousness at the required receptions and other official gatherings.

She soon demonstrated that while her husband was sponsoring a broad program of governmental reforms, she had her own agenda of changes. Like many other women of her time, Ellie was interested in reform in the nation's cities. Shocked by reports of disgraceful living conditions in alleys right near the Capitol, Ellie asked to be taken on a tour of these slums and then spent many hours conferring with congressmen about what action might be taken for the black families and immigrants occupying the tumbledown shacks.

Another of Ellie's special concerns was a campaign to install the first rest rooms for women workers in government offices. Along with her busy schedule of humanitarian meetings, she even planned an elaborate White House wedding when her daughter Jessie became engaged to a young professor: That gala near the end of 1913 marked the high point of her active life.

During the next several months Ellie's formerly inexhaustible energy deserted her. Although she found herself having to rest more and more often, it was not until March 1914, when she fell in her White House room, that she allowed anybody to see she was seriously ill. Doctors said she had a type of kidney ailment for which no cure existed.

That summer the assassination of Archduke Ferdinand of Austria in Sarajevo aroused tensions that led to the outbreak of World War I. But Woodrow Wilson could hardly attend to official business as the woman who had been "incomparably the greatest influence" on his life and career grew ever weaker.

Ellie remained conscious long enough to smile faintly when he told her that Congress had just passed "Ellen Wilson's Bill" approving clearance of the alley slums. While Congress cleared the alleys of the slum dwellings, sadly, they did not provide for new or better housing for the alley dwellers. Having been the nation's first lady for only seventeen months, Ellen Wilson died in the White House on August 6, 1914, at the age of fifty-four.

Edith Wilson

OCTOBER 15, 1872 – DECEMBER 28, 1961

Our first woman president?

In contrast to the first Mrs. Wilson, Edith Wilson thrived on the attention she received as first lady.

*N*ot long after the Civil War ended, a formerly wealthy plantation owner moved to the little town of Wytheville, in the southwestern corner of Virginia. Left almost penniless when the Southern cause was lost, William Holcombe Bolling built a new career as a respected though not very prosperous rural lawyer and judge. Meanwhile, his wife, Sallie White Bolling, presided over a shabby brick house filled with their own large brood in addition to several female relatives who had lost their husbands to the Civil War.

Edith, the seventh of William and Sallie's eleven children, became one of the most admired—and most controversial—first ladies in American history.

Edith Bolling, born on October 15, 1872, never spent a day in school during her childhood. But her father's mother, a woman who still regarded their family as upper-class gentlefolk despite the family's dire financial straits, felt a particular fondness for this lively granddaughter. So Edith was taught to love music and poetry, as well as more basic lessons in reading and writing.

At age fifteen Edith was sent to a boarding school called Martha Washington College, which proved to be an unethically run institution where the students were nearly starved. Edith looked so painfully thin when she returned home after only one semester that her parents did not send her back.

A year later, they tried another establishment, in Richmond. Edith spent only one winter there—by that time, her father was beginning to worry about the cost of educating her three younger brothers, and he sacrificed Edith's schooling for theirs.

Seventeen years old when her limited classroom experience ended, Edith had read only a few books and her handwriting was almost impossible to decipher. When Edith was eighteen, she received an invitation from her eldest sister, who had married into a family that owned one of the most fashionable jewelry stores in the nation's capital: Would she like to come to Washington for a Southern-style visit of several months? Edith enthusiastically agreed—and got her first taste of theater, opera, and Washington society.

Norman Galt, nine years her senior and manager of Galt's jewelry store, became enamored of Edith. To her, he seemed much too old for romance. But Norman refused to be discouraged by her lack of interest, and over the next few years he made repeated trips to Wytheville to continue courting her. At last, in 1896, when she was twenty-four, they married.

Becoming Mrs. Norman Galt opened a new life to Edith: She attended sophisticated dinner parties throughout the winter and took annual tours of Europe, becoming a client of the haute couture (high fashion) salons of Paris. Edith's life became increasingly connected to the influential men and women of Washington, as Galt's jewelry was worn by Washington's high society; Frances Cleveland was a frequent patron of the store.

In early 1903 Edith gave birth to a baby boy, but the infant lived only three days. Edith was told she could never have another child. She later wrote that although she was fond of her husband, she did not love him deeply. Even so, she felt that the main part of her youth was over when Norman died suddenly in 1908.

Age thirty-six when she became a widow, Edith was left with a comfortable house in Washington and no financial worries, and whether at home or on her trips to Europe, various relatives were always available to keep her company. In addition, her sympathetic warmth won her many friends in the nation's capital during her next seven years there.

An informal social encounter with Woodrow Wilson in March 1915 led swiftly to a new phase in Edith's life. Within just a few weeks of their meeting—at which, one witness reported, she had made him laugh for the first time since his first wife, Ellen, had died—Woodrow had fallen in love with Edith. His courtship of her was intense and secretive: Many of Wilson's political advisers counseled against his becoming romantically involved so soon after the death of his first wife—and at a time when the country was on the brink of entering a world war.

Although Edith hesitated to return his affections, expressing many doubts about the scrutiny she would receive as first lady, she soon became devoted to Woodrow. She told the president she would marry him after the November elections, which he won by a slim margin.

Woodrow trusted Edith implicitly and shared all details of his work with her, even classified information. Edith, who prior to Woodrow's victory could hardly have listed his opponents in the election, began to take a great interest in the running of the country. She started to form her own opinions about the president's decisions and about his advisers. "Much as I enjoy your delicious love letters," she told Woodrow early in their courtship, "I enjoy even more the ones in which you tell me . . . of what you are working on . . . for then I feel I am sharing your work and being taken into partnership as well."

On December 18, 1915, Edith and Woodrow's simple wedding took place in the parlor of her Washington home. She was forty-three then, and her boyishly elated husband would, ten days later, celebrate his fifty-ninth birthday. After an entirely private honeymoon at Hot Springs, Virginia, they returned to the White House together.

The new Mrs. Woodrow Wilson—she preferred that name to the title of first lady—quickly lifted the cloud of gloom that had hung over the mansion since her predecessor's illness and death. Edith's sociable nature, as well as her fondness for dressing in high style, allowed her to enjoy even routine gatherings. She presided with such verve that she won wide approval—a longtime observer of the capital scene called her "a first lady to be proud of."

Edith and Woodrow Wilson were rarely apart: She was the first presidential wife to accompany her husband to and from his inaugural swearing in. They golfed together, walked together, worked together; they even sat next to each other at state dinners. Edith worked with Woodrow as he answered important documents from "The Drawer" on his desk. And if visitors or guests wanted to see the president, they nearly always went through Edith first.

After being elected on the slogan "He kept us out of war," Woodrow Wilson regretfully led the country into the world war in Europe on April 6, 1917. Edith took up the mission of setting a good example for the nation's women: Besides spending many hours at her sewing machine turning out garments for soldiers, she donned a Red Cross uniform to serve coffee and doughnuts to men on troop trains passing through Washington's railroad station. She made sure that even the White House patriotically observed the meatless days that had been decreed to guarantee sufficient food for the armed forces. She even installed a herd of sheep on the White House lawn, whose grazing kept the grass trimmed and thereby freed groundskeepers for military duty. When it came time for the sheep to be shorn, Edith gave each state in the nation two pounds of wool to sell at charity auctions, raising fifty thousand dollars for the war cause.

Edith also contributed privately to American efforts in World War I. She became her husband's unofficial personal secretary, reviewing all the papers that came across his desk. In an unprecedented move, Edith decoded secret diplomatic and military messages sent to the president from Europe and encoded his replies. It was clear to the president's advisers, if not to the public, that Edith Wilson played a crucial role in the Wilson administration.

After the United States and its allies won the war in 1918, Edith sailed with Woodrow to Europe—the first first lady to accompany her husband on an overseas mission. There, millions of people turned out to cheer the American president whose desire to "make the world safe for democracy" had inspired the great victory. However, Wilson was not such a success diplomatically. Europe's leaders who had assembled to write a peace treaty at the high-level conference paid less attention to Wilson's idealistic vision of a League of Nations than to their own national interests.

Immensely disappointed, Woodrow became so tense that Edith began to worry about his health. Upon returning home, he began a nine-thousand-mile cross-country speaking tour to promote American support of the League, but the tour was cut short when Woodrow Wilson collapsed on September 15, 1918, during a speech in Colorado. Doctors counseled the president and his wife that the collapse was the result of exhaustion; the press was told the president simply needed some rest. In Washington a few days later, Woodrow suffered a severe stroke, which left

him blind in one eye and unable to move his left side. "My God," cried his doctor the moment he saw him, "the president is paralyzed."

However, it soon became clear to Woodrow's physicians that the president's mind was sound though his physical condition required complete rest. It was also clear that only one person could tend the spark of the president's flagging spirits—his wife Edith.

Edith became the gatekeeper to the president. She maintained that she did not take over the office of president but, she wrote later, "The only decision that was mine was what was important and what was not, and the *very* important decision of when to present matters to my husband." Woodrow's only contact was with his wife and his doctors. The cabinet, the president's advisers, and the press were not allowed to see the president.

Many historians now agree with Edith that she did not deliberately take the reins of power; her mission always appeared to be to keep her husband alive by not allowing the presidency to be taken from him. But her influence over Woodrow was immense. What Edith called "her stewardship," the president's opponents coined a "petticoat government." Though Woodrow was fully disabled for only six weeks, Edith's protection of her husband did not sit well with the press. Over and over they posed the question: Who is in charge? An editorial in the *Baltimore Sun* even asked, "Must we look for a woman in the case?" Only feminists—whose causes Woodrow had always opposed—applauded Mrs. Wilson's take-charge role.

The president's condition improved enough by the end of 1918 that he was able to resume at least a limited workload. Even though his left arm remained paralyzed and he was too weak for more than brief meetings with other officials, the messages he dictated were unmistakably in his own words.

During the year and a half from his collapse until his term ended, Woodrow Wilson continued to be a very sick man. Although he wished his party might draft him for another four years in office, Edith insisted that they were both more than ready for retirement. In March 1921 they moved into a house on Washington's S Street, where workmen, under her supervision, had installed an elevator and other conveniences for her husband's comfort.

Growing ever more frail, Woodrow died three years later. Edith was fifty-one then; she had been Mrs. Wilson hardly more than eight years, and she would live nearly thirty-eight years more. During the rest of her long life, she supported many projects to uphold her husband's high ideals. Even as a very old woman, she represented her husband at many ceremonial occasions.

One of Edith's last public appearances was as an honored guest at the inauguration of President John F. Kennedy. Near the end of that same year, on December 28, 1961, Edith Wilson died at her home on S Street, at the the age of eighty-nine.

Part IV

Modern Times
1920 to the Present

*I*n 1920, when women gained the vote, optimists hoped that this would begin a period of unprecedented progress for women in politics, business, and society. But the people who came together in the suffrage campaign had many different views about the kinds of lives women should lead. As the boom years of the twenties gave way to the Great Depression of the thirties, women's rights took second place to the very survival of the nation. Still, as America coped with the problems of the Depression and then a second world war, some women found new opportunities. They set examples that their daughters and granddaughters looked back to with pride when a new round of human rights struggles began in the sixties.

The Great Depression, which began in 1929 and lasted until the beginning of World War II, around 1940, was in many ways a setback for women. As unemployment rose, women were forced out of jobs. Men, people argued, needed to work to support their families. Women were falsely accused of holding jobs merely to buy frivolous items. At the same time, the difficulty of daily life made people focus on

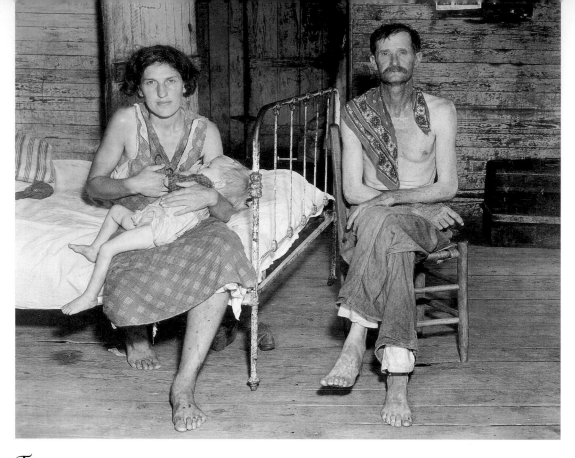

These sharecroppers—Bud Fields, his daughter-in-law, and his granddaughter—lived a grim existence in Alabama during the Great Depression.

family and survival, not broad questions about women and society. In the Roosevelt administration, though, women made new gains when Frances Perkins was named secretary of labor, the first woman to hold a cabinet post. Eleanor Roosevelt held her own press conferences at the White House, the first first lady to do so. Though African-American women held the lowest-paying jobs and gained little support from the federal government, they gained an advocate in Washington through activist Mary McLeod Bethune's ties to Mrs. Roosevelt.

World War II, beginning for the United States with the bombing of Pearl Harbor in December 1941, brought dramatic changes in women's lives. As hundreds of thousands of men went to war, women were actively recruited to take their places. Advertisements appealed to women to enter jobs formerly open only to men and stressed the importance of their work to the war effort. Child-care centers were set up across the country to care for the children of working mothers. At the same time, the All American Girls Professional Baseball Association gave women their first opportunity to compete as professionals in the "national pastime." Though the league was formed to make money, it served as a symbol of the possibilities open to women during the war.

After the war, many of these opportunities disappeared. Government, business, and even labor unions urged women to return to the home to make way for the men returning from war. Having survived the Depression and then World War II, many Americans were eager to create secure, prosperous, and conventional lives. In the postwar prosperity, cars, homes, and household appliances were built in record numbers. Women were encouraged to be housewives, mothers, and consumers. Movies, novels, women's magazines, advertising, popular songs, and the new medium of television all stressed the importance of femininity and motherhood, at least for white women.

Yet World War II had been a struggle against the worst of human tyranny, and after the war the barriers between men and women, and between blacks and whites, became harder to defend. After President Truman desegregated the armed forces in

When the United States entered World War II, millions of men—fathers, sons, husbands, and sweethearts—entered the armed forces to fight in Europe and the Pacific. This bittersweet good-bye kiss symbolized the feelings of millions of women as loved ones went off to war.

1948, pressure to integrate all of America began to grow. As African Americans fought for their rights in the 1950s and 1960s, they set a precedent women were eager to follow.

Inspired by Dr. Martin Luther King, Jr., and other civil rights leaders, college students, ministers, and thousands of others demonstrated and lobbied for the passage of the Civil Rights Act in 1964 and the Voting Rights Act in 1965. Finally the rights African Americans had been granted after the Civil War were actively protected by the government. The experience of the civil rights struggle, combined with the protest movement against American involvement in Vietnam, encouraged a generation of Americans to question many of the established rules and social norms of their nation. One of their main targets was the restricted role of American women.

Betty Friedan wrote *The Feminine Mystique* in 1963, arguing that a woman need not be only a housewife and mother but also should have access to other ways of expressing herself—in education, in work, in politics, in society. The book had a profound impact, and Friedan and other women launched the new women's rights movement in the mid-1960s. They formed the National Organization for Women (NOW) in 1966 to work for equality for women in every aspect of society. Women demanded that the Equal Rights Amendment (ERA) be passed by Congress. They wanted equal pay for equal work and equal access to education, jobs, sports, and the military.

On completion of their basic training, enlisted WAVES (Women Accepted for Volunteer Emergency Service) were sent to specialized schools to learn the skills that would enable them to replace men in all parts of the navy. These WAVES at the U.S. Naval Training School in Norman, Oklahoma, are learning to take apart airplane engines.

*S*upporters demonstrate for civil rights in the March on Washington in August 1963 to press for jobs, voting rights, better wages, and an end to discrimination against African Americans. This march featured the now-famous "I have a dream" speech given by civil rights leader Dr. Martin Luther King, Jr.

In the early 1970s women successfully lobbied Congress to pass the ERA and send it to the states for ratification. They formed the National Women's Political Caucus to develop an agenda to elect more women to political office and to put women's issues at the center of political concerns. The Women's Equity Action League and the Women's Legal Defense Fund brought legal challenges to discrimination against women. Despite laws passed to provide more equal pay, in the 1970s women still earned only fifty-nine cents for every dollar that men earned. Yet women gained entry into many areas of employment formerly closed to them, successfully ended quotas limiting women's acceptance to medical schools and law schools, and entered the professions in ever-increasing numbers. Indeed, in the seventies, college attendance by women surpassed that of men.

By 1977 conservative women, led by Phyllis Schlafly and her organization the Eagle Forum, had organized across the country to defeat the ERA and other reforms that they believed would damage the home and family and bring to an end the "traditional" role of women. They raised fears among many that equality would make women just like men, undermine laws supporting marriage, end men's financial support of wives and children, force women into military combat, and make men and women share the same public bathroom facilities. While no one could prove these things would happen—in fact, many legal opinions said they would not—enough states voted against ratification to defeat the ERA in 1982.

The Reagan administration, beginning in 1981, swept into the White House on a wave of conservative support that continued during the Bush administration. The Republican party, which had supported the ERA since it was first introduced in 1923, dropped its support. Civil rights and women's equal access to work, pay, and education lost support.

On the other hand, on Wall Street, in law firms, in business schools and other graduate programs, and in the arts and the media, women became ever more prominent. While Geraldine Ferraro's pioneering campaign for the vice presidency in 1984 was unsuccessful, in the 1990s both parties scrambled to find female candidates and to appeal to the now-crucial female vote.

In the 1990s the Clinton administration has tried to balance the expense of programs to assist children, health care, and education with the rising cost to taxpayers. This is a very difficult task. Women continue to work toward pay equity, equal education, equal access to jobs, and greater representation in state legislatures and Congress. For the first time in our history, two women—Diane Feinstein and Barbara Boxer—were elected as senators from California in 1992.

Women continue to carry the main responsibility for their homes and children. A soaring divorce rate indicates that many women choose not to remain in unhappy marriages, but many do not make enough money to support their families adequately. Trying to enforce child-support payments from divorced fathers or fathers who never married the mother of their children has become a national crisis.

As we near the end of the twentieth century, women's "proper place" in society is still hotly debated. As a younger generation of presidents and first ladies comes into the White House, we may see more professional women like Mrs. Clinton. Some presidential wives in the future may not wish to give up their professional careers to take on the duties of first lady. How will that affect the first lady's role? In the future we may also see the election of a woman as president. Will her husband assume the traditional responsibilities of a first lady or will he continue his own professional career? These interesting questions will be decided by the generation of young people who read this book, as they shape and are shaped by the changing definitions of the roles of women and men in American life.

Florence Harding

"Strange and rather difficult"

Florence Harding used her knowledge of modern journalism to advance her husband's political career. She was quoted as saying in 1921, "Well, Warren, I have got you the presidency; what are you going to do with it?"

Born in the central Ohio town of Marion on August 15, 1860, Florence Harding grew up as Flossie Kling, the only daughter of the richest man in town. Her father, Amos Kling, was a strong-minded banker so sure of his own opinions that he almost completely overshadowed his wife, Louisa Bouton Kling. Because Flossie patterned herself after him, not her mother, she often tried to defy his strict rules during her childhood.

Flossie showed no special ability while attending local schools. But she did put a lot of her energy into learning how to play the piano, displaying enough talent to be sent for a year of training at the Cincinnati Conservatory of Music. After she returned home, her attention turned to a handsome young man with a bad reputation.

Henry de Wolfe—Pete to his friends—was the son of a well-to-do coal dealer. Two years older than Flossie, he already had a serious problem with alcohol, so her father forbade her to attend parties where he was present. But she kept finding opportunities to meet him. In March 1880, a few months before her twentieth birthday and pregnant with de Wolfe's child, she convinced Pete to marry her. Their elopement stunned both their families.

That September, Flossie gave birth to a baby boy she named Marshall de Wolfe. By then Pete's alcoholism was uncontrollable, and he kept disappearing for longer and longer periods. Within another few months he had completely abandoned his wife and child. The marriage ended in divorce in 1886.

Flossie's unforgiving father refused to help her in any way. However, the de Wolfes took over the upbringing of their grandson while Flossie rented a small apartment, where she barely supported herself by giving piano lessons. Thanks to her mother's quiet efforts on her behalf, in a few years she was allowed to return to her family's comfortable home.

Not long after arrangements had been made to secure a divorce for her—a procedure that people like her parents regarded as disgraceful—Flossie became involved with another handsome man her father frowned upon.

Warren G. Harding, five years younger than she was, had arrived in Marion as editor of the local newspaper. He possessed a great gift for making political friends and for attracting female attention. Soon Flossie Kling de Wolfe began finding reasons for visiting his office. She even appeared at the railroad station whenever he was due to return from some trip.

Long afterward, many writers assumed that Harding—having started out as a poor farm boy—had been more favorably impressed by the wealth and social position of Flossie's father than by Flossie herself. He married her on July 8, 1891; she was a month short of her thirty-first birthday, and he was almost twenty-six. Although the bride's father refused to attend the ceremony, the bride's mother was noticed sitting alone in a back row of the church, and her presence stirred hopes that Amos Kling would eventually be won over.

In fact, over the next few decades the solidly Republican Mr. Kling became one of his son-in-law's warmest admirers. While Warren Harding used his newspaper

During the Hardings' "front-porch campaign" from their home in Ohio, Florence played a major role. She was expert at arranging what we would call "photo opportunities."

connection to achieve increasing political prominence, his wife used the business sense that she had absorbed from her father to make the *Marion Star* increasingly profitable. As she later told an interviewer: "I went down there for a few days and remained fourteen years."

Concentrating on the business side of the paper rather than its day-to-day contents, Florence Harding organized a reliable group of delivery boys and saw to it that local enterprises advertised regularly. After devoting many years and much energy to the paper, she gave up these responsibilities as her husband began advancing politically. Supported for a few lesser offices by Ohio's powerful Republican bosses, Warren Harding turned out to be such a popular candidate that in 1915 he won a seat in the U.S. Senate.

"Being a senator's wife suits me," Mrs. Harding assured reporters a few years afterward. Although the Midwestern twang of her voice, along with her small-town outlook, caused some Washington insiders to poke fun at her, she relished the elevated social status that her husband's post gave her—indeed, she felt that she herself had done much to spur his rise, and many political observers agreed with her.

Even though her "Wurr-rr-en" looked like a wise lawmaker and could speak impressively when somebody else told him what to say, he lacked the intellect to cope with complicated issues. If he had stayed in the Senate, where his fondness for playing poker endeared him to many of his colleagues, he and his wife might have continued to enjoy life in the nation's capital. As it was, some of his party's bosses decided that he should be nominated for the presidency in 1920.

Early in May 1920 Florence Harding visited a fortune-teller named Madame Marcia, who had gained a certain amount of fame among Washingtonians for making surprisingly accurate predictions. Told that her husband was destined to become president but was also doomed to die while in office, Florence didn't seem quite sure whether or not she believed in Madame Marcia's special powers. Even so, she consulted her repeatedly from then on and nervously reported every detail of these frightening forecasts to her acquaintances.

Florence assumed the role of first lady with a folksy style that pleased many ordinary citizens. For instance, on occasions when newspaper photographers crowded around her, she frequently said something like: "All right, boys. I always take a frightful picture and I hate this. But I know you've got to do it." She made a point of mingling with "the people" by personally greeting some of the groups of tourists admitted to the downstairs public rooms of the White House.

However, Washingtonians aware of her behind-the-scenes behavior as "the Duchess" (a name her husband called her) often made scornful remarks about her. One of them described Mrs. Harding as "a strange and rather difficult woman," while others ridiculed her high-pitched, strident voice and commanding ways.

Much more significantly, both Florence and her husband used very poor judgment in their choice of friends. Among the men in the administration were many high-level officials who took advantage of their connection to make a lot of money illegally. Although neither the president nor the first lady participated in any of these schemes, their innocent trust led to the worst series of high-level scandals the capital had yet experienced.

When hints of this corruption first began surfacing, the Hardings seemed bewildered. "I must say all the days are very trying," Florence wrote to an Ohio relative early in 1922. That year a severe attack of a kidney ailment made her an invalid for several months, and her husband started showing alarming symptoms of heart trouble.

By the summer of 1923 the full extent of the wrongdoing by presidential friends

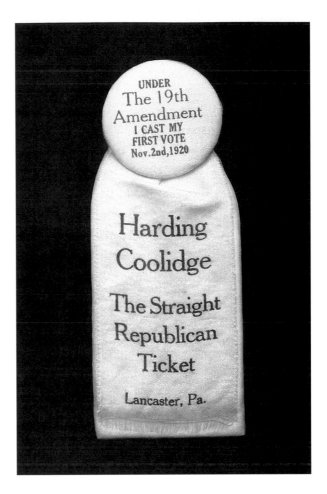

Florence Harding was a suffrage supporter, and her role may have been essential in the 1920 campaign—the first presidential race in which women could vote. This badge was made for women to wear after they had voted for the Republican candidates.

still had not been exposed. Doctors said the health of the president and the first lady would be improved by a long vacation, so the couple embarked on a train and boat trip to Alaska. Yet even in this remote area, Warren Harding could not escape his worries about what lay ahead. En route back to Washington, he had an attack of food poisoning; on August 2, 1923, he died in San Francisco.

After leaving the White House, a bewildered Florence returned to Marion. Growing ever weaker herself, she spent many hours going through her husband's papers and destroyed numerous private letters and files while the country was being shaken by exposure of the crimes of Harding cronies. Next came rumors that President Harding had actually committed suicide, and one writer even claimed that his wife had poisoned him, but these tales were completely unfounded. The detailed reports that began appearing in print about Harding's many extramarital affairs, however, were true.

Hardly more than a year after her husband's death, Florence Harding died in Marion on November 21, 1924, at the age of sixty-four.

Grace Coolidge

JANUARY 3, 1879–JULY 8, 1957

"A ray of sunlight"

Grace Coolidge's natural warmth and ease with people won political friends for her husband, who was known as "Silent Cal."

Except that they both were natives of Vermont and they both had moved to Massachusetts, Grace Goodhue could hardly have been more different from the extremely solemn lawyer she was to marry. Born in the small city of Burlington on January 3, 1879, Grace had been noted from her babyhood for her sunny disposition. An only child, she grew up cherished by both her parents: Her mother was Lemira Barrett Goodhue, a strong-minded homemaker; her father, Andrew Issachar Goodhue, made a comfortable living as an inspector of steamboats.

Burlington's location on the edge of Lake Champlain gave it a prosperous shipping industry, as well as a wonderful variety of outdoor activities. During her girlhood Grace eagerly looked forward to sailing and swimming every summer, then skating and sleighing in the winter. Indoors, too, she found something to enjoy.

After attending local schools, she enrolled at the University of Vermont in Burlington. "I still remember her sparkle," one of her college classmates wrote long afterward. Grace participated enthusiastically in many campus projects: She sang in the glee club, she acted in plays, and she helped to found the University of Vermont's chapter of Phi Beta Phi, one of the first national sororities for college women. On graduating in 1902, Grace decided to devote herself to work that would help others who were less fortunate than she.

One of the Goodhues' neighbors in Burlington was related to the founder of a pioneering school for the deaf—the Clark School, in Northampton, Massachusetts. Grace trained to become a teacher of deaf children and joined the staff of the school, where she later met her husband, Calvin Coolidge. Many of her friends couldn't understand how a happily outgoing woman had come to marry such an outwardly cold, taciturn man. In her later years one of her closest friends asked Grace the question directly. "Well, I thought I would get him to enjoy life and have fun," she replied, "but he was not very easy to instruct in that way."

At least while Calvin was courting her, he accompanied her on picnics and sightseeing expeditions. Silent as he was around other people, Grace assured her family and friends that he expressed himself freely during the long walks the two of them took almost daily. Despite the strong disapproval of her mother, on October 4, 1905, not much more than a year after the pair had met, they were married at a simple ceremony in Burlington; the bride was twenty-six then, and her husband thirty-three.

Calvin's views on married life were unshakably old-fashioned: He expected unquestioning obedience, believing that a wife should concern herself only with domestic duties. By agreeing to marry him, Grace was well aware that she had also agreed to accept whatever rules he set for her.

So she gave up her teaching even before she had two sons to care for: John, born a year after her marriage, and Calvin Junior, who arrived two years later. As her husband's income from his small-town law practice was not large, and he kept a tight grasp on every penny he earned, they lived very frugally in an unpretentious two-family house, where Grace did the cooking and cleaning without any assistance.

She felt amply rewarded for all her hard work by Calvin's unspoken appreciation.

His one extravagance was buying her beautiful and expensive clothing—without a word, he would present her with some stylish garment he had chosen himself. Calvin soon rose from being mayor of Northampton to the post of lieutenant governor of Massachusetts, and many of his official duties were in the state capital of Boston.

On the grounds that he couldn't afford keeping up two homes, Calvin left Grace and their sons in Northampton while he carried out his duties in Boston.

After the safely conservative Calvin won the governorship of his state, Grace did go to Boston whenever her husband requested her presence there. Her charming manner as she presided at official entertainments made a most favorable impression. Because Governor Coolidge won the approval of Republicans all over the country when he sternly settled a Boston police strike in 1919, the possibility of his becoming the next vice president of the United States began to be seriously discussed.

After graduating from the University of Vermont, Grace Goodhue Coolidge (shown here meeting Helen Keller) prepared to teach the hearing impaired at the Clark School for the Deaf.

"One of his greatest assets is Mrs. Coolidge," a leading Massachusetts Republican decided. "She will make friends wherever she goes and she will not meddle with his conduct of the office."

The governor's secretary expressed a similar opinion more picturesquely, describing the governor's wife as being "a ray of sunlight." So even though Grace continued to leave everything political to her husband, her presence by his side had a lot to do with his winning the vice presidency in 1920.

When Grace accompanied Calvin to Washington, she began playing a much larger part than she had ever imagined. By being herself, enjoying her new opportunities for meeting all sorts of people, she quickly earned popularity among the capital's social leaders. More important, by making a joke of her husband's many peculiarities in anecdotes she told wherever she went, she deftly accomplished the feat of turning him into a likably quirky Vermont character.

The most famous of Grace's stories described how a noted Washington hostess, seated beside Calvin at a dinner party, told him she had bet a friend of hers that she could make him say more than two words. "You lose," the vice president replied.

Outwardly, Grace wasn't fazed by her sudden elevation to the rank of first lady in the summer of 1923 when her husband became president following the death of Warren Harding. Yet she privately wrote to her closest college friends that being the wife of the chief executive was a very confining position.

Most of the additional restraints on her activities were actually decreed by her husband. Since he believed that the occupants of the White House had a particular responsibility for upholding conventional standards, he forbade Grace to shorten her skirts or cut her hair in keeping with 1920s trends. When she decided to take up horseback riding because she felt a need for daily exercise, he vetoed this plan; then when she took up hiking instead and bought some stylish skirt-length pants to wear while she walked, he told her to return the undignified garments.

Still, none of these edicts dimmed the sunny disposition Grace displayed at White House gatherings. Nor did she appear to mind her husband's invasion of what had always been considered female territory, such as his constant inspections of the mansion's kitchen to ensure not a penny was being spent unnecessarily. If she ever had any impulse to make political remarks herself, there is no record of it.

Happy as Grace seemed, she endured a great sorrow the summer after moving into the White House. By then the Coolidge boys were away at school, but while Calvin Junior was vacationing with his parents he developed a blister on one of his toes during a tennis game—and this small injury caused an infection doctors of the day could not cure. The death of their sixteen-year-old son deeply affected both of his parents.

Grace Coolidge often promoted women's groups, giving them national status by inviting them to the White House. Here representatives of the Visiting Nurse Association watch the first lady cut a cake to celebrate the group's twenty-fifth anniversary.

President Coolidge had already agreed to head his party's ticket in the 1924 election, and the nation's booming prosperity led to his winning a new term easily. Only a limited amount of official entertaining was done during the next four years because the loss of Calvin Junior continued to depress the boy's father. Grace occupied herself mainly in promoting charitable causes, particularly those involved with helping deaf children.

Gradually, though, she regained her own high spirits. Always fond of animals, she nurtured several dogs, cats, and canaries—and even a pet raccoon named Rebecca—in the family quarters of the White House. Grace continued doing her best to improve her husband's image.

Much relieved when Calvin announced his plans to retire from public life in 1928, Grace happily accompanied him back to their original home in Northampton. But life in the two-family house proved difficult for former residents of the White House because sight-seers often drove slowly past their front door. Since Calvin had managed to save a substantial amount of his presidential salary, he soon bought a more private dwelling on several acres near the edge of town.

There he occupied himself writing magazine and newspaper articles. But Calvin's health had never been very sturdy, and he soon developed serious heart problems. Nearly four years after leaving Washington, he died at the age of sixty.

Grace lived on another twenty-four years, mostly out of the public eye. Her independent personality came more into focus in the latter years of her life. She published poems and articles, and in 1935 she became president of the board of the Clark School for the Deaf, where she had taught as a young woman. The marriage of her son John brought her a pair of granddaughters to cherish, and she continued supporting several charitable causes.

After she could no longer go to see her beloved Boston Red Sox, she still spent many happy hours listening to their games on her radio. Grace Coolidge was seventy-eight when she died at her Northampton home on July 8, 1957.

Lou Hoover

MARCH 19, 1874–JANUARY 7, 1944

"Who would marry a woman geologist?"

A brilliant woman fluent in five languages, Lou Hoover was the first woman to earn a degree in geology from Stanford University.

Lou Hoover was a grandmother when she moved into the White House. But her staid appearance and her formal manner were really quite misleading. In fact, she deserves to be ranked among the most groundbreaking of the nation's first ladies.

As a girl, Lou Henry had been a fearless horseback rider who loved to explore rocky canyons. This special interest led her to study geology at college, where she was the only woman in most of her classes. Then, after marrying one of her fellow students, she repeatedly accompanied him on adventurous missions to isolated mining areas all around the world.

Lou had been brought up to believe that it was not proper for females to draw attention to their own activities. So she always shied away from personal publicity—even today just a few basic facts about her early life are available.

Born in Waterloo, Iowa, on March 19, 1874, she was the elder of the two daughters of a banker named Charles Henry and his wife, Florence Weed Henry. In an effort to improve her mother's failing health, the family moved to California when Lou was ten years old.

They settled in the beautiful coastal town of Whittier, south of San Francisco, where Charles Henry found a promising banking opportunity. Outdoor pursuits were his main interest, and he treated Lou like the son he never had, taking her often on camping trips into the nearby mountains. This tall, slender daughter became accustomed to being called a tomboy.

She had a lively mind too. Right after she graduated from high school Lou enrolled at a training school for teachers. During her second year there a series of lectures by a leading expert on rocks and minerals changed the whole direction of her life.

The speaker was Professor John Branner, head of the geology department at recently established Stanford University in Palo Alto. Lou asked him a crucial question: Would Stanford allow a woman student to major in geology? He replied that even though no woman had tried to do so since the university's founding three years earlier, he saw no reason why a female who met the entrance requirements should not be admitted.

When Lou entered Stanford in 1894, at the age of twenty, practically everybody she knew asked *her* a question: Who would marry a woman geologist? Her answer showed that she did not intend to give up her own interests if she did get married: "I want a man who loves the mountains, the rocks, and the oceans like my father does." She met just that sort of man even sooner than she imagined she would.

During her freshman year, one afternoon in the geology lab Professor Branner was showing her some rocks he thought were very old. Suddenly he called over a senior whom he considered his most promising student. "Isn't that your opinion?" he demanded. Blushing a deep pink, Herbert Hoover merely nodded.

Shortly afterward, Bert conquered the shyness that had kept him from approaching the blue-eyed young lady whose presence in the geology lab he had already noticed. He had been enchanted by her "broad grinnish smile," as he put it years later in his own story of his life.

Bert and Lou discovered that they both hailed from Iowa, where they had been born just a few months apart. By the time he graduated they had arrived at an "understanding" that they would marry as soon as he was able to support a wife and she had achieved her own aim of getting her Stanford diploma.

He started working at entry-level mining jobs while she completed her studies. During her junior year Bert was hired by a large company to search for gold in a remote part of Australia. From that distant land she received a cabled message soon after her graduation, saying he had just been offered a much better-paying assignment—in China. If he sailed home immediately, would she marry him and accompany him there?

Yes, Lou cabled back. Thus a simple wedding took place in Monterey, California, on February 10, 1899, with the twenty-four-year-old bride wearing a sensible gray traveling suit. Then she and her husband took a train to San Francisco, where they boarded a China-bound ship.

Lou's luggage contained numerous books about Chinese history and customs for them to read during their long voyage across the Pacific Ocean. But something wholly unexpected confronted them soon after their arrival in the Chinese city of Tientsin. It was the Boxer Rebellion, a fierce uprising against foreigners as well as Chinese supporters of foreign business interests.

Because the section of Tientsin set apart for Westerners became a prime target of the rebels, both Hoovers were caught up in something like a war. While Bert joined with other men in organizing a defense force, Lou helped to convert a club for international settlers into a hospital. Riding her bicycle back and forth from their house, she kept as close as possible to the buildings lining the road, but once a bullet hit one of her tires. Another time three shells burst around her, not hurting her at all.

After a month under fire, Lou was relieved when the fighting ended. But she firmly refused to accept her husband's decision that she should leave right away for the safer haven of Japan while he continued the mining exploration he had been hired to direct. Instead, setting a pattern for their future life together, she stayed with him almost constantly and helped him in so many ways that young engineers working on the same projects regarded her as her husband's chief assistant.

Better at learning languages than Bert was, Lou absorbed enough Chinese to translate letters and other documents for him. She rode along on expeditions to possible mining sites and used her Stanford training to prepare geological maps of the areas they visited. After a few years, when Bert became a partner in a major mining company based in London, Lou assisted him during trips around India and Egypt as well as several other countries.

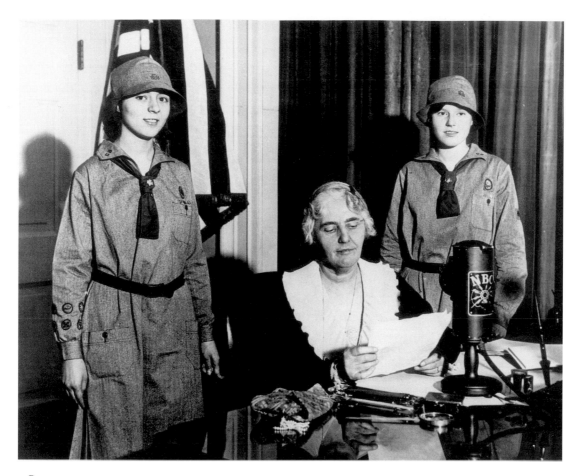

Lou Hoover made the first radio broadcast by a first lady from the White House.

In 1903, while in London, Lou gave birth to the first of the couple's two sons. When Herbert Junior was just five weeks old, his parents, accompanied by a nurse-maid, carried him in a basket aboard a ship departing for Australia. Then in 1907 his younger brother Allan sailed at the same age to Burma with the rest of his family.

Although Lou had comfortably furnished a fine house in London as their head-quarters, the Hoovers still considered California their home. With Lou's father they owned a bungalow on the Stanford campus, where they spent a month together every summer.

During these busy years, while Bert's mining expertise made him a millionaire, he and Lou also worked together on an ambitious sideline. Evenings and weekends they devoted many hours to producing the first English version of a book dating back to 1556, written by a man regarded as the father of mineralogy. His scholarly

Latin volume *De Re Metallica* was very difficult to translate because it contained numerous words its author had made up himself to describe chemical reactions unknown in ancient Rome. Lou used her gift for languages while Bert conducted chemical experiments to make sure she was on the right track. Their joint venture, published in 1912, was hailed as a great contribution to mining science.

Despite Lou's close involvement with Bert's career, as their boys grew older she felt a divided responsibility. Because the Hoovers wanted their sons to have an American education, she began spending winters in California with them and then shepherded them across the Atlantic come summer to be with their father. So the whole family was in London during the fateful August of 1914, when most of Europe was drawn into the terrible conflict of World War I.

Thousands of schoolteachers and other tourists from the United States had been stranded overseas by the outbreak of the war. Since they needed all sorts of help until ways could be found for them to return home, an emergency committee of Americans sprang up—with Bert as its chairman. His efficient direction of this group led to a series of other war-related assignments, opening a new phase in Lou's life too.

After Bert started devoting himself to public service, Lou no longer shared in his work the way she had, though she remained at his side as much as possible. She began to concentrate on entertaining and on decorating their homes tastefully. Such assistance was extremely important to her husband as he entered the world of politics, since he had never gotten over his youthful unease among strangers.

By the time he was elected president, in 1928, Lou pursued a traditional first lady role. As Herbert himself put it when he wrote his own memoirs, Mrs. Hoover believed that her role as first lady was to serve as "a symbol of everything wholesome in American life."

Within the White House, Lou very capably played the part of official hostess. All information regarding social events was provided to the press by a social secretary: The first lady herself merely posed for an occasional formal photograph. When the Hoovers took trips around the country, Lou usually stood quietly at her husband's side.

Once, though, during a campaign tour when she was presented with a particularly lovely bouquet of flowers before her husband addressed a large gathering, she let herself display a touch of humor. "I enjoy campaigning," Lou told a reporter, "because my husband makes the speeches—and I receive the roses."

Lou also continued to pursue active interests of her own. She strongly supported the Girl Scouts, even serving as the group's national president. Despite her distaste for publicity and speechmaking, she became fascinated by the possibilities of radio broadcasting, which had only recently begun on a national basis, and set up a "lab" on the second floor of the White House to "test her talkie technique."

Then in 1931 Lou began giving radio talks urging America's women to donate food and clothing for the needy. If the onset of the Great Depression in 1929 had not made Hoover a hated name all over the country, perhaps her own story would have had a happier ending. As it was, she left Washington bitterly disappointed by her husband's defeat in his 1932 bid for a second term.

Lou never ceased feeling that her cherished Bert had been unfairly blamed for the country's economic collapse. At their New York City apartment she died suddenly of a heart attack on January 7, 1944, two months short of her seventieth birthday. During the next twenty years Herbert Hoover won wide respect again as an eminent elder statesman.

Why Was It Hard for Women to Get an Education?

Until the end of the nineteenth century, women had no opportunity to acquire the type of education that had long been available to men. One factor holding women back was the deeply rooted prejudice that women's brains were somehow inferior to men's. Respected male members of society, such as teachers, ministers, and doctors, claimed that women weren't capable of higher learning or serious study. Some even asserted that the "smaller" brain of a woman simply could not store much information. Learning math or science, history or philosophy, could damage a woman's brain and body, cause her to become weak and sickly, and make her unable to have healthy babies! It would take many years, and fierce determination by women who were gifted with great intellect, to turn around such backward notions.

In the North and Midwest, towns and communities typically set up schools for the elementary grades that girls as well as boys could attend. But schools that taught subjects at what we would now call high-school level were almost always for boys. Girls born to wealthy and middle-class families might receive some additional lessons from tutors hired by their parents, but girls in poor families had very little education at all. Before the Civil War, few women received any higher education, because there were no colleges or universities open to women.

Frustrated in their attempts to get an education, some pioneering women opened their own schools for girls in the 1830s. As the nation's population grew, there was an increasing need for teachers. Women were thought to be good candidates, since teaching was seen as an extension of what women already did in their own families. Besides, women teachers were cheaper to employ than men. Emma Willard opened her school for girls in Troy, New York, in 1821, calling it the Troy Female Seminary. Mrs. Willard had asked to attend classes at Middlebury College before she opened her own school. She wanted to learn about a variety of subjects and to be educated in current teaching methods. Her request was denied. She set out to learn each subject herself and then trained the women teachers for her

In an era when most people considered women intellectually inferior to men, Emma Willard's father encouraged her to discard that idea. She obtained as much education as possible for a woman of her day and set up a series of schools offering women the same courses as men.

school, developing her own teaching methods. The Emma Willard School is still operating today.

Oberlin School in Ohio, founded in 1833, offered women an education almost the equal of men's. This was the first school (it later became a college) to welcome everyone who wanted an education, including African Americans and women. A woman named Catharine Beecher, a founder of modern teacher training, believed that professional training was needed for women teachers and began the American Women's Educational Association in 1852. In 1837 in Massachusetts, Mary Lyon started Mount Holyoke, now known as the oldest women's college in the United States.

After the Civil War (1861–1865), when more women sought the benefits of higher education, several important women's colleges opened in the Northeast. Vassar, in New York, was established in 1865; Smith and Wellesley in 1875; the "Harvard Annex" (later known as Radcliffe College) began in 1879; and Bryn Mawr in Pennsylvania opened in 1885. Still, it was the exception, not the norm, for a woman to attend college.

In the Midwest state colleges were established after the Civil War, and women were admitted if they could pass the entrance exams. Many women who became leaders of the women's movement and reform activists in the 1890s and 1900s graduated from these early colleges. Because women college graduates still faced prejudice or open hostility in completing their studies and finding work, a group called

An African-American educator of courage and vision, Anna J. Cooper was a highly intelligent woman who received her Ph.D. from the Sorbonne in Paris. An educator of African-American youth in Washington, D.C., she served as principal at the M Street High School, establishing a rigorous course of academic study and superior intellectual standards that earned her students acceptance in Northern colleges. At a time when black women were thought intellectually inferior, Cooper's achievements demonstrated the intellectual equality of black women and provided quality education to several generations of African-American students.

the Association of Collegiate Alumnae formed in 1881 to provide scholarships for women students and to offer a network of support for graduates. As more women attended college, each section of the country set up such groups. In 1921 they merged to become the American Association of University Women (AAUW), still a powerful force in seeking the best education for women.

Black women faced even more problems in getting an education. It was considered dangerous to teach slaves to read; they might learn too much and want freedom. After the Civil War, Congress established schools, called freedmen's schools, for African-American students. Still, most had no chance to attend high school, let alone college. Black women leaders such as Nannie Helen Burroughs, from Washington, D.C., set up schools that provided both high-school courses and job training. Anna J. Cooper was an outstanding teacher at one of the black high schools in Washington. Most black women who were fortunate and well schooled enough to go to college attended black colleges such as Howard in Washington, D.C.; Fisk in Tennessee; Atlanta University in Georgia; Hampton in Virginia; and Tuskeegee in Alabama. Kept from joining mostly white organizations such as the Collegiate Alumnae or the AAUW, African-American women worked through the National Association of Colored Women's Clubs to encourage education and promote racial equality.

Eleanor Roosevelt

OCTOBER 11, 1884–NOVEMBER 7, 1962

"First Lady of the World"

*E*leanor Roosevelt's long career as an advocate for
the victims of poverty, prejudice, and war made her
one of the most-loved women of her generation.

*D*uring her first year as first lady, Eleanor Roosevelt traveled 38,000 miles on
inspection trips around the country. The next year's total rose to 42,000 miles.
Then, because she kept making so many unannounced appearances all over the
country, reporters assigned to write about her decided that it really was impossible
to arrive at an accurate tally, and they stopped counting.

Far more than mere mileage set "Mrs. R." apart from every other presidential wife before her. Her vigorous support of countless efforts to improve the lives of ordinary people made her a symbol of hope throughout the world—looked up to as one of the most outstanding women who ever lived.

Anna Eleanor Roosevelt her parents had named her, and she seemed to have started life under a lucky star. Born into New York City's wealthy upper class on October 11, 1884, she was the first child of Anna Hall Roosevelt and Elliott Roosevelt: Both of them could trace ancestors back to colonial days. Her mother was a noted beauty, while her father was dashingly handsome. His older brother, Theodore, would become president of the United States in 1901, when Eleanor was seventeen.

Despite her social position, her early years were extremely unhappy. Being a solemn, serious child with large, protruding front teeth, she often heard relatives murmur what a shame it was that she looked like a little old lady. "Granny," her rather coldhearted mother called her.

Eleanor's father loved her, though, and she adored him. Yet he often forgot all about her. Once, while they were taking one of their wonderful walks together, he left her standing alone outside his club for several hours until a kind stranger brought her home. Only later did she learn that his alcoholism had made him totally unreliable.

Long before anybody told her this, when she was only eight, her mother suddenly fell ill and died. By then her father had been sent away "to recover his health," so she and her two small brothers went to live with their strict Grandmother Hall. A year later one of her brothers died of diphtheria. Around Eleanor's tenth birthday, her father died too.

Crushed by so much tragedy, she spent many hours spinning daydreams that her father would someday come and rescue her. To make sure he would not be disappointed when he arrived, she tried very hard to behave properly—as a result, people who knew her marveled at her sweet and thoughtful nature. Inwardly, though, she felt intense misery.

Outwardly, her life might have seemed far from miserable to many poor girls. Spending her summers at her grandmother's country mansion overlooking the Hudson River and her winters in a grand house near New York City's Madison Avenue, she was usually surrounded by relatives as well as servants. She had numerous aunts and uncles, some of them not much older than she was.

Eleanor always sensed that she was being pitied, not only because she was an orphan but also because she hadn't been born pretty. Although she made many friends at the elite private school she attended, she couldn't enjoy parties the way they did. The only lighthearted fun she had came when her grandmother allowed her to visit the Long Island home of her father's brother, where her uncle Ted managed to lure even this shy niece into boisterous games with his own lively children.

When she was fifteen, several of her aunts convinced Grandmother Hall that Eleanor needed special help. Today front teeth like hers could easily be straightened by a dentist, and the fact that she had grown to be nearly six feet tall wouldn't cause any great dismay. A hundred years ago, though, these things were thought to be handicaps for a girl. Eleanor was sent to an exclusive "finishing school" in England, with the hope that it might give her sufficient self-confidence to attract a suitable husband, still the main opportunity open to a woman at the time.

Allenswood, where the daughters of prominent European families received a high level of instruction in literature and the arts along with careful training in the social graces, was operated by a gifted teacher from France. Mademoiselle Marie Souvestre quickly sensed that this American pupil who had such a sad family history possessed exceptional qualities of mind and heart. Taking her under her own wing, she opened a whole world of new ideas to Eleanor—and Eleanor responded by becoming the school's top student.

Returning home after three years at Allenswood, Eleanor was poised and informed. Her aunts felt much more optimistic about her prospects as they began planning a series of parties at which she would be formally introduced to New York society following her eighteenth birthday that autumn. The purpose of such traditional "coming-out" festivities among the wealthy upper classes was to make sure that she met the right sort of young men, able to offer her a secure future as a wife and mother in the same privileged environment she had always inhabited.

Eleanor, however, had absorbed a broader outlook from Mademoiselle Souvestre. Seeking some worthwhile occupation in which to use her education, she decided upon working with the underprivileged. She began volunteer teaching a few afternoons a week at a settlement house for poor children. Still, she dutifully attended her aunts' parties and enjoyed talking with older men about the center where she taught.

Eleanor hadn't intended to charm her handsome cousin Franklin when she happened to encounter him during a train ride up to her grandmother's country house; he lived nearby, in the Hudson Valley community of Hyde Park. Much to her surprise, he seemed interested in what she told him about the poverty of the area where she was working, and he said he would like to accompany her there some afternoon.

Franklin Delano Roosevelt, at the age of twenty, was a Harvard student more

noted for his sociability than his attention to his studies. He and Eleanor were actually fifth cousins, and they hardly knew each other. In a hazy way she remembered visiting Hyde Park when she had been only about three years old—and being given a rather alarming piggyback ride by a laughing boy there—but since then she had seen Franklin only at large family parties.

Even though Franklin had always struck Eleanor as quite frivolous, he did come with her to the center soon afterward, and he appeared truly shaken by the horrifying conditions she showed him in nearby buildings. When he confided that he hoped someday to enter politics, she thought the reason he started showering her with attention was just that he felt grateful to her for opening his eyes to the sort of problems he would have to deal with in his future career: It never occurred to her that he could have the least interest in her personally.

So Eleanor was astounded, soon after she turned nineteen, by Franklin's asking her to marry him. Only when he assured her that he had fallen deeply in love with her did she let herself admit that she loved him too. But a very powerful force opposed them—Franklin's mother.

Sara Delano Roosevelt, a widow who doted on her only son, insisted that he and Eleanor were much too young even to think of marrying. As Franklin had always managed to get his own way by amiably coaxing his mother rather than fighting with her, he made a compromise: The couple would keep their engagement secret for a year if she promised to withdraw her objections after the year was over.

While Sara Roosevelt clearly believed the youthful romance would not survive such a delay, she was mistaken. When the year ended, Eleanor joyfully wrote dozens of notes informing relatives and friends about her impending marriage. From the White House, Uncle Ted dashed off an enthusiastic reply telling her he felt as fond of her as if she were his own daughter.

When she and Franklin spoke their vows on March 17, 1905, hundreds of people hoping for a glimpse of the president (who had "given away" his niece) stood outside the Manhattan home of one of Eleanor's cousins, where the ceremony took place. Wearing the same splendid satin-and-lace wedding gown that had once been her mother's, the twenty-year-old bride looked amazingly beautiful.

Married life brought Eleanor many happy moments. At first, somewhat overwhelmed, she said she was always either expecting a baby or getting over just having had a baby. From 1906 to 1916 she and Franklin became the parents of Anna, James, Elliott, Franklin Junior, and John, besides another boy who died in infancy.

Because Franklin's mother made the outrageous outlandishly protest that she might bring home dreadful germs if she kept on with her teaching, Eleanor gave up her work at the settlement house. While Franklin finished law school and started rising politically, she came to feel more and more useless: Nursemaids cared for her children, and Franklin's bossy mother even hired them.

Fearing that her husband would become angry and reject her if she opposed his mother, Eleanor did not begin to assert her independence until the young Roosevelts moved to Washington, following Franklin's appointment as assistant secretary of the navy. In her early thirties, when the United States was drawn into World War I, she showed exceptional organizing ability at a Red Cross canteen that fed soldiers on trains passing through the capital.

Then, shortly after the war ended, Eleanor was shocked to discover that Franklin had become involved in a love affair with her social secretary, Lucy Mercer. Devastated by this knowledge, Eleanor offered to divorce Franklin, but a divorce in those days would have ruined his political career. Even after he promised never to see Lucy again, Eleanor found it hard to forgive him—although her marriage still seemed intact outwardly, she felt betrayed. In spite of the fact that they maintained an affection for each other and shared mutual interests, especially in politics, their marriage was never the same, and Eleanor felt an urgent need for some kind of useful work. She returned to her earlier interest in social reform.

As America's women had finally gained the right to vote in 1920, Eleanor joined the new League of Women Voters and several other reform organizations such as the Women's Trade Union League. Soon she was very busy attending meetings or writing reports about laws of special interest to women: equal-pay laws and laws to end child labor. Then came a terrible new crisis.

In 1921, at their summer home in Maine, Franklin woke up one morning unable to move his legs. This vigorous man of thirty-nine had been paralyzed by the crippling disease polio, which usually attacked young children. No doctor could say whether he would ever walk again.

*I*n her many years as a social activist and political worker, Eleanor Roosevelt formed close working relationships with female journalists. As first lady she gave a boost to women reporters by holding press conferences like this one, exclusively for them, giving them serious information about New Deal policies and political programs.

Years afterward, Eleanor Roosevelt insisted that she deserved no credit for her husband's eventual triumph over his illness. She said it was Franklin himself who had kept striving, month after month, until, wearing heavy leg braces, he could stand and take at least a few steps. However, it was his wife who fiercely fought his mother's efforts to make him give up any further thought of politics—and spend the rest of his life in a wheelchair at Hyde Park, puttering with his stamp collection.

To keep his name before the public, Mrs. Franklin D. Roosevelt became active in the women's division of New York's Democratic party, which she organized to support Franklin's run for the governorship of the state. She tried hard to conquer her fear of facing large groups and, despite being nervous, began making speeches all over the state. In addition, while supervising complicated households in the city and up in Maine, as well as five nearly grown children, she helped to operate a private school for girls and regularly taught classes there.

Eleanor became busier than ever after Franklin was elected governor of New York in 1928. At the age of forty-four, her energy seemed boundless: Every Sunday evening she strode out of the governor's mansion in Albany with a briefcase under her arm on her way to her school in New York City, and then she would take another three-hour train ride Wednesday afternoon back to Albany for a hectic four days as her husband's official hostess.

During the summer Eleanor accompanied Franklin on trips throughout the state. Because of his inability to walk any distance, they evolved a very effective travel partnership. While he welcomed local officials to private conferences in his car, his wife would stride through hospitals, prisons, and other institutions, carefully observing the way they were being operated. Instead of relying on what she was told, she questioned and determined for herself: She even lifted the lids on the pots in the kitchens to make sure the menus described to her were really being served.

After the collapse of the Wall Street stock market in 1929 brought the worst economic depression in the country's history, more and more people began hoping that New York's optimistic governor would become the nation's next president. Although Eleanor did all she could to help Franklin win the 1932 election—directing activities for the women's division of the Democratic party, organizing thousands of women to vote for Franklin—his victory caused her great personal anguish. She was concerned that she would only be able to act as a social hostess and not continue her reform and political work.

But during her initial week as first lady, Eleanor Roosevelt scrawled a note to a woman reporter who had become one of her closest friends. "I begin to think there may be ways in which I can be useful," she wrote. Soon she was showing the whole country what she meant.

Wherever she heard of human suffering, this presidential wife offered compassion. Any program that promised to improve life for the underprivileged was likely to win her enthusiastic support. Poor people, young people, black people—they all came to regard Mrs. R. as their particular friend because of the sympathy she felt for their problems.

For instance, after the organization called the Daughters of the American Revolution would not allow the great black singer Marian Anderson to give a concert in its Washington auditorium, Mrs. R. resigned from the group. Then she helped to plan a free outdoor concert at the Lincoln Memorial at which a huge audience, both white and black, demonstrated that the bigotry of the past could not be tolerated much longer.

Even though this first lady's human-rights concerns made her immensely popular among many Americans, she infuriated many others. They ridiculed her as an interfering busybody and spread nasty "Eleanor jokes." Radio comedians imitated her distinctive, high-pitched voice in a cruel way.

Despite ridicule and opposition, she kept giving her compassionate speeches all over the country. She talked to the people of the United States by radio about social and political issues and gave them reassurance during the Depression and, later, during the war. She took up writing too—composing a column called "My Day," which appeared in hundreds of newspapers. She also wrote numerous magazine articles as well as a book about her early life that, much to her own amazement, became a best-seller. "I think you are a kind of genius," an experienced writer told her.

After the threat of U.S. involvement in World War II gave Franklin Roosevelt an unprecedented third term in 1940, even some of his wife's severest critics found themselves joining the ranks of her admirers because of her morale-building efforts. Immediately following the attack on Pearl Harbor that plunged the country into the conflict, Eleanor flew to California to dispel rumors that enemy planes were about to bomb the West Coast. "I seem to have a calming effect," she admitted.

Throughout the war years Eleanor tirelessly visited American troops—smiling warmly and jotting down names and addresses so she could send reassuring notes to soldiers' parents on her return home. Her wartime role as her husband's unofficial ambassador certainly made an important contribution to the nation's war effort.

When Franklin died on April 12, 1945, just a few months after starting his fourth term and just a few weeks before the war in Europe ended, Eleanor was sixty years

In 1940 Franklin Roosevelt decided to seek an unprecedented third term as president. Because he did not wish to appear to be pressuring the delegates into nominating him, he sent his wife as his stand-in, knowing that her influence in the party and her political skill would accomplish his goal.

old. Packing up personal belongings accumulated during twelve incredibly busy White House years, a very subdued first lady told friends that she felt more than ready to retire to her own cottage at Hyde Park. At last she would have plenty of time for enjoying her grandchildren, and perhaps she would even take up gardening.

It didn't happen. The new president, Harry Truman, appointed her a U.S. delegate to the new United Nations. On her own, Eleanor Roosevelt won more fame than ever: She fundamentally shaped the Universal Declaration of Human Rights, the UN's cornerstone document, adopted in 1948.

Although almost seventy when she gave up her UN post, she still continued to speak out and travel all over the globe. "The First Lady of the World," President Truman called her.

Though she had repeatedly refused to run for any office herself, her word carried so much weight that candidates often asked her to endorse them. In 1960 a young man named John F. Kennedy went to see her before he began campaigning for the presidency. (Once elected, Kennedy appointed her chairperson of his newly formed Commission on the Status of Women, where she continued to promote changes for women.) Throughout American history, no other woman has ever had as much political influence as she did.

Eleanor Roosevelt died of a blood disease on November 7, 1962, shortly after her seventy-eighth birthday. A great assemblage of world leaders attended her funeral in Hyde Park, where a leading Democrat summed up her career most movingly. "She would rather light a candle than curse the darkness," Adlai Stevenson said. "And her glow has warmed the world."

Bess Truman

FEBRUARY 13, 1885–OCTOBER 18, 1982

"A full partner in all my transactions"

Although she was closely involved in her husband's career, Bess Truman chose not to accept the public spotlight and refused all requests for interviews.

Soon after the Trumans had moved out of the White House, former President Truman came into the living room of their Missouri home and found Bess seated beside the fireplace. All around her were piles of old letters. As she finished reading one of them, she threw it into the flames.

"Bess," he said, "what are you doing?"

"Burning our letters."

"Bess," he repeated. "Think of history."

"I have," she replied, tossing another letter into the blaze.

Not too surprisingly, Bess saved most of Harry Truman's letters to her—and destroyed practically all of her letters to him. Even though no presidential marriage had ever been more of a partnership than hers was, no presidential wife has ever been more determined to keep her life private than she was. This very strong desire for personal privacy could be traced to a tragic event during her youth.

Until her eighteenth year, she had seemed particularly fortunate. Born in the pleasant Missouri town of Independence on February 13, 1885, she had been named Elizabeth Virginia Wallace by her loving and comfortably well-off parents. Bess, as everybody called her, was also a notably pretty child.

Indeed, when she was only five her energy, blue eyes, and golden curls made a firm friend of a six-year-old boy who briefly attended the same Sunday school. From that time on, there was no other girl in the world for Harry Truman. Because he soon moved to an outlying farm, though, they didn't really get acquainted until they were much older.

Bess displayed her own spirit of independence by energetically going out for sports in a period that did not support or approve of female athletes. She got so good at baseball that she batted regularly for a team of neighborhood boys, and she took up tennis with such vigor that she soon ranked as the town's best young player. Winters, her favorite activity was ice skating.

Bess's mother made sure that her daughter also learned more traditional, ladylike behavior. Margaret Gates Wallace had grown up in one of the richest families in the area; her father owned a thriving flour mill. She saw to it that Bess took dancing lessons with the children of the town's leading citizens and then learned other social graces at an elite boarding school in nearby Kansas City.

It was Bess's father who cast a terrible shadow over her youthful happiness. Handsome and charming, David Willock Wallace somehow couldn't find any career that suited him. Depressed by his failures as a breadwinner, in 1903 he killed himself with a bullet from his own revolver.

His suicide had a profound effect on his eighteen-year-old daughter. In addition to the immediate shock and grief it caused, Bess was afflicted by a lasting dread of any gossip about her father's death. Her horror at the possible exposure of his business and psychological problems undoubtedly lay behind her lifelong aversion to personal publicity.

David Wallace's death also influenced Bess's day-to-day routine during the next decade. Because her mother relied on her more and more, soon Bess had taken over most of the family's housekeeping responsibilities. Then in 1910, when she was twenty-five, Harry Truman turned up in Independence again.

Harry at this time seemed set in life as just a plain dirt farmer. Although Bess appeared happy to see him, the gap between their social positions had grown very wide. She didn't like to picture herself giving up her own comfortable existence to become a hardworking farm wife.

Yet Harry persisted in courting Bess after long days of plowing or other chores. Traveling an hour each way by train and streetcar, he gradually won her heart—by 1913 she told him that if she ever did get married, he would be the man. Then in 1917, right after the United States entered World War I, Bess informed him that she wanted to marry him before he went off to fight overseas.

Harry said he would rather wait till he came home safely. So it was on June 28, 1919, that Bess at last became his bride, at the age of thirty-four. Despite all her previous uncertainty and despite some hard times financially during the next several years, their marriage proved exceptionally happy.

With their daughter Margaret, born in 1924, they created an oasis of warm and close family life wherever they went. Bess never did speak publicly about her own feelings, but her daughter would write very perceptively about them years afterward.

According to Margaret, her mother felt that the only sort of marriage worth having was an equal partnership, with both husband and wife sharing in every important decision. Bess even seemed to believe that her own father's tragedy might have been avoided if he had confided in her mother, instead of hiding his business worries from her.

As a result Bess was fully involved with every step along Harry's remarkable career. To start with, when he and a wartime buddy opened a men's clothing store, she helped with the bookkeeping. When the business failed during a period of hard times, she briskly cut down family expenses so every penny they owed could be paid back.

Then when Harry started taking an active part in Missouri politics, he talked over every issue with Bess. When the opportunity unexpectedly arose in 1934 for him to run for U.S. senator, she had very mixed feelings. Knowing that he had always dreamed of such a chance, she raised no objection—and yet she herself would have much preferred remaining in Independence.

The election won, Bess enjoyed Washington at first. She shopped, drove her car where she pleased, played bridge, and met other Senate wives. But the capital's social life didn't appeal to her much, so she soon started helping Harry officially as a paid staff member, working in his Senate office answering mail or assisting him with speechwriting chores.

On campaign tours, Harry Truman would call out, "Now, do you want to meet 'The Boss'?" and Bess would appear. The crowds loved it.

Bess's enjoyment ended abruptly in 1944, when President Franklin Roosevelt decided that he wanted Missouri's popular Senator Truman as his running mate in his campaign for an unprecedented fourth term. Right after Harry's nomination for the post of vice president at the Democratic National Convention, he and his wife tried to depart from the crowded hall. Mobbed by a cheering crowd, blinded by the flashbulbs of photographers, the Trumans finally reached their car, where Bess exploded.

"Are we going to have to go through this for the rest of our lives?" she demanded, her daughter later reported. Margaret did not record her father's reply.

After the Democratic victory in the election that autumn, the wife of Vice President Truman found herself expected to attend a constant round of luncheons, cocktail parties, receptions, and formal dinners. Bess detested this sort of social whirl, much preferring the company of her family and friends. With them she was always talkative, witty, and relaxed. At large gatherings, ill at ease, she became stiffly sedate, often looking grim or even angry.

Life for the Trumans changed still more drastically on April 12, 1945, when President Roosevelt died. Moving into the White House during the final months of

World War II, Harry faced the enormous challenge of taking over after the country had been led for more than twelve years by an extraordinary man. Bess, too, confronted a somewhat similar problem.

If Washington reporters expected the new first lady to follow in Eleanor Roosevelt's footsteps, they quickly found they were mistaken. Although Bess Truman let herself be convinced that she should hold a press conference shortly after the great change in her status, almost immediately she reconsidered and canceled it. A secretary explained that this presidential wife did not intend to play any public role, so there would be nothing for her to tell them.

After several reportorial protests, Bess agreed to meet a group of women correspondents at an off-the-record tea. When one of them said they were hoping to get to know her, she had a sharp reply ready: "You don't need to know me." As a result, newspapers and magazines carried articles complaining that President Truman's wife was "a hard person to write about."

Nevertheless, Bess did carry out traditional first lady duties conscientiously: She greeted White House visitors, she appeared at charity events, she even aroused smiles all over the nation when pictures showed her vigorously battering a wine bottle against the hull of a new ship. The no-nonsense image of her that photographers captured made many people admire her as real and old-fashioned.

Her complete silence on public issues didn't mean she had no opinions about them. She expressed them very forcefully, where they counted most. After Harry Truman left the White House, he himself would say that his wife had been his "chief adviser" as well as "a full partner in all my transactions—politically and otherwise."

Both Bess and Harry were greatly relieved, however, when they left Washington, following the inauguration of his successor early in 1953. Back in Independence they enjoyed almost ten peaceful years of retirement together, enlivened by frequent visits from their four grandsons, Margaret's four children.

After Harry died at the age of eighty-nine, Bess survived him nearly another decade. Behind the tall fence surrounding her lifelong home on Delaware Street, she spent much of her time following baseball games on radio and television and reading her favorite detective stories.

By the time her health failed, she had outlived every other first lady in the nation's history. As much as Bess had always hated personal publicity, she might have relished the headline that appeared in the *New York Times* the day after her own death on October 18, 1982: BESS TRUMAN IS DEAD AT 97; WAS PRESIDENT'S "FULL PARTNER."

Mamie Eisenhower

NOVEMBER 14, 1896–NOVEMBER 1, 1979

Pink ribbons and "a spine of steel"

The image of Mamie Eisenhower as a loving, loyal wife made her very popular with the American people.

As an army wife, Mamie Eisenhower had lived in everything from shacks to palaces. So moving into the White House didn't faze her at all. Unlike many other first ladies, she thoroughly enjoyed her years there, and she directed the staff in charge of running the mansion with her own style of military precision.

Every morning, while having her breakfast in bed, she operated her private command post very efficiently. Wearing her favorite pink robe and a matching pink ribbon in her hair, she gave her orders for lunch and dinner menus to a procession of aides. Using a little stand-up bed tray as her desk, she paid bills, answered letters, and arranged her personal schedule.

Although the American public never saw this behind-the-scenes performance, Mamie's enjoyment of her role during her husband's presidency was no secret. Wherever she went, her beaming smile gave clear evidence that she was having the time of her life. But few people suspected the strength of her will: Despite Mamie's fondness for pink ribbons, a White House assistant would later declare that she had "a spine of steel."

Born in Boone, Iowa, on November 14, 1896, Mamie Geneva Doud had such a charming manner that her father, in particular, couldn't help spoiling her a little.

John Sheldon Doud had made enough money from his meatpacking business by the time he was in his mid-thirties to retire and use his leisure to promote the happiness of his family. When his wife, Elivera Carlson Doud, worried over the fragile health of one of Mamie's older sisters, he decided to move his entire household to the more bracing climate of Colorado.

Denver became the main scene of Mamie's girlhood. She attended dancing school there, as well as a private school for the daughters of the city's leading families. During her teens she began going to frequent dances or other gatherings, and she often entertained her friends at home by playing the piano in the Douds' billiard room.

Mamie also had plenty of opportunities to meet handsome young soldiers because John Doud took his wife and daughters to Texas every autumn—and they spent several months in balmy San Antonio, near the army base called Fort Sam Houston. One Sunday afternoon in October 1915, while the nearly nineteen-year-old Mamie and her mother were sitting outside the officers' club with a group of military wives, a lieutenant emerged from a nearby building.

"Ike," a major's wife called to him, "won't you come over here? I have some people I'd like you to meet."

Mamie would always remember thinking, at her first sight of twenty-five-year-old Lieutenant Dwight Eisenhower: "He's about the handsomest male I have ever seen." Ike himself, till then much more interested in games such as football than in young ladies, would recall that "a vivacious girl, smaller than average, saucy in the look about her face and in her whole attitude" attracted his eye "instantly."

By February they both were sure of their feelings. On Valentine's Day, Ike asked Mamie to marry him—and she immediately said yes. Her father, however, had some questions of his own on hearing the couple's news. Did Mamie realize that the wife of a junior officer must not expect to live in luxury? And could she be happy without the comforts to which she had become accustomed?

Although his daughter assured him that she was willing to face whatever hardships might be involved, Mr. Doud urged that any wedding plans be delayed at least until after Mamie turned twenty that November. But with the increasing likelihood that Ike might be sent to Europe to fight in World War I, she didn't want to wait. At the Doud home in Denver on July 1, 1916, while still only nineteen, Mamie became Mrs. Dwight Eisenhower.

Back at Fort Sam Houston, the newlyweds found their tiny apartment packed with wedding presents. Ike, with his enormously appealing grin, was one of the most popular young officers on the post. When American troops began fighting in the European war the following year, his superiors assigned him to supervise the training of new recruits on this side of the ocean—much to his own disappointment and Mamie's relief.

Right from the start, Mamie demonstrated exceptional ability as a hostess. Every Sunday evening the Eisenhowers gave an informal buffet dinner, with Mamie playing the piano and all the guests singing. Because of the friendly atmosphere their quarters became known as Club Eisenhower.

During the next twenty years, as the army transferred Ike from post to post,

Mamie Eisenhower's approving and supportive demeanor during a televised interview created an image of the devoted family at a time when a strong American family was seen as a defense against the threat of Communism.

Mamie Eisenhower and Pat Nixon, the wives of the 1952 and 1956 Republican candidates, became famous and popular with the American people as they helped their husbands' campaigns.

Mamie established a Club Eisenhower wherever they went. But these years brought sorrow, too. In 1920 a baby son they adored died of scarlet fever, and neither of them could ever forget this tragedy—even though they soon had another boy, a sturdy infant they named John, who eventually would be a soldier like his father.

While Ike slowly rose through the ranks of the peacetime army, Mamie endured all sorts of difficult living conditions at military posts in the jungles of Panama, in isolated areas of the United States, and in the Philippine Islands. It was during those wandering years that she changed her appearance by having her hair cut with a fringe of bangs across her forehead—a distinctive style that made a big hit with Ike, and later with the American public.

The American entry into World War II in 1941 lifted Mamie's husband to international fame as the general in command of the Allied forces in Europe. Unable to accompany him overseas, Mamie spent several very lonely and worried years in a Washington hotel apartment.

With her husband's rise, Mamie blossomed under the blaze of publicity. The country's favorite war hero received one important peacetime post after another. When the Republican party made him its presidential candidate in 1952, she waved to crowds of voters wearing "I Like Ike" buttons with such obvious enthusiasm that soon Ike himself began wearing one proclaiming "I Like Mamie." She became a celebrity in her own right as her husband's most enthusiastic and visible supporter.

Regarding the second floor of the White House as her private domain, Mamie furnished it to her own taste—with pink-flowered patterns on the chair covers and pink towels in the bathrooms. She felt that her main task as first lady was to make a cozy home for her husband, where he could relax from the awesome pressures of his office, so she saw to it that she and the president often had dinner alone. As television had recently overtaken radio as America's favorite evening entertainment, they usually dined on trays in front of their TV set. Many evenings they watched movies in the White House screening room.

Of course, there were also state dinners, at which Mamie delighted in wearing elaborate gowns, as well as countless receptions where she cheerfully shook thousands of hands. Yet she much preferred the company of old friends—and most of all, visits from John and his wife and their four children.

Indeed, Mamie's White House years focused her attention on the fact that she and Ike had actually never had a home of their own where they could freely welcome their cherished grandchildren. So she spent much of her time as first lady planning the remodeling and furnishing of a fifteen-room house on a farm she and Ike bought in Gettysburg, Pennsylvania, only a few hours' drive from Washington.

Mamie had the traditional view of a woman brought up in the early years of this century. She avoided making public political comments. She counseled her husband in private—strongly urging him to distance himself from and discredit the investigations of Senator Joseph McCarthy, for instance. Yet her attitude toward interviewers was very friendly, and they treated her with kindness even though what she told them was hardly stop-the-press news. "Being a wife is the best career that life has to offer a woman," she often said.

Such time-honored sentiments pleased many voters, and Mamie's wifely devotion when Ike had a major heart attack toward the end of his first term further increased her popularity. For nineteen days she never left the hospital where he had been taken, occupying the room next to his. Then, on his recovery, she insisted that he must not risk running for a second term.

Doctors assured her, however, that for a man like her husband retirement could be more dangerous than working, so Mamie withdrew her objection. Yet she did all she could to encourage a slower pace during his second term—and when it ended early in 1961, she felt immensely relieved.

At their home in Gettysburg, Mamie and Ike enjoyed eight peaceful years before he had another heart attack. Following his death in 1969, Mamie continued to live there quietly, leaving only occasionally to appear at ceremonies honoring her husband. "I miss him every day," she told friends who visited her.

Mamie died on November 1, 1979, two weeks before she would have marked her eighty-third birthday. She was buried alongside Ike and their first son on the grounds of the Eisenhower Library in his boyhood hometown of Abilene, Kansas.

Jacqueline Kennedy

"Vive *Jackie!*"

*T*he Kennedys were young, rich, intelligent, and well educated. They embodied a certain American ideal, and the first lady's beauty, glamour, and sophistication made her enormously popular with the public.

*P*eople everywhere were captivated by her. In the French capital of Paris, such huge crowds turned out to see her that her husband wryly told a gathering of international leaders: "I do not think it altogether inappropriate to introduce myself. I am the man who accompanied Jacqueline Kennedy to Paris."

Jackie, as all the world called her, might almost have been a movie star. Her picture appeared on countless magazine covers, and "the Jackie look" was widely imitated. But in spite of the enormous amount of publicity the wife of President John F. Kennedy received because of her youthful beauty and her great sense of style, she remained a very private person.

This first lady's background, as well as her appearance, could hardly have been more glamorous. Her father was a rich and handsome New York stockbroker named John Vernon Bouvier III; her mother, Janet Lee Bouvier, besides being beautiful, was also a skilled and daring horsewoman who frequently won prizes at society horse shows.

Born in the fashionable Long Island resort of East Hampton on July 28, 1929, Jacqueline Lee Bouvier had a seemingly perfect childhood. By her second birthday she already had her own pony to ride. At the family's beach estate or at the spacious apartment on New York City's Park Avenue where they spent their winters, her parents and numerous servants treated her like a little princess.

Not surprisingly, therefore, Jackie developed a great deal of self-confidence. Once, when she was only four, while playing in Central Park she looked around and couldn't see any familiar face. Walking up to the nearest policeman, she said firmly, "My nurse is lost."

Beneath the surface of her luxurious surroundings, trouble was brewing. When Jackie was eight, her parents separated after bitter quarrels over money problems and John Bouvier's habits of drinking too much and seeking the companionship of other women. Adoring her father, Jackie felt deeply torn by the divorce that left her and her younger sister, Lee, living with their mother somewhat less luxuriously.

Jackie continued to attend private schools along with other daughters of the wealthy. Having the sort of quick mind and lively wit that made ordinary classroom topics seem boring, she began writing poems or stories for her own entertainment and drew pictures to illustrate them. Because she showed such an interest in the fine arts, she received a variety of special lessons.

Then when Jackie was thirteen, her mother remarried. Her stepfather, a rich and amiable gentleman named Hugh Auchincloss, had a mansion known as Merrywood overlooking the Potomac River not far from Washington, which became her winter home. He also owned one of the most pleasant waterfront estates in Rhode Island's exclusive vacation community of Newport, where she spent her summers.

Whether in Virginia or Rhode Island or at Miss Porter's School for young women in Farmington, Connecticut, Jackie kept up her favorite sport of horseback riding. She even insisted on bringing her own sleek mare Danseuse to board at a nearby stable while she attended Miss Porter's classes. But after she turned seventeen, the thrill of winning first prize at horse shows was overshadowed by the excitement of a new sort of triumph.

In her elite world, every girl's advancement into adulthood was celebrated at a series of elaborate "coming-out" parties. While descriptions of such festivities had fascinated many outside this circle, personal publicity about any young woman making her debut had until recently been quite limited. However, a new breed of gossip columnists had begun making celebrities of the most notable debutantes—so Jackie got her first taste of fame during the summer of 1946.

"Queen Deb of the Year Is Jacqueline Bouvier," the writer who called himself Cholly Knickerbocker proclaimed in the *New York Journal-American*. He called her "a regal brunette who has classic features and the daintiness of Dresden porcelain," then added: "She has poise, is soft-spoken and intelligent, everything the leading debutante should be."

Jackie turned her back on the social whirl that autumn, enrolling at Vassar College to major in art history. After her freshman year she toured Europe with some of her classmates, and she enjoyed this first exposure to Old World culture so much that she arranged to spend her entire junior year studying in France. She even thought of settling there permanently.

On completing her college course at George Washington University in Washington, twenty-one-year-old Jackie entered a writing contest sponsored by *Vogue* magazine. Competing with more than a thousand other hopeful graduates, she won the first prize—the opportunity to work for the magazine's Paris edition—and then turned it down. She couldn't explain why: "I guess I was scared to go," she mused years later.

Yet her success in the contest turned Jackie's thoughts toward journalism, and with the help of a family friend she got a job at the *Washington Times-Herald*. She became the newspaper's "Inquiring Camera Girl," wandering around the capital interviewing people and taking their pictures, then preparing a daily column giving their answers to questions she asked them.

If her mind had begun dwelling on the subject of marriage, it was because she had already met a man who interested her more than any previous suitor. At a dinner party some newspaper friends had introduced her to a young congressman from Massachusetts who was regarded as the capital's most eligible bachelor. Tall and good-looking, with a keen mind and a wonderfully dry wit, John F. Kennedy also had a very rich father.

Not until a few years later, when he advanced into the Senate and started aiming for the presidency, did he seriously begin courting Jackie. Politics had never appealed

*M*rs. Kennedy's pregnancy during her husband's presidential campaign limited her public appearances. She contributed to the campaign in other ways: Here she is shown writing a newspaper column called "The Candidate's Wife."

to her, and everybody in Washington knew that Senator Kennedy had been involved with many other women. Even so, she told a friend who warned her about him, "What I want more than anything else in the world is to be married to him."

Their marriage took place on September 12, 1953, when Jackie was twenty-four and Jack thirty-six, with thousands of reporters and spectators gathered outside St. Mary's Roman Catholic Church in Newport, where Boston's Archbishop Richard Cushing conducted the ceremony. Then came a festive reception at the Auchincloss estate, Hammersmith Farm, attended by 1,700 invited guests from high society as well as the less elegant world of politics.

In old-time fairy tales, after the beautiful princess finally married the handsome prince, all that was left to say was that they lived happily ever after. But even though Jackie's next ten years were filled with glowing moments, they also brought much tension—and then tragedy.

Despite her dislike of politics, she did try to play the part of a political wife by the accepted rules of the game. When asked for her views about her role in her husband's career, she gave conventional answers such as "I'm an old-fashioned wife, and I'll do anything my husband asks me to do." Quitting her job, she saw to it that Jack stopped skipping meals, got stylish haircuts, developed more polished manners.

Jackie also wanted to become a mother. After several miscarriages, in 1957 she gave birth to a little girl, Caroline, and three years later to a baby son they named John F. Kennedy, Jr.

Jackie really was anything but an old-fashioned wife—she was an independent woman with a very definite mind of her own. As Jack's drive to win the presidency became front-page news, many rumors about marital difficulties caused by his love affairs and her spending of huge sums on her clothing were spread by Washington insiders. Yet the prevailing journalistic policy of not delving into the personal lives of political figures kept the American public unaware of any problems.

On January 20, 1961, when John F. Kennedy and his wife moved into the White House, it seemed as if a magic aura had settled over the old mansion. At forty-three, Jack was the youngest man ever elected president of the United States. At thirty-one, Jackie possessed an awesome combination of beauty and high style that made her greatly admired.

The Kennedy publicity team cannily took full advantage of how photogenic she was. Young women everywhere took to copying Jackie's hairdo, and less expensive versions of her every outfit were widely sold.

When she accompanied her husband to Europe in the spring of 1961, even Parisians, who ordinarily scoffed at everything American, stood along her route shouting, "*Vive* Jackie!" Despite her enormous popularity, she carefully preserved much of her time for private activities.

Jackie often refused to greet groups of White House visitors who didn't interest her. She remained independent from her husband, who pursued affairs with other women while he remained in Washington. She took several foreign vacation trips with her sister—including a Mediterranean cruise aboard the luxurious yacht of one of her sister's friends, the millionaire Greek shipping tycoon Aristotle Onassis.

Jackie won much approval by achieving three goals she had set for herself as first lady: She renovated the White House in keeping with its historical past, raised the tone of official entertaining by inviting America's best artists to perform there, and also gave strong support to all sorts of artistic and cultural endeavors largely neglected by previous administrations.

Having studied art and history, she brought a wealth of knowledge to her White

Eight first ladies attended the inauguration of John F. Kennedy, including (from far left) Pat Nixon, Mamie Eisenhower, Lady Bird Johnson, Edith Wilson (behind Mrs. Johnson), and Jackie Kennedy. Present but not pictured were Eleanor Roosevelt, Bess Truman, and Betty Ford.

House restoration project. She brought together a team of experts and scholars to advise her on what artworks and antiques should be brought into the mansion, saying, "It would be sacrilege merely to 'redecorate' it—a word I hate. It must be restored—that has nothing to do with decoration. That is a question of scholarship." She was aware that her plans and ideas promoted the preservation of architecture and historic furnishings from America's past.

She also used the glittering entertainments that she held at the White House to make her home a national stage, showcasing the best in American culture and performing arts.

In September 1961 she persuaded her husband to have a law passed that made the White House an official museum and protected its historic furnishings and artworks for the American people. Even staunch Republican enemies of her husband's political program admitted that she succeeded brilliantly in all of these areas. Millions of Americans gathered around their television sets on February 14, 1962, when she starred in an unprecedented program showing off the new elegance of the restored White House.

The following summer, the death of her third child only a few days after his birth aroused much personal sympathy for her. The private grief she and her husband shared as a result of this loss seemed to bring a closer relationship between them. Democratic political leaders rejoiced when they heard that Jackie had agreed to campaign by Jack's side throughout his drive to win a second term in 1964.

Late in November 1963 she flew to Texas with her husband for some preliminary politicking there. Wearing a stylish pink suit, she was sitting next to him as the presidential motorcade drove through the streets of Dallas—and an assassin's bullet killed him. No American old enough to watch television would ever forget the sight of the dazed Jackie, in her bloodstained pink suit, standing beside Vice President Lyndon B. Johnson just a few hours later when he was sworn in as the country's new chief executive.

Indeed, her dignity and courage throughout the somber funeral ceremonies for her slain husband made an indelible impression. After Jackie moved to New York City with her two children, a Gallup poll called her the most admired woman in the world. Pursued by photographers wherever she went, she still tried hard to bring up Caroline and John away from the constant glare of publicity.

In 1968, when Jackie was forty, she shocked millions of people by announcing her engagement to marry sixty-year-old Aristotle Onassis. A friend warned her, "Jackie, you're going to fall off your pedestal." "That's better than freezing there," she replied. To another friend, she said, "You don't know how lonely I have been."

After becoming Mrs. Onassis, she remained at her apartment on New York's Fifth Avenue while her children went to school, although she flew to Greece frequently with her new husband. At first she enjoyed being the wife of one of the richest men in the world, but their vastly different backgrounds brought many strains to the marriage, which ended with his death in 1975.

Then Jackie found a job in New York as an editor at a leading book-publishing firm. Settling into an office routine, she tried to live a quiet life with her children and her friends in the world of art and literature. But she still couldn't escape constantly being photographed and treated like a celebrity.

To some observers, it seemed that Jackie actually relished being the center of attention just as much as she liked her interludes of isolation at her secluded vacation home on the Massachusetts island of Martha's Vineyard. In her sixties, still a remarkably beautiful woman, she became a grandmother. However, her performance of that role remained entirely private.

On May 19, 1994, Jacqueline Bouvier Kennedy Onassis died of cancer at her Manhattan home. She was surrounded by close friends and family. Her funeral was a private affair, though hundreds of mourners gathered outside the church where the service was held and millions more all over the world watched tributes to her on television.

Lady Bird Johnson

DECEMBER 22, 1912–

"What did you do for women today?"

A woman of great intelligence and business skill, Lady Bird Johnson promoted early childhood education for children from poor families through the Head Start program.

"Why, she's as pretty as a ladybird!" the nursemaid who worked for her family exclaimed right after her birth. That was how Claudia Alta Taylor came to be called Lady Bird—shortened just to Bird by those who knew her best. Years later, though, Lyndon Baines Johnson would exuberantly claim that some higher power really must have given them both the same first two initials.

Lady Bird was a dainty little girl with two older brothers. Born on a farm near the small eastern Texas town of Karnack on December 22, 1912, she lived in a fine brick house, the first in the area to have electricity and indoor plumbing.

Lady Bird's father, besides prospering as a cotton grower, also ran a thriving general store: "T. J. Taylor, Dealer in Everything" the sign outside read. Her mother, Minnie Patillo Taylor, who came from a well-to-do Alabama family, loved to read to her daughter in the wood-paneled library that was another unusual feature of their rural Texas residence.

When Lady Bird was five, her mother fell and hurt herself so severely that she died a few days later. Then the child's unmarried aunt Effie moved in to supervise her upbringing. Although Aunt Effie was as fond of reading books and listening to classical music as her sister had been, she didn't teach many of the basic lessons that mothers usually provided. As Lady Bird herself tactfully put it years later, "She opened my spirit to beauty, but she neglected to give me any insight into the practical matters a girl should know about . . . such as how to dress or learn to dance."

At the one-room grade school Lady Bird attended near her home, her fellow students were all the children of her father's tenant farmers, and a great social gulf separated her from them. So she often felt lonely. She grew up shy and spent much time alone, reading.

When Lady Bird was thirteen and her father decided it was time she entered the high school in the town of Marshall, eighteen miles away, she showed that she possessed true Texas spunk. There were no school buses in those days, nor were there many of the rules and regulations that have since become universal. Mr. Thomas Jefferson Taylor just gave his thirteen-year-old daughter a little car, and after only a few casual lessons she started driving fearlessly in any sort of weather.

Being younger than most of her classmates had added to her shyness, so Lady Bird concentrated on her studies to the extent that she received A's in every subject. When her senior year opened, it appeared that she would surely rank either first or second in her class on graduation day.

The top two students would be expected to make speeches at the ceremony. Lady Bird later recalled feeling that she "would just as soon have smallpox as open my mouth" in front of an audience. While she never said she purposely let up on her studying, she remembered feeling delighted when she finished third after all.

With a brand-new car as a graduation present from her father, Lady Bird went off that autumn to the University of Texas in the state capital of Austin. In addition, Mr. Taylor provided a generous allowance as well as a card letting her charge whatever she wished at the region's most expensive department store. Despite all this, she wasn't careless about money throughout her college years.

Dressing plainly, eating simply, Lady Bird did so well at her studies that in 1933 she graduated in the top tenth of her class. Having received a bachelor of arts degree six months before her twenty-first birthday, she decided to stay on at the university for another year of advanced study in journalism. Even though she wouldn't need to earn her keep, she looked forward to finding satisfying work on a newspaper or perhaps as a schoolteacher.

After she got her journalism degree the following spring, Lady Bird received another present from her father—a trip to the nation's capital. By this time her gentle manner and unfailing kindness had won her many friends, and one of them urged her to look up a lively young man working as secretary to the area's congressman when she got to Washington.

But Lady Bird didn't telephone Lyndon Johnson. "I would have felt mighty odd calling an absolute stranger," she later explained. There were also plenty of Washingtonians who'd graduated from the university a year or two earlier ready to take her sight-seeing. When she stopped off in Austin after her trip, late in August 1934, however, she encountered the man who would change her life.

Lyndon Baines Johnson, twenty-six years old then, was a tall and lean dynamo of energy, with a tremendous drive to get ahead politically. From a respected but poor ranching family in the hill country about an hour's ride west of Austin, he made up his mind the minute he was introduced to Lady Bird that he wanted her to be his wife. Beyond the similarity of their initials, he instantly sensed in her the same combination of feminine sweetness and intelligence that his cherished mother possessed.

He waited till the second time she went out with him to ask her to marry him. Stunned as Lady Bird felt, she had to admit he was "terribly, terribly interesting . . . very good looking . . . the most determined young man" she had ever met. Less than three months later, on November 17, 1934, an impromptu wedding took place, a few weeks before the bride's twenty-second birthday.

Following their brief honeymoon in Mexico, Lady Bird embarked on a far more exciting—and demanding—career than she had ever imagined. Always too modest to claim any credit for Lyndon's rise, she pictured herself as merely the background figure who gave her husband a serene refuge from political pressures. But some shrewd political observers thought that without her, he might never have achieved fame.

Undoubtedly it was her money that paid the bills during his first election campaign: Lady Bird asked her father for $10,000 from her future inheritance when

*L*ady Bird Johnson's four-day train trip through the South on the Lady Bird Special was the first independent whistle-stop tour by a candidate's wife.

twenty-nine-year-old Lyndon saw an opportunity to win a seat in Congress. But both before and after this victory, at every step along his path to national prominence, she smoothed away the many irritations that his brash and sometimes uncouth manner constantly aroused.

Despite her shyness, Lady Bird had a remarkable ability to make people like her. Bidding visitors good-bye, her warmth when she said, "Y'all come back real soon, hear now?" gave the feeling that she really meant it. During the early 1940s, as

Lyndon kept winning reelection, she efficiently ran his congressional office while he was away from Washington on wartime naval duty.

Following his return, she used her managerial talent to increase their financial security. Hearing that a small radio station in Austin was for sale, she bought it and, dividing her time between Texas and the national capital, she turned it into a highly profitable business. Also, in those years she became the mother of two baby daughters, whom Lyndon insisted on endowing with the same initials—Linda Bird (who later changed the spelling to Lynda Bird), born in 1944, and Lucy Baines (who also renamed herself, Luci), born in 1947.

As if motherhood, a demanding husband, a radio station, and a beautiful new home near Lyndon's Texas birthplace were not enough to keep her busy, in 1948 Lady Bird plunged into active politics. With Lyndon involved in a tense campaign to move up to the U.S. Senate, she began appearing at women's meetings on her own instead of just smiling or waving at his side.

Two days before the election, while Lady Bird was driving herself to San Antonio, her car overturned. She climbed out into a muddy ditch, hitchhiked a ride, borrowed a dress, shook several hundred hands, made a brief speech—and then went to a hospital for X rays and bandages. Lyndon won that election by such a narrow margin that his wife's unprecedented efforts may have made the difference.

Lady Bird was still very nervous every time she had to speak in public. Finally in 1955 Lyndon's elevation to the leadership of the Senate's Democratic majority made her decide that the wife of such an important person simply had to conquer this old fear. So she enrolled in a public-speaking course, and "it turned out to be one of the most delightful, expanding experiences I've ever had."

Lady Bird's new confidence enabled her to play a major role in 1960 when her husband became John F. Kennedy's vice-presidential running mate. She traveled 35,000 miles throughout the nation that autumn, speaking at hundreds of political breakfasts, lunches, and dinners. After the Kennedy-Johnson ticket's victory, the new president's brother, Robert Kennedy—who made no secret of his lack of affection for Lyndon—commented that "Lady Bird carried Texas for us."

Yet Lyndon himself could never feel unappreciated at home. "My husband comes first," Lady Bird told her household staff repeatedly. When she was asked about her own aims as the second lady of the land, she listed them as: "Helping Lyndon all that I can, helping Mrs. Kennedy whenever she needs me, and becoming a more alive me."

Because first lady Jackie Kennedy often declined at the last minute to appear at ceremonial occasions, Lady Bird found herself filling in for her much more frequently than she had anticipated. "Washington's number one pinch hitter," one capital reporter called her.

In November 1963 both of the Johnsons flew to Texas with the Kennedys for what was supposed to be a cheerful preview of their joint campaign for reelection the following year. On November 22, when President Kennedy was assassinated in Dallas, Lady Bird did her best to comfort Jackie as her own husband took the oath of office, making him the new president—and she herself became the nation's first lady.

Quietly but confidently, Lady Bird proceeded to put her own stamp on the position. She devoted much of her time to advancing the cause of women in government, holding special luncheons for women of achievement, suggesting women for top official posts, and attending meetings of women's groups. When her husband returned to the White House living quarters in the evening, she often asked him, "Well, what did you do for women today?"

Many Johnson aides considered Lady Bird the president's indispensable partner, giving him not only love and companionship but also advice on almost every important issue. When he ran for reelection in 1964, she went out campaigning on her own, too—until that time Eleanor Roosevelt was the only first lady to have done so. Touring the South, she managed with her gracious Southern ways to disarm many enemies of the strong civil rights law her husband had recently signed.

Indeed, the wife of a leading Republican said she had never met anyone who did not admire Mrs. Johnson, and Democrats were even more effusive. "The greatest woman I have ever met," Speaker of the House Sam Rayburn called her. "She's good and she's kind and she doesn't have a mean thought." Another old political friend added: "This is the problem with Bird. When you talk about her, you make her too good to be true."

During her husband's second term Lady Bird made a cause that had always been close to her heart the focus of national attention. Largely because of her efforts, Congress passed a new law aimed at protecting the natural environment and beautifying the country's highways by limiting billboards and promoting the planting of wildflowers.

Lady Bird also sponsored a program to beautify Washington itself, emphasizing the close connection between ugliness, oppression, and crime. Throughout the land she dedicated many new parks and gardens.

When the Johnsons left the White House in 1969, Lady Bird was in her late fifties. She and Lyndon returned to their LBJ Ranch on the Pedernales River in Texas, where she used her new leisure to prepare a book based on the daily record

Lady Bird Johnson was able to make "beautification"—the name given to her focus on environmental protection—a national issue. Here she greets bicyclists amid daffodils planted as part of the program in Washington, D.C.

she had dictated during her busy years in the executive mansion. Her book, *A White House Diary,* was published the following year.

Despite revelations of Lyndon Johnson's love affairs—which were made public after his death in 1973 and no doubt caused Lady Bird pain and embarrassment—she continued her work with the Johnson Presidential Library and her support of environmental awareness.

Besides supervising the ranch and enjoying frequent visits from her children and grandchildren, she continues to make occasional public appearances even in her advancing years.

How Have First Ladies Contributed to Campaigning?

*C*ampaigning developed as a male activity in the 1800s as political parties grew and battled each other to elect candidates and to enact their policies. Campaigning and voting brought together all classes of white men and gave them a common bond. Politics took place outside the home and was considered too rough and corrupt for women. Popular ideas such as "a woman's place is in the home" and laws that kept women from voting made their direct participation in campaigns seem improper. Still, women had always supported party politics by sewing banners, holding fund-raisers, and attending campaign speeches and rallies.

In the 1880s and 1890s new campaign styles appeared. "Front-porch" campaigns, where the candidate spoke to the press from his home, and "whistle-stop" campaigns, where candidates traveled around the country on a train, brought candidates' wives directly into the campaign. Since the front porch was the place where women often met and entertained guests, the wife of a candidate running a front-porch campaign could take part without leaving her home and seeming improper. When a wife went with her husband on a whistle-stop campaign, she could appear helpful and supportive and not be viewed as "meddling in politics." Candidates' wives began to use these new styles to promote their husbands' campaigns, and by the 1950s campaigning by a candidate's wife had become an expected part of American political life.

James Garfield waged the first front-porch campaign in 1880 from his home in Ohio. Benjamin Harrison and his wife, Caroline, received three hundred thousand party supporters at their home in Indianapolis in 1888. By 1920, the year that women gained the vote, Florence Harding actually helped her husband, Warren Harding, run his campaign for president.

Franklin D. Roosevelt's wife, Eleanor, had been brought up to think that campaigning by the candidate's wife was not proper. But her husband's polio often made him weak and tired. She agreed to accompany him on some campaigns to ease the

Eleanor Roosevelt campaigned for her husband during his presidency, both with him and on her own. Here she shakes hands from a train during a whistle-stop tour.

strain, and later became a very effective campaigner on her own. Mrs. Roosevelt was a smart politician in her own right and a driving force in many policies of her husband's presidency, opening new paths for other candidates' wives to follow.

By the 1950s women were voting in almost equal numbers with men. Political parties often didn't want to run women for political office but felt they had to have a strategy to attract women to vote for their party. Mamie Eisenhower and Pat Nixon, the wives of the Republican candidates, were presented to the public as candidates for first and second lady. The public loved Mamie and Pat. In fact, at the close of his campaign speeches Eisenhower would tell the eager crowds, "And now I want you to meet my Mamie." Since that time the candidate's wife has been a central part of the campaign.

Both parties appealed to women to be grassroots workers in the campaigns of 1952 and 1956—by promoting dresses, skirts, scarves, and perfume with their candidate's name. These "I Like Ike" stockings could be worn by the well-dressed Republican woman. Democrats also produced women's stockings for their candidate that read "Madly for Adlai" (Stevenson).

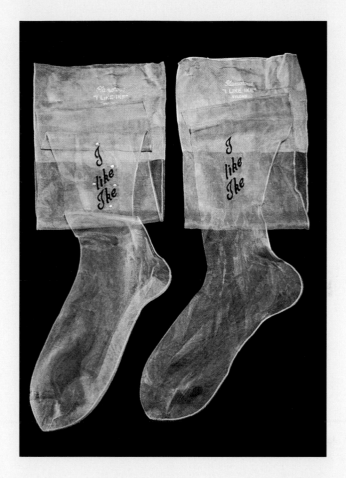

In 1964 Lady Bird Johnson had her own campaign train, the Lady Bird Special, and traveled through the South in the first independent whistle-stop campaign by a candidate's wife.

Campaigning has changed radically since the 1960s. The ability of a candidate's wife to campaign effectively is now an integral part of every modern race for the White House. She must be able to speak well and be persuasive and informed on the issues. She is also expected to have an important project of her own once she gets to the White House—yet the public still thinks she shouldn't seek power for herself.

Pat Nixon

MARCH 16, 1912–JUNE 22, 1993

"I've never had it easy"

$\mathcal{P}$at Nixon entered the White House at a troubled time in U.S. history. Privately spontaneous and lively, her controlled public behavior made her seem stiff and withdrawn.

$\mathcal{E}$ven the mere matter of her name was a little confusing. After she grew up, everybody called her Pat—and it was widely assumed that she had been named Patricia. Actually, though, she had been christened Thelma.

Two very different impressions of this first lady's personality spread around the world. Was she a wonderfully warm and friendly woman? Or a pretty blond "robot," obediently playing the part assigned to her?

Of course, both of these opinions of her were politically inspired: Voters who supported her husband tended to admire her, and his opponents were her severest critics. But because Richard Nixon aroused extremely bitter hatred among his political enemies, his wife received far more than an ordinary amount of partisan ridicule.

All the evidence from people who knew her during her early life indicates that she had been an especially likable young woman—bright, cheery, and adventurous. What's more, her spirit of optimism had survived outright poverty in her childhood, as well as the loss of both of her parents before she reached her eighteenth birthday.

Born in the gold-mining town of Ely, Nevada, on March 16, 1912, Thelma Catharine Ryan had mixed ancestry. Her mother, Kate Halberstadt, had come to America from Germany and was a young widow when she married William Ryan from Ireland. With his loyalty to old Irish traditions, he enthusiastically welcomed their daughter's arrival on the eve of St. Patrick's Day by nicknaming her Pat.

Bill Ryan worked hard as a miner, and the dusty job already gave him symptoms of the dreaded lung disease called silicosis. So while Pat was still an infant, the family moved to a ten-acre farm in California, not far from Los Angeles. Living in a tiny house without electricity, they grew tomatoes, peppers, and other vegetables for sale in the city about twenty miles away.

"It was a good kind of life when you look back on it," Pat once recalled. "I worked right along with my brothers in the field, really, which was lots of fun. When I was real tiny, I just tagged along. But when I got older, I drove the team of horses."

Pat attended school regularly, walking a mile back and forth every day. On advancing into high school, she began riding a bus—but not long afterward, her mother became very ill. Pat was fourteen when her mother died of cancer, and then she herself took charge of housekeeping for her father and two older brothers.

Not that she quit school: After preparing breakfast, she ran for the bus, and on returning home, she cleaned and did laundry and prepared supper. Somehow she found time to study and even joined the school's debating team. But her favorite outside activity was acting in school plays.

After graduation she got a job first as a cleaning woman and then as a clerk for the bank in the nearest town. She took some classes at the local junior college while she cooked and cleaned and cared for her ailing father. When he died in 1930, she decided to change her name from Thelma to Patricia because she thought that would keep his memory alive.

The following year, when she was nineteen, Pat seized an unusual opportunity to earn money for her college education. An elderly couple with an old Packard car asked her if she would drive them all the way to New York City, and, unfazed by coping with thousands of miles of old-fashioned highways, she delivered them there safely. In the East Coast metropolis she found an office job, then managed to get hired for better-paying work as an X-ray technician.

"The world is just what we make it," she wrote home to her brother Tom, "so let's make ours a grand one. Too, it's fun to work and then enjoy the fruits of the success. I love to learn new things, no matter how difficult—also go to new places."

After two years in New York, Pat returned to California to complete her education. Moving into a Los Angeles apartment with her brothers, she enrolled at the University of Southern California. Between the ages of twenty-two and twenty-five, she went to classes and also held a variety of part-time jobs: library aide, store clerk, telephone operator, cafeteria helper, even movie extra.

Despite having to spend a good part of every week working to pay her bills, Pat did well at her studies. She graduated in 1937 with honors and a degree in merchandising as well as a teaching certificate. In those Depression days, she took the first full-time job offered to her, teaching typing and shorthand at the high school in Whittier, about fifteen miles east of Los Angeles.

One of her pupils later described Miss Ryan: "She looked so young to us. She was very attractive, red hair, a very slim face." Despite her youthful appearance and enthusiasm, she conducted her classes firmly and expected "clockwork punctuality" as well as a high level of achievement from her students.

Since teachers at her school were encouraged to participate in community activities, Pat tried out for a part in a play being put on by a local drama group. She got the part (as a minor character in a mystery called *The Dark Tower*) and in so doing, she drew the attention of an ambitious young lawyer also planning to join the play's cast.

Although Richard Nixon's face and manner were so solemn that he had earned the nickname "Gloomy Gus," he displayed a surprising streak of romance. On the evening he first met Pat, he told her that someday she was going to marry him. "I thought he was nuts or something," she remembered long afterward.

After two and a half years during which Pat gradually came to admire Dick Nixon more and more, she did marry him—on June 21, 1940; she was twenty-eight then, and so was he. Moving into his small apartment over a garage near his law office, she continued teaching to help pay their expenses. Soon, as the United States drew closer to involvement in World War II, the national emergency uprooted the couple.

W*earing African dress, Pat Nixon attended the inauguration of the new president of Liberia. She excelled at this kind of personal diplomacy.*

Dick worked briefly for a government agency in Washington. Then after Pearl Harbor, when he began serving as a naval officer, Pat got a job in the San Francisco branch of the wartime Office of Price Administration. With the return of peace, in 1946 her husband received an intriguing invitation: Would he run for Congress on the Republican ticket in his hometown of Whittier?

Pat had no particular interest in politics, but she strongly believed that it was a wife's duty to help her husband any way she could. As Dick clearly yearned to triumph over his Democratic opponent, she worked long hours in his campaign office and then celebrated with him joyfully when the election returns gave him the victory. Years later he would recall: "Pat and I were happier on November 6, 1946, than we were ever to be again in my political career."

Congressman Richard Nixon's hard-driving political style quickly won him national attention. While his efforts to expose Communist sympathizers brought him many supporters, some of the ruthless methods he used made his opponents label him "tricky Dick." Pat felt that her husband's critics were terribly unfair.

The same year he entered Congress, she gave birth to a daughter they named Patricia, shortened to Tricia. Then two years later their second little girl, Julie, was born. Raising the two children, rather than politics, absorbed most of Pat's energy from then on.

Indeed, she felt so distressed by the controversies constantly swirling around Dick that on four separate occasions over the next several decades, she obtained written promises from him that he would never run for office again. Each time, when circumstances of overriding importance made him break his promise, Pat loyally appeared on platforms with him and smiled for photographers. But by 1952, when his election as vice president first brought her into national prominence, she had already developed her own way of dealing with unwanted celebrity.

"She chatters, answers questions, smiles and smiles, all with a doll's terrifying poise," an English newspaper reported during a London visit by Vice President Nixon and his wife. Some American writers called her "plastic Pat." Her stiff, impersonal manner astonished a television correspondent who could remember the warm friendliness of Miss Ryan back in Whittier High School.

After eight vice-presidential years, Pat dutifully traveled with her husband throughout his 1960 campaign to succeed Dwight Eisenhower as president. Although disappointed when John F. Kennedy won that election, she was also relieved—and she had the same mixture of emotions following Dick's defeat in a subsequent drive to become governor of California.

Then came a short interval Pat later looked back on as a wonderful vacation. Dick accepted a job with a New York law firm, the family moved into a large Fifth Avenue apartment, and she and their daughters were at last free to enjoy life privately. That freedom ended, though, when her husband ran again for the presidency in 1968. This time he won.

Pat's anger over the way some reporters treated her in print burst forth once during this campaign. Asked about her dreams and goals as a girl, she had astonished her questioner by replying passionately: "I never had time to think about things like that—who I wanted to be or who I admired, or to have ideas. I had to work . . . I've never had it easy."

Much to her own surprise, though, Pat at first enjoyed being first lady. While she still struck many observers as artificially stiff at large gatherings, she often relaxed when greeting small groups of visitors. "She had more ways to say that someone had a pretty hat than anyone else I ever knew," one of her friends commented, acknowledging Pat's skill at talking to people. Also, the challenge of continuing on Jackie Kennedy's renovation of the White House appealed to her. She brought more than 500 pieces of antique furniture and works of art into the White House while first lady.

Most of all Pat relished the adventure of flying all over the world on goodwill missions. With her husband, or sometimes on her own, she paid official visits to a total of eighty-two countries, she once calculated. "I do or die," she told an interviewer awed by her stamina. "I never cancel out."

Favors picturing the "Nixon team"—Dick; Pat; their daughters, Tricia and Julie; and their dog, Checkers—decorated tables at Republican women's luncheons. Direct appeals to women were part of a major Republican campaign theme in the 1950s and early 1960s.

But all the pleasant aspects of public life she relished were overshadowed during her husband's second term by the Watergate scandal. During the tense months that led to Richard Nixon's becoming the first president of the United States ever to resign his office—rather than face being impeached and possibly prosecuted for the crime of obstructing justice—even many of his political enemies felt increasing sympathy for his wife.

Totally absorbed with his own troubles, Dick had seemed completely unaware of Pat's presence by his side. Walking ahead of her, never showing any affection in public, he seemed not to realize she deserved better treatment. The climax of this apparent indifference came during his tearful farewell to his staff just before leaving the White House in disgrace, when he repeatedly praised his "saintly" mother but did not even mention his wife.

The pained look on Pat's face was unforgettable—but cameras ceased focusing on her after she boarded the helicopter on the White House lawn that ended this awful chapter in American history. After the Nixons returned to their California home in the summer of 1974, she stayed completely out of the public eye. "The lonely lady of San Clemente," a sympathetic biographer called her.

Two years later Pat suffered a stroke that reportedly left her partly paralyzed. In time, her husband published several books about his political career, and after he and Pat moved to secluded homes in New Jersey and then New York, he began venturing forth to defend his record and play the part of elder statesman.

The Nixons' daughter Julie, who had married former president Eisenhower's grandson David, wrote a warmly loving book about her mother titled *Pat Nixon: The Untold Story*. Pat herself spent her later years reading, gardening, listening to music, and enjoying visits from her children and grandchildren. She died at her home on June 22, 1993, at age eighty-one.

Betty Ford

AUGUST 8, 1918–

"She's a gutsy lady"

*B*etty Ford said of her outspoken public comments: "Being ladylike does not require silence."

You can't help liking her!" exclaimed a writer for the *Washington Post.* One of her White House aides called her "the most up-front person I ever knew." And a noted photographer said she was "the most refreshing character we've had in public life for some time."

Although Betty Ford spent only two and a half years as the nation's first lady, her informal way of speaking out about both personal and political matters made her widely popular. Her frank discussion of her own case of breast cancer—at a time when a hush-hush attitude toward the disease still prevailed—was credited with encouraging thousands of other women to take steps toward securing prompt medical attention that might save their lives.

Betty often seemed cheerfully surprised by the attention paid to her every remark. As she once explained to an interviewer, moving into the White House gave her a wonderful opportunity to emerge from being just a background figure and say, "Look, I'm important too!" However, both before and after her husband's unexpected elevation to the presidency, she had some difficult private problems that were painful by-products of his political career.

Born in Chicago on April 8, 1918, she was the daughter of a machinery salesman named William Stephenson Bloomer and his wife, Hortense Neahr Bloomer. Even though her birth certificate referred to her as Elizabeth Ann, everybody called her Betty, and with a name like Betty Bloomer, she would laughingly say many years later, how could she help looking forward to changing it by getting married?

Betty grew up in Grand Rapids, Michigan, with two older brothers. She had what she later described as a "sunny childhood," despite the teasing she received because of her name. The only serious sorrow she experienced came with her father's death when she was sixteen.

By then Betty already had a career picked out for herself. Since the age of eight she had been taking dance lessons—ballet, tap, acrobatic: "I signed up for everything, I adored it." At fourteen she had even started giving younger children lessons on Saturday afternoons. The idea of becoming a famous dancer made her enroll, after she graduated from high school in 1936, in a summer program offered by Bennington College in Vermont.

At Bennington one of Betty's teachers was the great Martha Graham, who had organized a highly acclaimed modern-dance group in New York. Although Graham hardly noticed her pupil from Grand Rapids, Betty was strongly influenced by her teacher's brilliance and daring. As money was scarce during those Depression years, she realized that she would have to work while seeking further training, and after two winters of holding assorted jobs in Grand Rapids, interrupted by another summer in Vermont, Betty at the age of twenty bravely went off to New York.

Sharing a small apartment with another aspiring dancer, she spent two exciting years there. Daytimes she worked as a model in the clothing showrooms of the garment industry—so that she could afford to pay for evening classes at Martha Graham's dance school. Dedicated as Betty was, she couldn't win a place in Graham's main company, which performed a regular schedule of concerts.

Betty Ford campaigns in 1976. Women especially loved Mrs. Ford, and many wore buttons reading "Betty's Husband for President."

Yet she did have the thrill of dancing onstage with one of Graham's secondary groups. Ready then to admit she couldn't become a professional dancer, she accepted her mother's suggestion that she come home for six months before deciding whether she wanted to stay in New York. At the end of those six months Betty chose to pursue a career teaching Graham's experimental technique in Grand Rapids.

Besides starting her own dance group and teaching dance classes, she worked as a fashion coordinator at a local department store. But she still had plenty of energy to enjoy an active social life with old friends. One of them, who had taken her to her first prom at the age of twelve, was a lively insurance salesman named Bill Warren.

Practically all Betty's friends already had husbands. Popular as Betty had always been, she had not yet met a man who more than briefly appealed to her. Right after the United States was drawn into World War II, in 1942, she decided that she did want to become Betty Warren.

Very soon after her wedding, though, the twenty-four-year-old bride began to feel that she had made a mistake. Increasingly unhappy, Betty secured a divorce in 1947, and at twenty-nine she went back to work at the department store.

She had already made the acquaintance of a lawyer of thirty-five, a former football hero at the University of Michigan. Gerald Ford told her in February 1948 that he wanted to marry her, and in her own words, "I took him up on it instantly."

However, Jerry rather mysteriously informed her that they couldn't be married till the fall because there was something else he had to do first. It turned out he was planning to run for Congress and wanted to concentrate on securing the approval of local Republican leaders before taking time off for a wedding. Right after he won a primary assuring him of his party's nomination, Betty donned a blue satin dress for a brief church ceremony on October 15, 1948.

Yet there still remained a hard struggle to defeat Jerry's Democratic opponent in the actual election a few weeks later. The day after their wedding he hurried off to resume shaking hands with voters, and he kept up a hectic schedule of politicking until he won the seat in the national House of Representatives. It was a fitting start for Betty's new life as the wife of a longtime congressman.

Happy as Betty and Jerry were together, his political career over the next quarter of a century often separated them. Although she moved to Washington with him only a few weeks after they got married and traveled back to Grand Rapids with him whenever he spent any length of time there, his heavy schedule of meetings kept him away from home many evenings until midnight.

Betty very soon began having children, giving birth to three boys and a girl during the first seven years of their marriage, so her own domestic duties filled most of her time. As much as possible, though, she helped out in Jerry's office. She thoroughly enjoyed whatever hours she managed to spend at gatherings of the social club made up of other congressional wives.

Betty's enjoyment of life in Washington faded as her husband rose in the Republican ranks. After Jerry was elected as his party's leader in the House of Representatives in 1965, Betty would ruefully recall: "The Congress got a new minority leader, and I lost a husband." One year she kept a count showing he didn't have dinner at home on 258 evenings. "I had to bring up four kids by myself."

Betty's dissatisfaction with the course of her life reached a critical point as a result of an injury she suffered. One day while she was home alone, reaching to open a window, she strained her neck. Her injury later resulted in severe arthritis. To ease her discomfort, a doctor prescribed painkilling drugs, and she soon became dependent on them.

Feeling increasingly depressed, Betty finally consulted a psychiatrist. The counseling she received gave her the self-confidence to have a serious talk with Jerry, and he promised that for her sake, he would retire from public life when his current

*D*uring her time as first lady, Betty Ford strongly supported women's rights and passage of the Equal Rights Amendment. Here women have gathered on the Mall in Washington, D.C., in support of the ERA.

term of office ended in 1974. But two of the most bizarre occurrences in American history prevented him from keeping his word.

In 1973 Vice President Spiro Agnew resigned after being accused of taking bribes, and President Richard Nixon chose Gerald Ford, one of the most respected Republicans in Washington, as the nation's new vice president. Then, less than a year later, Nixon himself resigned rather than face impeachment for his part in the Watergate scandal, making Jerry the new president.

Instead of returning to a quiet life in Grand Rapids, Betty moved into the center of national attention with her husband. The role of first lady thoroughly delighted her. At her first press conference she gave reporters a sample of what to expect: She would not only support the creative arts and encourage better treatment of ailing elderly Americans, but she would also work for ratification of the controversial Equal Rights Amendment.

Even though her husband continued to oppose this feminist measure, the undaunted Betty "used everything, including pillow talk at the end of the day," in her effort to make him change his mind. Despite the fears of some staunch Republicans that all the outspoken comments by the first lady would hurt her husband politically, Jerry himself did not share these worries. "If I could just get my rating up to hers!" he joked.

Indeed, polls showed that she was one of the most popular presidential wives of modern times, especially after she spoke openly about her treatment for breast cancer. Her doctor summed up the prevailing opinion: "She's a gutsy lady." To Betty, all the applause she received was tremendously invigorating. Continuing her speaking to the public with great honesty about controversial issues, Betty Ford angered some segments of the public by her openness during an appearance on *60 Minutes.* She spoke frankly with interviewer Morley Safer about abortion, premarital sex, and women's health issues. The interview brought a flood of mail from the public, much of it critical. Yet because of her honesty, her ratings in the press and public opinion polls remained high.

But her husband, a solid yet undramatic president, never could erase the tarnish of the Nixon years. Running in 1976 to win a term of his own in the White House, he was defeated by Jimmy Carter, the Democratic candidate. Then the Fords retired to a luxurious new home in Palm Springs, California, where Jerry had plenty of opportunity for playing golf, his favorite recreation.

For Betty, though, retirement meant a sudden end to the excitement and the sense of purpose she had gained as first lady. Her use of painkillers and alcohol to get her through the White House years increased after her husband's retirement from public office. "The truth is," she said several years later, "I was at the end of my rope."

In 1984 Betty's family convinced her to seek professional help. As a result she entered the alcohol and drug rehabilitation wing of the U.S. naval hospital in Long Beach, California. But in typical Betty Ford style, she didn't do so quietly. She told the public about her problems and her treatment, urging others with similar problems to seek help too. Once again her candor brought understanding, sympathy, and praise from many people.

After Betty left the hospital, she helped to found the Betty Ford Center for Drug and Alcohol Rehabilitation in Rancho Mirage, California, where many celebrities as well as less famous people now go to conquer their addictions. She made speeches on behalf of numerous causes she supported and wrote a book about her life that sold widely.

When a television network presented a program called *The Betty Ford Story* late in the 1980s, her husband was asked why his rise to the presidency hadn't been the subject of a similar film. He replied with a smile, "My wife is much more interesting."

Rosalynn Carter

AUGUST 18, 1927–

"A steel magnolia blossom"

*R*osalynn Carter's years as the wife of Georgia's governor prepared her well, both socially and politically, for her role as first lady.

W hile her husband presided over meetings of his cabinet, first lady Rosalynn Carter sat quietly taking notes. Besides working very actively for several causes of her own, she also served as his most trusted adviser. She even represented him officially during a trip to seven Central and South American countries a few months after moving into the White House.

Although previous presidential wives had sometimes traveled abroad alone, their missions had been mainly ceremonial. When it became clear that the purpose of her Latin American tour was to talk about important matters with the leaders of other lands, a reporter challenged her:

"You have neither been elected by the American people nor confirmed by the Senate to discuss foreign policy with the heads of [other countries]. Do you consider this trip an appropriate exercise of your position?"

President Jimmy Carter's wife replied a little sharply, "I am the person closest to the president of the United States, and if I can explain his policies and let the people of Latin America know of his great interest and friendship, I intend to do so."

Her expansion of the traditional activities of first lady came at a time when women everywhere were starting to take larger and larger roles in business and government. So Rosalynn aroused much admiration as well as criticism—she seemed to be a symbol of the great changes resulting from the women's movement of the late 1960s and 1970s.

"A steel magnolia blossom," one interviewer called her, aptly summing up both the charm and the determination shaped by Rosalynn's rural Georgia girlhood. Born on a farm near the small town of Plains on August 18, 1927, she had started life as Eleanor Rosalynn Smith. Nobody ever paid much attention to the first name she had been given, though, until some people years later compared her to Eleanor Roosevelt.

Rosalynn was the eldest of four children. Her father, William Edgar Smith, in addition to running their small farm, operated an auto repair shop and also drove the bus that brought outlying students to the high school in Plains. That was how he had originally met Frances Allethea Murray, who took schooling seriously enough to insist on earning a teaching certificate before she married him.

Although times were hard during Rosalynn's growing-up years, she and her younger brothers and sister didn't feel particularly poor. The Smiths grew their own food and made their own clothes. Even if the family had very little money, the Great Depression scarcely affected them.

At school Rosalynn was an outstanding student. While she later recalled being the sort of shy and quiet girl who could wear a white dress all day without getting it dirty, she also remembered relishing many lively games with her brothers and their friends. As she entered her teens, she was inspired by a young teacher to start reading newspapers and listening to news reports on the radio—and she discovered a whole new world of interesting people and faraway places that made her dream about leaving her small town.

Not long after Rosalynn entered high school, her father became seriously ill. She was fourteen when he died of leukemia, and she felt deeply bound to help her mother as much as she possibly could. Besides taking over many household chores, she worked part-time in the beauty parlor her mother opened.

Even so, she managed to get straight A's at school: Her high marks made her the valedictorian of her class on her graduation day in the spring of 1945. Wearing a beautiful store-bought long dress of white organdy, she managed, despite her trembling knees, to deliver her speech without missing a word.

Early that summer, while she was still only seventeen, Rosalynn received an exciting summons from her closest friend in high school. Ruth Carter's older brother had been away for the past several years at the U.S. Naval Academy in Annapolis, and now he was home on a visit. Rosalynn had always known Jimmy Carter in just the casual way everybody in the Plains vicinity knew everybody else, but at Ruth's house she had fallen in love with a picture of him wearing his midshipman's uniform—"I thought he was the most handsome young man I had ever seen."

When Ruth invited her to a picnic at which the twenty-year-old Jimmy would be present, Rosalynn worried that she would be too tongue-tied to say a word to him. "But I wasn't." And he asked her to a movie that evening; then, on the way home, he kissed her.

"I couldn't believe it had happened," Rosalynn wrote years later. "I had never let any boy kiss me on a first date. My mother told me she hadn't even held hands with Daddy until they were engaged! But I was completely swept off my feet."

Plans were soon made for a wedding after Jimmy graduated from Annapolis and Rosalynn finished a year at Georgia State College for Women in Americus, about twenty miles from Plains. The ceremony took place on July 7, 1946, a few weeks before the bride's nineteenth birthday.

During their year apart Jimmy had sent Rosalynn a little book titled *The Navy Wife,* which provided all kinds of helpful hints for women whose husbands were on active duty. (At that time the regular navy was open only to men.) As Jimmy expected to make the navy his career, it was likely that he would be assigned to many different places—and he had teased Rosalynn that her secret longing to leave Plains was the only reason she had agreed to marry him.

In the next seven years Rosalynn repeatedly thought back to how starry-eyed she had been when she had first read the small book he sent her. With Jimmy away on duty much of the time, she faced new challenges almost daily and yet, "I loved our life in the navy and the independence that I had finally achieved."

From Norfolk, Virginia, all the way to Hawaii, she set up housekeeping at six different naval bases during those seven years. As she soon began having children, giving birth to their sons Jack, Chip, and Jeff, she had to cope with a great variety of problems on her own. Yet she kept finding new achievements to enjoy, and as Jimmy received increasingly important assignments, she looked forward to many even more interesting new experiences.

Then came a phone call from Plains: Jimmy's father had cancer and was dying. After going home for several weeks of emergency leave, Jimmy made a major decision without consulting Rosalynn—to resign from the navy so he could take over the family's peanut business. Rosalynn felt so crushed by the prospect of returning to Plains for good that they had the only serious dispute of their marriage.

"I argued," she wrote later. "I cried. I even screamed at him." Then, during their first several months back, she felt that both her mother and Jimmy's mother were constantly looking over her shoulder. "I was miserable," she recalled, though another telephone call soon cured her misery.

It was during the summer of 1955 that Jimmy called Rosalynn at home and asked her to come and help out in the office while he went to see some farmers. She brought the children with her, first for one day a week, then two days, and finally full-time. She kept the books, sent out bills, and gradually learned so much that within a few years Jimmy thought she knew more about the business than he did.

"We grew together as full partners," Rosalynn herself put it more tactfully. Then, after the couple's involvement in community projects led to Jimmy's running for a seat in Georgia's state senate, the partnership extended to politics too. In keeping with the established pattern, it was Jimmy who actually sought office—but both of them felt that his political career rested on Rosalynn's efforts no less than his own.

By 1970, when Jimmy won election as Georgia's governor, Rosalynn had learned to speak informally at all sorts of gatherings, without any trembling of the knees. While she went out campaigning for Jimmy, his mother took care of little Amy, their cherished daughter born three years earlier. Even the social part of being a political wife didn't faze Rosalynn after she studied a helpful book called *Gracious Entertaining,* but she much preferred working with committees to improve state programs for groups that needed special help, particularly mentally retarded children.

When Jimmy decided to run for president in 1976, Rosalynn was ready. In a difficult, uphill battle for nomination by the Democratic party, the Carters felt they could cover more ground if they campaigned separately. Every Monday through Friday, month after month, Rosalynn traveled in her own chartered airplane, making countless speeches and giving hundreds of interviews to newspapers and on radio and television.

*M*rs. *Carter held weekly working lunches with the president, participated in policy discussions, and attended cabinet meetings.*

Her soft-spoken Southern manner, combined with her iron determination, impressed reporters. One referred to her as "a Sherman tank in a field of clover." Rosalynn didn't object to this kind of journalistic treatment. "I don't mind being called tough," she said. "I am strong. I do have definite ideas and opinions. In the sense that 'tough' means that I can take a lot, stand up to a lot, it's a fair description."

In the White House the Carters' political partnership continued to flourish. Once a week Rosalynn and her husband met at a "business lunch" to coordinate their schedules and talk over administration policies. However, after her official trip to Latin America stirred a great deal of criticism, the couple didn't try any similar experiments.

Rosalynn kept extremely busy with her own agenda as first lady. At the top of her list was mental health reform, and she became honorary chairperson of the President's Commission on Mental Health, created to propose new programs in this

Rosalynn Carter at a meeting of the President's Commission on Mental Health, which she had lobbied hard to create.

field. She also actively supported legislation to reform Social Security, hosted discussions about the problems of the aging, and urged approval of the Equal Rights Amendment.

One newspaper made a tally showing that as an activist first lady, Rosalynn Carter had no peer. During her first fourteen months in the White House, she visited eighteen foreign nations and twenty-seven American cities, attended two hundred fifty-nine private and fifty public meetings, made fifteen major speeches, gave thirty-two interviews, held twenty-two press conferences, and also was the hostess at eighty-three official receptions.

When Jimmy Carter ran for reelection in 1980, Rosalynn's role as campaigner increased because the president thought he should remain in Washington to keep close track of the Americans then being held hostage by Iran. She spoke so often, she almost lost her voice. Nevertheless, her husband was defeated by Republican Ronald Reagan.

Right after the election results became clear, a reporter watching the returns with the Carters said: "Mr. President, you're a great example. You don't seem bitter at all." Rosalynn burst out: "I'm bitter enough for both of us." Gradually, though, she began to accept the defeat more philosophically.

Only fifty-three when she and Jimmy returned to their home in Plains, she still felt far from ready for retirement. He too wanted to keep on working, so their long-time partnership continued during those post–White House years. Besides writing several books about their own experiences, they started the Carter Center, associated with the Carter presidential library, where they devoted much of their energy to promoting humanitarian causes close to their hearts. They were especially involved with a group called Habitat for Humanity, which renovated homes for the poor, and sponsored immunization programs for children, both at home and abroad.

Yet Rosalynn never stopped missing the excitement of her life in Washington. "I won't say it's a relief not to be the first lady," she told one interviewer, "because I enjoyed every minute of it."

Nancy Reagan

"He is my hero!"

Nancy Reagan was a close confidante of her husband's during the Reagan presidency.

*H*ow much influence did Nancy Reagan really have over her husband's decision making?

This question was repeatedly raised during the eight years of Ronald Reagan's presidency—and then it stirred more controversy two years later, when a book about her claimed that she had exercised more power than any previous first lady.

Yet all the furor struck many people, including Nancy herself, as very unfair. For she always held that she actually was an old-fashioned wife whose main concern was promoting her husband's health and welfare. "My life began when I got married," she liked to say. "My life began with Ronnie."

Thirty years before her marriage in Hollywood, she had been born in New York City, on July 6, 1921. Her parents were an actress, Edith Luckett, and Kenneth Robbins, an automobile salesman. They named their daughter Anne Francis Robbins but called her Nancy.

At the age of two Nancy found herself uprooted when her parents divorced. Her mother returned to the stage and traveled around the country with various touring groups, leaving her little girl with an aunt and uncle in Bethesda, Maryland. Although Nancy would later say that she had "wonderful memories" of the five years she spent there, it was a period of her life she rarely spoke of.

When Nancy was seven, her mother married again and gave up acting. She brought Nancy to live with her and her new husband, Dr. Loyal Davis, a prominent surgeon in Chicago. The rest of Nancy's girlhood was spent in a spacious apartment on that city's Lake Shore Drive, where she grew accustomed to mingling with Chicago's rich and fashionable elite—and where she also met the stars of touring theater companies who came to visit her mother.

At the age of fourteen Nancy was formally adopted by Dr. Davis, a strict but kindly man with strong conservative political opinions, whom she had come to consider her real father. Known thereafter as Nancy Davis, she attended the highly regarded Girls' Latin School, at which she acted in school plays and served as president of the Dramatic Club.

Yet the entry beside her picture in her senior yearbook gave evidence of her wider accomplishments: "Nancy's social perfection is a constant source of amazement. She is invariably becomingly and suitably dressed. She can talk and listen intelligently to anyone from her little kindergarten partner of the Halloween party to the grandmother of one of her friends."

In 1939, when Nancy was eighteen, she went to Smith College in Northampton, Massachusetts, where she majored in English and drama—and, as she herself said, boys. Besides acting in many college plays, during vacation periods she worked as an apprentice at New England summer theaters.

After graduating in 1943, while World War II was raging, Nancy worked briefly as a nurse's aide. Then, thanks to the help of some of her mother's acting friends, she secured small parts in a few Broadway plays. These led to a screen test in Hollywood in 1949, and at the age of twenty-eight she was hired as a "starlet" by MGM, one of the major movie companies.

Nancy appeared in around a dozen films. "Most of them are best forgotten," she would say when she looked back on her movie career. But the year she arrived in Hollywood, she met a handsome leading man ten years older than she was, whom she liked immediately. Ronald Reagan had recently been divorced from actress Jane Wyman and seemed happy to be a bachelor again.

Hollywood gossips soon noted that he and Nancy Davis made a most attractive couple, however. Nobody was very surprised when it became known that they had gotten married on March 4, 1952. For a time they both continued their film careers, even making one picture together, *Hellcats of the Navy,* in 1957. After that Nancy bowed out to devote herself to caring for her husband and children, Patricia, born in 1952, and Ronald, born in 1958.

In those same years her husband's career changed too. He became host for a popular television series, the General Electric Theatre, and traveled around the country making speeches about the virtues of big business and the sins of big government. Although Nancy had never been much interested in politics, some people thought that the outlook she had absorbed from her stepfather had much to do with turning "Ronnie," who had started out as a liberal Democrat, into a conservative Republican.

The Reagans became part of a stylish circle of rich Californians—and got involved in politics. A fine speaker, Ronnie soon became a star on the speechmaking circuit for Republican candidates everywhere. In 1966 his friends urged him to run for governor of California.

During this campaign Nancy got her first taste of the pleasures and pains of being a political wife. Even if appearing with Ronnie at crowded rallies could be very tiring, she found the excitement so thrilling that she later said: "I wouldn't have traded it for anything." Yet she couldn't help feeling distressed when reporters made fun of the fond way she gazed at her husband while he was speaking.

"The Look," they called it. "Her eyes sparkle as if she were in some kind of trance," a writer for the *Chicago Tribune* told the paper's readers. "Hearing a one-liner for the one-hundredth time, she laughs on cue and then resumes the adoring gaze." Even Nancy's friends admitted that her stare upset them. "Nancy," one of them dared to say to her, "people just don't *believe* it when you look at Ronnie that way—as though you are saying, 'He's my hero.'" "But he *is* my hero!" she exclaimed.

On becoming California's first lady, Nancy tried to prove that she was a traditional wife devoted to making a pleasant home for her husband and children, including his daughter and son from his previous marriage. She made sure that Ronnie got good food, sufficient rest, and time to watch his favorite television shows. She frequently overruled his aides when they scheduled too many public appearances for him.

*P*hotographs depicting the Reagans' devotion to each other promoted the image of "family values," an important political tactic with the president's conservative supporters.

At the same time Nancy herself emerged as a glamorous figure because of her perfect grooming and the fashionable clothes she wore. One writer called her a Republican version of Jackie Kennedy, with "the same spare figure, the same air of immaculate chic." Also, her insistence on renting a fine home in Sacramento, instead of living in what struck her as the ugly old governor's mansion, contributed toward the aura of hauteur surrounding her.

Following her husband's election as president in 1980, Nancy gave the whole country a similar impression. But her initial efforts at redecorating the family living quarters in the White House and planning lavish official entertainments aroused widespread criticism. When it became known that she had spent $200,000 for a new set of china—in the same week a government program to provide school lunches for poor children had been drastically cut—a storm of protest arose, which raged undiminished even after explanations that the china had been paid for not with government funds but by money donated by wealthy Reagan friends.

In addition, the many splendid gowns this first lady wore at formal White House gatherings brought further negative comment. One of the best-selling postcards at Washington souvenir stands depicted her elaborately dressed, wearing a crown on her head—and the card was captioned "Queen Nancy." Soon the president's advisers began to fear that his political agenda might be affected by all the adverse comment about his wife.

Then Nancy herself responded to the criticism with unexpected humor. At a dinner in New York she referred to the postcard lightly. "Now that's silly," she said. "I'd never wear a crown—it would mess up my hair." She also announced her new pet charity: "The Nancy Reagan Home for Wayward China." And at a newspaper party in Washington she converted some of her sharpest critics by making a surprise appearance on the stage wearing clownish old clothes and singing a comic song starting:

> *I'm wearing secondhand clothes,*
> *Secondhand clothes;*
> *They're quite the style*
> *In the spring fashion shows.*

At the same time, she began to devote herself to promoting causes she adopted as her own, particularly a campaign on behalf of drug rehabilitation centers. Nancy traveled all over the country making appearances aimed at convincing children to "Just say NO!" to drugs. Gradually her frivolous image changed, and by 1985 public opinion polls showed that she had risen from being the least popular presidential wife of modern times to "the most popular first lady of the last seven, topping even Jacqueline Kennedy."

Within the White House, Nancy regarded herself as her husband's chief protector, not only of his health but of his place in history. Soon after Ronald Reagan took office an assassination attempt was made on his life. During her husband's recovery, Nancy was adamant about guarding his health and insisted to his staff that his working schedule be kept light. Again, during his second term she stepped in often, just as she had in California, to prevent his aides from overworking him, especially when he was recovering from surgery.

That led to a bitter controversy, which was played out in the press, between Nancy and Donald Regan, the president's chief of staff. "I told Ronnie repeatedly that he should be fired," she admitted later. After Regan finally resigned, he found a way to tell his side of the story.

In a book about his White House experiences, Regan reported that the first lady had frequently consulted an astrologer for advice regarding her husband's schedule of appointments. This disclosure exposed Nancy to a new storm of criticism—and focused new attention on charges that had come up ever since Ronald Reagan's entry into politics.

The charges that Nancy forcefully set official policy behind the scenes were ridiculed by many Reagan supporters. Nevertheless, some members of her own staff fed the rumors by privately referring to her as "Mrs. President." And countless thousands of words were written by political pundits attempting to assess the weight of her influence.

To help fight drug abuse, Nancy Reagan hosted the two-day First Ladies' Conference on Drug Abuse in 1985. Eighteen wives of world leaders attended the event.

Amid all this speculation, Nancy herself tried to set the record straight in a speech at the end of her husband's second term. She started by jokingly telling her audience of newspaper publishers that she had almost had to cancel her appearance at their meeting.

"You know how busy I am," she told them. "I'm staffing the White House and overseeing the arms talks. I'm writing speeches." Then she turned serious.

"Although I don't get involved in policy," she said, "it's silly to suggest that my opinion should not carry some weight with a man I've been married to for thirty-five years. I'm a woman who loves her husband and I make no apologies for looking out for his personal and political welfare. . . . I have opinions, he has opinions. We don't always agree. But neither marriage nor politics denies a spouse the right to hold an opinion and the right to express it."

Even after Ronald Reagan's second term ended early in 1989 and he and Nancy retired to a luxurious new home in California, the issue would not die.

Indeed, Nancy herself helped to keep it alive with a book titled *My Turn,* in which she attempted to pay back her political enemies for their unkind words. Then came an unauthorized biography of her, accusing her of a variety of scandalous behavior.

Although she refused to dignify any of the charges by replying to them, friends of hers pointed to a passage in a preretirement speech of hers, offering some advice to future first ladies: "Once you're in the White House, don't think it's going to be a glamorous, fairy-tale life. It's very hard work with high highs and low lows. Since you're under a microscope, everything is magnified, so just keep your perspective and your patience."

Barbara Bush

JUNE 8, 1925–

"Everybody's grandmother"

Barbara Bush used her "grandmotherly" image to support her husband in the White House.

Just before Barbara Bush became the nation's first lady, she laughingly described herself as a role model for many American women.

"I mean, look at me!" she urged a group of reporters, referring to her matronly figure and no-frills style of dressing. "My mail tells me a lot of fat, white-haired, wrinkled ladies are tickled pink."

Then after she moved into the White House, her warmth and wit and down-to-earth manner endeared her to practically the entire population, male as well as female, regardless of whether or not they had voted for her husband. As she herself sometimes put it, she was considered "everybody's grandmother."

Unlike her recent predecessors, Barbara Bush was careful not to show herself taking part in public controversies or private power struggles among presidential aides. She defined her role as the president's wife this way: "I don't fool around with his office, and he doesn't fool around with my household."

She did, however, have an influence on her husband behind the scenes. "I tell him what I think, he tells me what he thinks, and then we are united," she explained. Barbara devoted most of her time and energy to traditional wifely occupations and to volunteer work on behalf of noncontroversial causes, such as campaigns to promote literacy.

Her rather traditional role led to the one major controversy in her public life. Following her selection as commencement speaker at Wellesley College in 1990, some of the seniors protested that Mrs. Bush, as just a wife and mother, did not represent women who had achieved goals in their own right whom they believed the college sought to produce.

Despite this criticism, she delivered the speech, gently confronting the Wellesley graduates and telling them that family values were more important than careers.

"As important as your obligations as a doctor, lawyer, or business leader may be, your human connections with spouses, with children, with friends are the most important investment you will ever make," she said. "At the end of your life you will never regret not having passed one more test, not winning one more verdict, or not closing one more deal. You will regret time not spent with a husband, a child, a friend, or a parent."

Recognizing the strong feminist element among the graduating seniors, however, she softened her lecture. "Who knows," she said, "somewhere out there in this audience may even be someone who will one day follow in my footsteps and preside over the White House as the president's spouse."

She paused briefly before adding: "And I wish him well." The audience roared with laughter, then applauded loudly. George Bush's wife charmed her critics that day, as she had on many occasions during her husband's long career.

Their story started back in 1941, at a Christmas dance at a country club. Just sixteen then, Barbara Pierce was slim and rather tall with reddish brown hair. When seventeen-year-old George caught a glimpse of her, he walked over to make her acquaintance. They sat out a waltz together, and from then on they were constantly in each other's thoughts.

Barbara, born in New York City on June 8, 1925, had grown up in the affluent

During her years in the White House, Barbara Bush visited many schools, where she read to children. Her literacy campaign was her major project during her term as first lady.

suburb of Rye, with two brothers and a sister. Her parents were Marvin Pierce, a magazine executive, and Pauline Robinson Pierce, the daughter of an Ohio supreme court justice. In their comfortable home, books were highly regarded.

"I think of my dad sitting in his chair by the fireplace and my mother on the couch reading, and after we children read, everyone was curled up with something," Barbara later recalled for an interviewer.

But World War II interrupted the pleasant life of the Pierces and the Bushes, who lived in nearby Connecticut. Barbara was a third-year student at the elite Ashley Hall boarding school in Charleston, South Carolina, home for her Christmas vacation, when she and George met. That summer, following his own prep school graduation, he enlisted in the navy—and during her senior year he took flight training.

In September 1943, shortly after Barbara turned eighteen, she entered Smith College in Northampton, Massachusetts, and soon became captain of its freshman soccer team. Meanwhile, George at nineteen was assigned to pilot a fighter plane on which he had painted the name "Barbara." During a South Pacific air battle only a few months later, his plane was shot down—but George was rescued from the ocean by an American submarine and returned to the United States in 1944.

Throughout this period Barbara and George wrote many letters to each other. "I didn't like to study very much," she admitted afterward. "The truth is, I just wasn't interested. I was just interested in George." At the beginning of her sophomore year, around the time his plane was shot down, she dropped out of college. As soon as he arrived home Barbara married George at the First Presbyterian Church in Rye, on January 6, 1945.

Only nineteen when she became a bride, Barbara in later years liked to joke, "I married the first man I ever kissed." More seriously, she called her marriage "the biggest turning point" in her life. But did she have any regrets about dropping out of college and never completing her degree?

"No regrets," she replied. "If I had, I could have gone back to school. I think people who tell you they have regrets are dumb."

What Barbara chose to do instead was to accompany her husband to naval bases in Michigan, Maine, and Virginia, where he taught student pilots until the war's end in September 1945. Then she moved with him to New Haven, Connecticut, where he enrolled at Yale University. The first of their six children was born the following summer. Before becoming a mother, Barbara worked for nearly a year at the Yale bookstore—the only job outside her home that she ever held.

Barbara willingly went to Texas with George when he decided, after graduating, to go into the oil business. Altogether, she once calculated, during the next forty years she set up housekeeping in twenty-nine different homes as he advanced in business and then in politics. At least in the early years, her domestic duties sometimes overwhelmed her.

The hardest time came in 1953, when the Bushes' second child—a little girl named Robin—died of leukemia. This tragedy is said to have caused Barbara's hair to begin turning white, even though she was only twenty-eight then. But she already had two boys, and she gave birth to two more sons, plus another daughter, within the next several years.

In a speech Barbara summed up her life in Texas during the 1950s and 1960s as a period of "diapers, runny noses, earaches, more Little League games than you could believe possible; and those unscheduled races to the hospital emergency

Barbara and George Bush, walking beside General Norman Schwarzkopf, visit American troops in the Middle East in November 1990, during the Persian Gulf War.

room; Sunday school and church; of hours of urging homework, of short chubby arms around your neck and sticky kisses."

It was also a period, she added, "of experiencing bumpy moments—not many, but a few—of feeling that I'd never, ever be able to have fun again, and coping with the feeling that George Bush, in his excitement of starting a small company and traveling around the world, was having a lot of fun."

But things began to change for Barbara when her husband put aside his business interests to enter politics. On his election to the House of Representatives in 1966, they moved to Washington. There she found time for volunteer work and entertaining as well as for raising her family.

As George held increasingly important jobs, Barbara traveled with him—and started having the fun she thought she had missed earlier. During the 1970s she presided over an elegant apartment at New York City's Waldorf-Astoria Hotel while her husband served as U.S. ambassador to the United Nations, and she also had an exciting time in China when George was appointed American envoy to that country. In between were lively interludes in Washington during her husband's assignments there.

Barbara was thoroughly familiar with capital social life by the time George became the nation's vice president in 1980. As second lady of the land, she decided that her own cause would be promoting literacy. In 1984 she wrote a book, *C. Fred's Story: A Dog's Life,* about the golden cocker spaniel that lived in the vice-presidential residence with the Bushes, and donated her share of the proceeds to two national literacy organizations.

When George was elected president in 1988, she didn't change. In contrast to her predecessor, Nancy Reagan, she showed no interest in designer clothes, preferring to buy her dresses from department-store racks. But she did have one impact on fashion. Almost everywhere she went, she wore multiple strands of artificial pearls around her neck—and sales of similar beads increased notably.

Unlike many other first ladies, Barbara Bush left all the details of formal entertaining to the White House staff. That gave her more time for her five grown children and their spouses, her eleven grandchildren, and her volunteer activities.

She always found time to read to her grandchildren. Believing that reading was a tremendously important accomplishment for all children, she organized the Barbara Bush Foundation for Family Literacy. She also donated many books received by the president to the public library in Kennebunkport, Maine, where the Bushes maintained a summer residence.

Although slowed down by Graves' disease, a thyroid condition, Barbara Bush remained active, still playing tennis, jogging, and walking her English springer spaniel, Millie. Millie made the headlines twice, once when she gave birth to a litter of six puppies in 1989, and later when, with some help, she wrote a book called *Millie's Book,* whose earnings also went to the literacy cause.

Despite what she called the "fishbowl" aspects of life in the White House, with staff members and tourists always wandering around, this first lady made no secret of her enjoyment of her position. "I love living here," she often said. "You'd be an awfully spoiled person if you didn't love this life."

Hillary Rodham Clinton

OCTOBER 26, 1947–

"A first lady of many talents"

*H*illary Rodham Clinton came into the White House after serving twelve years as the first lady of Arkansas. Following the path she established there, she continues to be an advocate for family and children's issues.

---

*S*he is better at organizing and leading people from a complex beginning to a certain end than anybody I've ever worked with in my life," President Clinton said when he appointed Hillary Rodham Clinton to head the Task Force on National Health Care Reform. The nation, he said, would soon find out that "we have a first lady of many talents."

People had high expectations for the new first lady from the start. Like many women of her generation, Hillary is a career woman: She had a very successful law practice and a long history of prestigious jobs. She also has a different perspective on issues. She belongs to the baby-boom generation—people born in the years immediately after World War II—and she went to college in the 1960s. Her opinions on politics and social issues continue to evolve and shape her approach to health care, children and families, and education, three of the first lady's major concerns.

Born Hillary Diane Rodham on October 26, 1947, in Park Ridge, Illinois, a suburb of Chicago, she had an early life that was quiet and predictable. Her father, Hugh Rodham, worked his way up from curtain salesman at the Columbia Lace Company to owning a drapery-making business in Chicago. Dorothy Howell Rodham, Hillary's mother, met Hugh in 1937 when she applied for a secretarial job at the lace company. As a child Hillary played cards and baseball with her parents and two younger brothers, Hugh and Tony. She became a lifelong Chicago Cubs fan.

From a young age, Hillary was a neighborhood leader. "She just took charge," her mother remembers. Hillary's father kept an eye on her grades, which were excellent. When she brought home a report card covered with A's, all he said was, "You must go to a pretty easy school." Hugh Rodham wanted to prepare his daughter for a tough world. Hillary's mother encouraged her to stand up for herself too. "No daughter of mine was going to have to go through the agony of being afraid to say what was on her mind," she said.

In the ninth grade Hillary's life took a new direction when she met the Reverend Donald Jones, the youth minister at the First Methodist Church, to which Hillary belonged. He took the white, middle-class teenagers in Hillary's youth group to Chicago's notorious South Side, where they were introduced to black and Latino kids and gang members. Hillary also saw the shacks where migrant farmworkers and their children lived. Her passion to help provide a better life for all children began then.

Hillary went to college at Wellesley, majoring in political science. There she encouraged students to become politically active, helped teach poor children to read, and tried to get Wellesley to increase the number of black students enrolled. She was president of the student government and graduated in 1969 with high honors. Her fellow students held her in such esteem that they asked her to be a commencement speaker.

Hillary said in her commencement speech that she and other people her age thought America was about to begin a great "experiment in human living." More would be expected from government. "The challenge now is to practice politics as the art of making what appears to be impossible, possible."

Hillary applied to Yale University to study law after a Harvard professor told her, "We don't need any more women at Harvard Law." She viewed the law as a tool for helping and protecting children and the family. She was one of just thirty women in Yale Law's class of 1972—and ten dropped out before graduating.

Always a serious student, Hillary met her husband-to-be in the library at Yale. In the fall of 1970 William Jefferson Clinton had just arrived back in the United States after studying at Oxford University in England. Hillary was reading in the library when she felt someone looking at her. Finally Hillary got up and walked over to Bill Clinton. "If you're going to keep staring at me and I'm going to keep staring at you, we might as well know each other's names," she said. "I'm Hillary Rodham."

Bill just grinned. He was so surprised, he had forgotten his name. But soon he was telling Hillary all about his home state of Arkansas: how beautiful it was and how friendly the people were, and that they grew the biggest watermelons in the world. Before long he and Hillary were seeing each other often.

A friend of Hillary and Bill's thought they were made for each other. One of the traits they shared was a passionate interest in politics. "I had a sense that this was a couple who would have made it across the West in a covered wagon," she said.

During a state visit to Japan in the early part of the Clinton presidency, Mrs. Clinton spent time with children, whose well-being remains at the center of her interests as first lady.

At Yale, Hillary became involved in the Children's Defense Fund, a nonprofit organization set up to help children and families. She spent an extra year at Yale to specialize in law about children.

After Hillary graduated from Yale Law in 1973, she traveled to Washington, D.C., to join the legal staff investigating President Nixon's involvement in the Watergate scandal. Bill Clinton returned to Arkansas to teach law. Hillary then announced to her friends that she was moving to Arkansas to join Bill.

Many of her friends were horrified. After Hillary's exciting work in Washington, they were sure she would be burying herself in Arkansas. A friend drove her south. "Why are you throwing your life away for this guy?" she asked.

"I decided to follow my heart," Hillary said. She took a job teaching law in Fayetteville, Arkansas. On October 11, 1975, she and Bill were married, when Hillary was just shy of her twenty-eighth birthday.

Bill was elected attorney general of Arkansas in 1976, and he and Hillary moved to the capital of Arkansas, Little Rock. In 1977 Hillary joined the prestigious Rose law firm there. At the young age of thirty-two she was promoted to partner. Meanwhile Bill was elected governor of Arkansas, and Hillary became Arkansas's first lady. The new first lady didn't suit all Arkansas voters.

For one thing, she had kept her own name—Rodham—when she married, instead of taking her husband's name.

Bill lost his second bid for the governorship. Wondering if it was in part because of her image, Hillary began to call herself Hillary Rodham Clinton. "It just meant more to the voters than it did to me," she explained.

Motherhood presented a new challenge. The Clintons' daughter, Chelsea Victoria, was born on February 27, 1980. One day while she was rocking Chelsea, Hillary said to her: "Chelsea, you have never been a baby before, and I've never been a mother before. We are just going to have to help each other get through this together."

As governor again in 1982, Bill appointed Hillary chairperson of the new Arkansas Education Standards Committee. In that role she traveled throughout the state, talking to parents and teachers. Some of the changes she recommended were controversial, such as testing teachers to make sure they could competently teach their subjects. Most people liked the educational reforms she proposed. The state adopted them.

When Bill entered the race for president of the United States in 1991, Hillary campaigned for him all over the country. "She's a spectacular candidate in her own right," commented an assistant secretary of state. Bill Clinton agreed. "I've

Hillary Rodham Clinton testified before Congress about the plan to reform health care. The first lady headed the president's task force on health care and played the leading role in developing the plan.

always liked strong women," he said. "It doesn't bother me for people to see her and get excited and say she could be president. I always say she could be president, too."

But some people expressed misgivings about having a strong, successful business-woman for first lady. When Hillary remarked to a group of reporters that "I suppose I could have just stayed home and baked cookies and had teas," the resulting uproar lasted for months. Had she insulted homemakers?

Actually, as first lady of Arkansas, Hillary had sat through plenty of teas. She had only meant to say that women should have a choice about their occupation.

Bill Clinton was elected to the presidency in 1992. He acknowledged Hillary's contributions to his campaign in his acceptance speech. "I believe she will be one of the greatest first ladies in the history of this republic." He signaled the importance of the role Hillary would play by putting her office in the West Wing of the White House, not the East Wing, where every other first lady had her office. The West Wing is near the president and other senior White House advisers.

Hillary's organizing and political skills were quickly put to the test when she began the task of overhauling the nation's health-care system. She set up her operation with her usual thoroughness.

Again Hillary traveled across the country for months, talking to doctors, hospital officials, and hundreds of other people in the health-care field. Perhaps most important, she listened to the stories of many people who had lost their health insurance because of illness or because they couldn't afford it. Finally Hillary, working with a team of administration health experts, submitted a health-care plan over one thousand pages long for Congress to consider. Under this plan all Americans would get affordable, quality health coverage.

The plan did not pass, but Hillary was praised for her ability to make complicated issues understandable and for the thoroughness of the team's research. She had also charmed some of the prickliest members of Congress. At the end of her testimony she received a standing ovation.

"It's kind of nice. She finally gets to be judged on substance instead of on her hair or her proximity to power," said a senior White House official.

"Our lives are a mixture of different roles," Hillary said once. "Most of us are doing the best we can to find whatever the right balance is for our lives. For me the elements of that balance are family, work, and service.

"If people will stop and think, this is what women do."

The Smithsonian's First Ladies Collection and the Exhibition

The Smithsonian's First Ladies Collection was begun in 1912 by Mrs. Cassie Myers James and Mrs. Rose Gouverneur Hoes, two women who volunteered their services to the Institution. Saving the gowns and belongings of first ladies was part of a national movement to preserve our country's history and culture. The Smithsonian, and other museums at that time, presented the lives of notable people as a way to teach history through exemplary models of achievement and good citizenship. Most of the worthy people whose lives and deeds the museum celebrated were important white men.

Mrs. James, a leading Washington society woman, introduced the idea of women as historical role models by building a collection of clothing that showed "the fashions of the women of the United States from colonial times . . . and their sphere in home life." When Mrs. Hoes, a descendant of President Monroe, was asked to contribute clothing (called "costume" by museum professionals) to the collection, the idea of conserving and exhibiting the first ladies' dresses was born.

Though first ladies represented only upper-class role models, the new collection at the Smithsonian was a radical step in its day. It established that women's lives and their accomplishments were an important part of our history by making them visible in the nation's museum. It also paved the way for future collections about women.

First ladies' gowns were displayed in rows of museum cases in the Arts and Industries building from 1914 until the 1950s. In the mid-1950s, the Smithsonian opened the new First Ladies Hall, grouping gowns by time period in beautiful room settings from different eras of White House history. Room settings enhanced the gowns and displayed many objects saved from the White House when it was restored during the Truman presidency.

In 1964 the new Museum of History and Technology opened (now called the National Museum of American History), and the first ladies' gowns were again displayed in elegant settings that resembled White House rooms at different periods

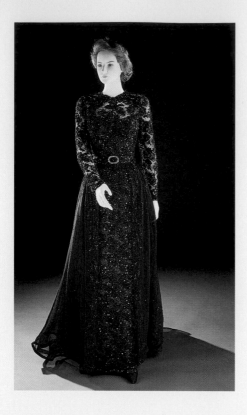

of history. In 1987 the first ladies exhibition was taken down for a museum renovation. People who specialize in saving clothing, called conservators, found that many of the gowns were deteriorating from long years on display. Conservators and curators agreed not to display all the gowns at the same time but to rotate them, keeping some on exhibit and letting others rest and be repaired.

Between 1987 and 1992 curators and researchers, conservators and designers worked to create a new exhibition. They read about the first ladies' lives, located portraits and photographs, chose objects for the exhibit, and repaired many of the gowns. The new exhibition, called "First Ladies: Political Role and Public Image," opened in March 1992.

In addition to gowns, the new exhibition displays many other objects used by first ladies, such as White House invitations and menus; first ladies' calling cards (similar to our business cards today) and calling-card cases; visiting schedules; recipe and etiquette books; political campaign materials; and jewelry, fans, capes, and shawls. The new exhibit also provides information about the first ladies' lives, families, and projects while in the White House. It gives museum visitors a new look at each first lady's role in the politics and life of the nation and shows how changing media technology continues to play a part in making first ladies more visible, popular, and politically powerful.

Bibliography

The factual framework of most of the life stories related in this book is drawn from the authoritative multivolume biographical dictionary *Notable American Women,* published by the Belknap Press of Harvard University Press. In the cases of several of the most recent presidential wives, not included in its latest supplement, birth dates and the like have been taken from such publications as the *New York Times* and *Current Biography,* issued regularly by the H. W. Wilson Company of New York.

As to the anecdotal material illuminating each subject's personality, a great variety of sources were consulted. Here are some of the most helpful memoirs and biographies, organized by chapter. A brief selection of other books about women's history, Washington life, and first ladies in general follows.

PART I: THE NEW NATION, 1775–1830

Martha Washington

Faber, Doris and Harold. *The Birth of a Nation: The Early Years of the United States.* New York: Scribner's, 1989.

Fleming, Thomas J., ed. *Affectionately Yours, George Washington: A Self-Portrait in Letters of Friendship.* New York: Norton, 1967.

Flexner, James T. *Washington, the Indispensable Man.* New York: Signet, 1984.

Tebbel, John. *George Washington's America.* New York: Dutton, 1954.

Abigail Adams

Akers, Charles W. *Abigail Adams.* Boston: Little, Brown, 1980.

Butterfield, L. H., ed. *The Book of Abigail and John: Selected Letters of the Adams Family, 1762–84.* Cambridge: Harvard University Press, 1975.

Faber, Doris. *The Presidents' Mothers.* New York: St. Martin's, 1978.

Nagel, Paul C. *The Adams Women: Abigail and Louisa Adams, Their Sisters and Daughters.* New York: Oxford University Press, 1987.

Withey, Lynne. *Dearest Friend: A Life of Abigail Adams.* New York: Macmillan, 1981.

Martha Jefferson

Malone, Dumas. *Jefferson the Virginian.* Boston: Little, Brown, 1948.

Schachner, Nathan. *Thomas Jefferson.* New York: Thomas Yoseloff, 1960.

Dolley Madison

Anthony, Katharine. *Dolly* [sic] *Madison: Her Life and Times.* Garden City.: Doubleday, 1949.

Brant, Irving. *The Life of James Madison.* New York: Macmillan, 1970.

Meare, Virginia. *The Madisons.* New York: McGraw-Hill, 1979.

Elizabeth Monroe

Ammon, Harry. *James Monroe.* Charlottesville: University of Virginia Press, 1990.

Cresson, William P. *James Monroe.* Chapel Hill: University of North Carolina Press, 1946.

Louisa Adams

Adams, James Truslow. *The Adams Family.* Boston: Little, Brown, 1930.

Nagel, Paul C. *The Adams Women: Abigail and Louisa Adams, Their Sisters and Daughters.* New York: Oxford University Press, 1987.

Shepherd, Jack. *Cannibals of the Heart:* A Personal Biography *of Louisa Catherine and John Q. Adams.* New York: McGraw Hill, 1981.

PART II: GROWING PAINS, SLAVERY, AND THE CIVIL WAR, 1830–1865

Rachel Jackson

Marquis, James. *Andrew Jackson: The Border Captain.* New York: Literary Guild, 1933.
————. *Andrew Jackson: Portrait of a President.* Indianapolis: Bobbs-Merrill, 1937.
Remini, Robert V. *Andrew Jackson.* New York: Harper & Row, 1969.

Hannah Van Buren

Holmes, Alexander. *The American Talleyrand: The Career and Contemporaries of Martin Van Buren.* New York: Harper & Brothers, 1935.
Niven, John. *Martin Van Buren.* New York: Oxford University Press, 1983.

Anna Harrison

Cleaves, Freeman. *Old Tippecanoe: William Henry Harrison and His Time.* New York: Scribner's, 1939.
Green, James A. *William Henry Harrison.* Richmond: Garret and Massie, 1941.

Letitia Tyler and Julia Tyler

Seager, Robert. *And Tyler Too: A Biography of John and Julia Tyler.* New York: McGraw-Hill, 1963.

Sarah Polk

Bergeron, Paul H. *The Presidency of James K. Polk.* Lawrence: University Press of Kansas, 1987.
Sellers, Charles G. *James K. Polk,* 2 vols. Princeton: Princeton University Press, 1957 and 1966.

Margaret Taylor

Hamilton, Holman. *Zachary Taylor,* 2 vols. Indianapolis: Bobbs-Merrill, 1941.

Abigail Fillmore

Rayback, Robert J. *Millard Fillmore*. Buffalo: Buffalo Historical Society, 1959.

Jane Pierce

Nichols, Roy Franklin. *Franklin Pierce*. Philadelphia: University of Pennsylvania Press, 1931.

Harriet Lane

Klein, Philip Shriver. *President James Buchanan*. University Park: Pennsylvania State University Press, 1962.

Mary Lincoln

Baker, Jean H. *Mary Todd Lincoln*. New York: Norton, 1987.
Randall, Ruth P. *Mary Lincoln: Biography of a Marriage*. Boston: Little, Brown, 1953.
Ross, Ishbel. *The President's Wife: Mary Todd Lincoln*. New York: Putnam, 1973.
Turner, Juston G., and Linda Levitt Turner. *Mary Todd Lincoln: Her Life and Letters*. New York: Knopf, 1972.

PART III: POST–CIVIL WAR ERA, AGE OF REFORM, AND WORLD WAR I, 1865–1920

Eliza Johnson

Trefousee, Hans L. *Andrew Johnson*. New York: Norton, 1989.
Winston, Robert W. *Andrew Johnson: Plebian and Patriot*. New York: Henry Holt, 1928.

Julia Grant

McFeely, William S. *Grant*. New York: Norton, 1981.
Ross, Ishbel. *The General's Wife: The Life of Mrs. Ulysses S. Grant*. New York: Dodd, Mead, 1959.
Simon, John, ed. *The Personal Memoirs of Julia Dent Grant*. New York: Putnam, 1975.

Lucy Hayes

Barnard, Harry. *Rutherford B. Hayes and His America.* Indianapolis: Bobbs-Merrill, 1954.

Geer, Emily Apt. *First Lady: The Life of Lucy Webb Hayes.* Kent: Kent State University Press, 1984.

Lucretia Garfield

Brown, Harry J., and Frederick D. Williams, eds. *The Diary of James A. Garfield.* Lansing: Michigan State University Press, 1967.

Leech, Margaret, and Harry J. Brown. *The Garfield Orbit: The Life of President James A. Garfield.* New York: Harper & Row, 1978.

Ellen Arthur

Howe, George F. *Chester A. Arthur.* New York: Frederick Ungar, 1957.

Frances Cleveland

McElroy, Robert. *Grover Cleveland,* 2 vols. New York: Harper & Brothers, 1933.

Nevins, Allan. *Grover Cleveland.* New York: Dodd, Mead, 1932.

Caroline Harrison

————. *Benjamin Harrison: Hoosier President.* Indianapolis: Bobbs-Merrill, 1968.

————. *Benjamin Harrison: Hoosier Statesman.* New York: New York University Publishers, 1954.

Sievers, Harry J. *Benjamin Harrison: Hoosier Warrior.* New York: New York University Publishers, 1952.

Ida McKinley

Leech, Margaret. *In the Days of McKinley.* New York: Harper & Brothers, 1959.

Morgan, Howard Wayne. *William McKinley and His America.* Syracuse: Syracuse University Press, 1963.

Edith Roosevelt

Hagedorn, Hermann. *The Roosevelt Family of Sagamore Hill.* New York: Macmillan, 1954.

Morris, Edmund. *The Rise of Theodore Roosevelt.* New York: Coward, McCann & Geoghegan, 1979.

Morris, Sylvia Jukes. *Edith Kermit Roosevelt: Portrait of a First Lady.* New York: Coward, McCann & Geoghegan, 1980.

Putnam, Carleton. *Theodore Roosevelt: The Formative Years.* New York: Scribner's, 1958.

Helen Taft

Anderson, Judith Icke. *William Howard Taft.* New York: Norton, 1981.

Pringle, Henry F. *The Life and Times of William Howard Taft.* New York: Farrar & Rinehart, 1939.

Ross, Ishbel. *The Tafts: An American Family.* Cleveland: World Publishing, 1964.

Taft, Helen H. *Recollections of Full Years.* New York: Dodd, Mead, 1914.

Ellen Wilson and Edith Wilson

Hatch, Alden. *Edith Bolling Wilson.* New York: Dodd, Mead, 1961.

McAdoo, Eleanor Wilson. *The Woodrow Wilsons.* New York: Macmillan, 1937.

Ross, Ishbel. *Power with Grace: The Life Story of Mrs. Woodrow Wilson.* New York: Putnam, 1975.

Saunders, Frances Wright. *Ellen Axson Wilson: First Lady Between Two Worlds.* Chapel Hill: University of North Carolina Press, 1985.

Smith, Gene. *When the Cheering Stopped.* New York: Morrow, 1964.

Wilson, Edith Bolling. *My Memoir.* Indianapolis: Bobbs-Merrill, 1938.

PART IV: MODERN TIMES, 1920 TO THE PRESENT

Florence Harding

Murray, Robert K. *The Harding Era.* Minneapolis: University of Minnesota Press, 1969.

Russell, Francis. *The Shadow of Blooming Grove: Warren G. Harding in His Times.* New York: McGraw-Hill, 1968.

Sinclair, Andrew. *The Available Man.* New York: Macmillan, 1965.

Grace Coolidge

Fuess, Claude M. *Calvin Coolidge.* Boston: Little, Brown, 1940.
McCoy, Donald R. *Calvin Coolidge.* New York: Macmillan, 1967.
Ross, Ishbel. *Grace Coolidge and Her Era.* New York: Dodd, Mead, 1962.

Lou Hoover

Burner, David. *Herbert Hoover: A Public Life.* New York: Knopf, 1979.
Hinshaw, David. *Herbert Hoover.* New York: Farrar Straus, 1950.
Hoover, Herbert. *The Memoirs of Herbert Hoover,* 3 vols. New York: Macmillan, 1951.
Pryor, Helen B. *Lou Henry Hoover: Gallant First Lady.* New York: Dodd, Mead, 1969.
Smith, Gene. *The Shattered Dream: Herbert Hoover and the Great Depression.* New York: Morrow, 1970.

Eleanor Roosevelt

Cook, Blanche Wiesen. *Eleanor Roosevelt, Vol. 1: 1884–1933.* New York: Penguin Books, 1992.
Faber, Doris. *The Life of Lorena Hickok: E. R.'s Friend.* New York: Morrow, 1980.
Goodwin, Doris Kearns. *No Ordinary Time: Franklin and Eleanor Roosevelt: The Home Front in World War II.* New York: Simon & Schuster, 1994.
Lash, Joseph. *Eleanor and Franklin.* New York: Norton, 1971.
————. *Eleanor: The Years Alone.* New York: Norton, 1972.
Roosevelt, Eleanor. *This Is My Story.* New York: Harper & Brothers, 1937.
————. *This I Remember.* New York: Harper & Brothers, 1949.

Bess Truman

Ferrell, Robert H., ed. *Dear Bess: The Letters from Harry to Bess Truman, 1910–1959.* New York: Norton, 1983.
Truman, Harry. *Memoirs,* 2 vols. New York: Doubleday, 1955, 1956.
Truman, Margaret. *Bess W. Truman.* New York: Macmillan, 1986.

Mamie Eisenhower

David, Lester, and Irene David. *Ike and Mamie.* New York: Putnam, 1981.
Eisenhower, Dwight D. *At Ease: Stories I Tell to Friends.* Garden City: Doubleday, 1967.

Eisenhower, Dwight D. *Letters to Mamie.* Edited by John S. D. Eisenhower. New York: Doubleday, 1978.

Hatch, Alden. *Red Carpet for Mamie.* New York: Henry Holt, 1954.

Jacqueline Kennedy

Birmingham, Stephen. *Jacqueline Bouvier Kennedy Onassis.* New York: Grosset & Dunlap, 1978.

Faber, Harold, ed. *The Kennedy Years.* New York: Viking, 1964.

Heymann, C. David. *A Woman Named Jackie.* New York: Carol Publishing Group, 1994.

Thayer, Mary Van Rensselaer. *Jacqueline Bouvier Kennedy.* Garden City: Doubleday, 1961.

————. *Jacqueline Kennedy: The White House Years.* Boston: Little, Brown, 1971.

Lady Bird Johnson

Caro, Robert. *The Years of Lyndon Johnson: The Path to Power.* New York: Knopf, 1982.

Johnson, Claudia Alta. *A White House Diary.* New York: Holt, Rinehart & Winston, 1970.

Kearns, Doris. *Lyndon Johnson and the American Dream.* New York: Harper & Row, 1976.

Montgomery, Ruth. *Mrs. LBJ.* New York: Holt, Rinehart & Winston, 1964.

Valenti, Jack. *A Very Human President.* New York: Norton, 1976.

Pat Nixon

Abrahamson, David. *Nixon vs. Nixon.* New York: Farrar Straus Giroux, 1976.

Brodie, Fawn. *Richard Nixon: The Shaping of His Character.* New York: Norton, 1981.

David, Lester. *The Lonely Lady of San Clemente.* New York: Crown, 1978.

Eisenhower, Julie Nixon. *Pat Nixon: The Untold Story.* New York: Simon & Schuster, 1986.

Parmet, Herbert S. *Richard Nixon and His America.* New York: Little, Brown, 1990.

Betty Ford

Ford, Betty, with Chris Chase. *The Times of My Life.* New York: Ballantine, 1979.

Weidenfeld, Sheila R. *First Lady's Lady: With the Fords at the White House.* New York: Putnam, 1979.

Rosalynn Carter

Carter, Jimmy. *Why Not the Best?* New York: Bantam, 1976.
Carter, Rosalynn. *First Lady from Plains.* Boston: Houghton Mifflin, 1984.
Neyland, James. *The Carter Family Scrapbook.* New York: Grosset & Dunlap, 1977.

Nancy Reagan

Cannon, Lou. *Reagan.* New York: Putnam, 1982.
Duggen, Ronnie. *On Reagan.* New York: McGraw-Hill, 1983.
Leamer, Laurence. *Make Believe: The Story of Nancy and Ronald Reagan.* New York: Harper & Row, 1983.
Reagan, Nancy, with William Novak. *My Turn: The Memoirs of Nancy Reagan.* New York: Simon & Schuster, 1989.

Barbara Bush

Bush, Barbara. *A Memoir.* New York: Macmillan, 1994.
Klapthor, Margaret B. *The First Ladies.* Washington: White House Historical Association, 1989.
Radcliffe, Donnie. *Simply Barbara Bush.* New York: Warner, 1989.

Hillary Rodham Clinton

Guernsey, JoAnn Bren. *Hillary Rodham Clinton: A New Kind of First Lady.* Minneapolis: Lerner, 1993.
Milton, Joyce. *The Story of Hillary Rodham Clinton: First Lady of the United States.* New York: Dell, 1994.
Radcliffe, Donnie. *Hillary Rodham Clinton: A First Lady for Our Time.* New York: Warner, 1994.

Further Reading

Anthony, Carl Sferrazza. *First Ladies: The Saga of the Presidents' Wives and Their Power,* 2 vols. New York: Morrow, 1990, 1991.

Bassett, Margaret. *Profiles and Portraits of American Presidents and Their Wives.* Freeport: Bond & Wheelwright, 1969.

Boller, Paul F., Jr. *Presidential Wives.* New York: Oxford University Press, 1988.

Caroli, Betty Boyd. *First Ladies.* New York: Oxford University Press, 1987.

Carpenter, Frank. *Carp's Washington.* New York: McGraw-Hill, 1960.

Degler, Carl N. *At Odds: Women and the Family in America from the Revolution to the Present.* New York: Oxford University Press, 1980.

Ellett, Elizabeth. *The Queens of American Society.* Philadelphia: Porter & Coates, 1867.

Flexner, Eleanor. *Century of Struggle: The Women's Rights Movement in the United States.* Cambridge: Belknap Press of Harvard University Press, 1959.

Furman, Bess. *White House Profile.* Indianapolis: Bobbs-Merrill, 1951.

Hoover, Irwin H. *Forty-two Years in the White House.* Boston: Houghton Mifflin, 1934.

Means, Marianne. *The Woman in the White House.* New York: Random House, 1963.

Norton, Mary Beth. *Liberty's Daughters.* Boston: Little, Brown, 1980.

Parks, Lillian Rogers. *My Thirty Years Backstairs at the White House.* New York: Fleet Publishing Corporation, 1961.

Smith, Margaret Bayard. *The First Forty Years of Washington Society.* New York: Scribner's, 1906.

West, J. B., with Mary Lynn Kotz. *Upstairs at the White House: My Life with the First Ladies.* New York: Coward, McCann & Geoghegan, 1973.

Acknowledgments

Abbreviations

LOC	Library of Congress
NGS	National Geographic Society
NMAA	National Museum of American Art
NPG	National Portrait Gallery
SI	Smithsonian Institution
WHHA	White House Historical Association

pp. ii–iii WHHA/photo by NGS; p. x The White House; p. xviii The Daughters of the American Revolution Museum, Washington, D. C.; pp. 4, 5 LOC; p. 7 © SI/NPG; p. 10 Mount Vernon Ladies' Association; pp. 14, 16 © SI; p. 21 WHHA/photo by NGS; p. 24 courtesy of the Museums at Stony Brook, Stony Brook, NY; p. 25 Visiting Nurse Association; pp. 26, 29 WHHA/photo by NGS; p. 31 LOC; p. 33 The Daughters of the

American Revolution Museum, Washington, D.C.; p. 35 © SI; p. 37 LOC; p. 39 © SI/NMAA; p. 43 © SI; pp. 46, 47 LOC; p. 48 © SI; p. 53 courtesy of the American Antiquarian Society; p. 56 LOC; p. 58 LOC/Rinhart Collection; p. 60 LOC; p. 63 WHHA/photo by NGS; p. 65 © SI/NPG; p. 66 Smith College/Sophia Smith Collection; p. 67 © SI; pp. 68, 70 The James K. Polk Memorial Association; p. 72 George Eastman House; pp. 74, 78 © SI; p. 81 The Pierce Brigade, Concord, N.H.; p. 84 © SI/NPG/photo by Matthew Brady Studio; p. 89 R. B. Hayes Presidential Center; p. 90 LOC; pp. 94–95 WHHA/photo by NGS; p. 97 © SI; p. 100 LOC; p. 102 George Eastman House/photo by Lewis Hine; p. 104 National Archives; p. 106 WHHA/photo by NGS; p. 109 National Park Service/Andrew Johnson National Historic Site, Greeneville, Tenn.; p. 111 LOC; p. 113 Chicago Historical Society; p. 115 © SI/NPG; p. 117 WHHA/photo by NGS; p. 121 © SI; p. 123 LOC; p. 124 © SI; pp. 125, 128, 131, 133, 135, 137 LOC; p. 141 National Society Daughters of the American Revolution/NSDAR Archives; p. 142 LOC; p. 145 © SI; p. 147 The White House/Office of the Curator; p. 150 © SI/NPG; p. 152 WHHA/photo by NGS; pp. 153, 154, 156 LOC; p. 159 © SI; p. 160 LOC; pp. 163, 164 © SI; p. 165 LOC; p. 167 George Eastman House/photo by Lewis Hine; pp. 169, 173 LOC; p. 176 LOC/photo by Walker Evans; p. 177 UPI/Bettmann Newsphoto; p. 178 Culver Pictures; p. 179 © SI/photo by Jim Wallace; p. 181 LOC; pp. 183, 185 © SI; pp 186, 188 LOC; p. 190 Visiting Nurse Association; p. 192 © SI; p. 195 Herbert Hoover Library; p. 199 Private Collection; p. 200 Scurlock Studio, Washington, D.C.; p. 201 © SI/NPG; pp. 204, 206 © SI; p. 209 UPI/Bettmann Newsphoto; p. 211 LOC; p. 214 AP/Wide World Photos; p. 216 LOC; p. 218 National Archives; p. 219 © SI/photo by Eric Long; p. 221 The White House; p. 224 *Washington Star*/AP; pp. 226-227 © *Washington Post*/reprinted by permission of Washington, D.C., Public Library; p. 230 LOC; p. 233 © *Washington Post*/reprinted by permission of Washington, D.C., Public Library; p. 236 courtesy of the Lyndon Baines Johnson Library/photo by Robert Knudsen; p. 238 UPI/ Bettmann/Franklin D. Roosevelt Library; p. 239 © SI/photo by Eric Long; p. 240 WHHA/photo by Bachrach; p. 243 National Archives/Nixon Presidential Materials; p. 245 © SI; p. 247 WHHA/photo by David Hume Kennerly; p. 249 courtesy Gerald R. Ford Library; p. 251 UPI/Bettmann Newsphoto; p. 253 The White House; pp. 257, 258 courtesy Jimmy Carter Library; p. 260 WHHA/photo by Michael Evans; p. 263 courtesy Reagan Presidential Library/photo by Michael Evans; p. 265 courtesy Reagan Presidential Library; p. 267 The White House; p. 269 The Bush Presidential Materials Project/photo by Carol T. Powers; p. 271 The Bush Presidential Materials Project; pp. 273, 275, 277 The White House; p. 280 © SI/photo by Eric Long.

Index

(Page numbers in *italic* refer to illustrations.)

Abolitionism. *See* Anti-slavery movement
Adams, Abigail, 5, *16,* 16–21, 41, 42, *53,*
    69
    family background and upbringing of,
      17–18
    as first lady, 20
    letters of, 16–17, 18, 20, 21, *53*
    political interests of, 16–17, 20, 21
Adams, Charles Francis, 41, 42, 44
Adams, Henry, 44
Adams, John, 16–21, 40, 41
Adams, John Quincy, 19, 20, 39–44
Adams, Louisa, *39,* 39–44, *43*
    European adventures of, 42
    family background and upbringing of, 40
    as first lady, 2, 39, 43–44
    women's position as envisioned by, 43–44
African-Americans, 46, 47, 52, 168, 176
    in abolition movement, 65

civil rights movement and, 178, *179*
educational opportunities for, 199, 200,
    200
legal rights of, 99, 110, 178
segregation and, 99–100
see also Slavery
Agnew, Spiro, 251
Alcoholism, 103, 122
Alcott, Louisa May, 49
All American Girls Professional Baseball
    Association, 176–78
American Anti-Slavery Society, 64
American Association of University Women
    (AAUW), 200
American Philosophical Society, 18–19
American Women's Educational Association,
    199
Anderson, Marian, 208
Antebellum period, 45–49

Anthony, Susan B., 162, *163*

Anti-Slavery Convention of American Women (1837, 1838, and 1839), 64

Anti-slavery movement (abolitionism), 6, 21, 44, 47, 49, 64–67, *67,* 104, 162

Arthur, Chester, 130

Arthur, Ellen, 130

Assassinations, 62, 96, 125–26, 129, 130, 146, 148, 150–51, 228, 235, 264

Association of Collegiate Alumnae, 200

Atlanta University, 200

Baltimore Sun, 174

Barton, Clara, 49

Beecher, Catharine, 199

Bethune, Mary McLeod, 176, *204*

Birthrate, 23

Blackwell, Elizabeth, 103

Bliss, Mary Elizabeth ("Betty"), 76, 77

Boxer, Barbara, 180

Boxer Rebellion, 194

Brady, Mathew, *90*

Branner, John, 193

Bryan, William Jennings, 167

Bryn Mawr College, 199

Buchanan, James, 33, 84–87

Burr, Aaron, 28, 30

Burroughs, Nannie Helen, 200

Bush, Barbara, *267,* 267–72, *269, 271,* 277
    family background and upbringing of, 268–69
    as first lady, 267–68, 270–72

Bush, George, 180, 268–72, *271*

Barbara Bush Foundation for Family Literacy, 272

Cabinet, U.S., 70–71
    first woman appointed to, 176

Campaigns
    first ladies' activities in, 207, *209, 233,* 234, 235, 237–39, *238, 251,* 256, 258, 276–77
    memorabilia from, *145, 185, 219, 239, 245*

Carter, Jimmy, 251, 253–59, *257*

Carter, Rosalynn, *253,* 253–59, *257, 258*
    family background and upbringing of, 254–55
    husband's partnership with, 253–54, 256–59
    as navy wife, 255–56

Celebrity endorsements, *60*

Century of Dishonor (Jackson), 100

Chapman, Maria Weston, 64–65

Child, Lydia Maria, 64

Child-care centers, 176

Child labor, *102,* 206

Children
    infant mortality rates and, 23–25
    mourning rituals for, 24, *24*
    "republican motherhood" notion and, 15

Children's Defense Fund, 276

China, 194, 270
    immigrants from, 101

China services, presidential, *121,* 137, 151, 263–64

Civil Rights Act (1964), 178, 235

Civil rights movement, 178, *179*

Civil Service Commission, U.S., 150

Civil War, 62, 73, 93–96, 99, 104, 107–8, 119, 127, 130, 138–39, 144, 169
    forces leading to, 45, 86
    Grant's campaigns in, 114, 116
    women's roles in, 49

Clark School for the Deaf, 187, 191

Clay, Henry, 71, 91

Cleveland, Frances, 105, *131,* 131–36, *133, 135,* 153, 170
    family background and upbringing of, 132
    as first lady, 131–32, 134–36
    wedding of, 131, 133–34

Cleveland, Grover, 131–36, 141

Cleveland, Rose, 133

Clinton, Hillary Rodham, *x,* xi, 180, *273,* 273–78, *275, 277, 280*
    family background and upbringing of, 274–75
    as first lady of Arkansas, 276, 277
    as first lady of U.S., 273–74, 277–78

Clinton, William, 180, 273, 275–78
Colleges, 103
    first first lady to have graduated from, 117,
        119
    for women, 199
Colonial period, 3–6, 7–10
Commission on the Status of Women, 210
Congress, U.S., 25, 28, *31,* 33, 36, 103, 120,
        122, 168, 180, 200, 235, 278
    future presidents' service in, 19, 30, 44,
        69–70, 92–93, 119, 127, 128, 145,
        233–34, 243–44, 249–50, 270
    presidential widows and, 32, 62, 97, 129
    Reconstruction and, 99, 110
    slavery and, 64, 67
    White House and, 140, 151
    women's rights and, 104, 163, 164, 178
    see also Senate, U.S.
Constitution, U.S., 11, 28
    amendments to, 67, 99, 104, 123–24,
        164
    women's rights and, 13–14, 104, 162,
        164
Constitutions, state, 13–14
Consumer movement, 103
Contracts, women's legal rights and, 13
Coolidge, Calvin, 186, 187–91
Coolidge, Grace, *186,* 186–91, *188, 190*
    family background and upbringing of,
        186–88
    as first lady, 190–91
Cooper, Anna J., 200, *200*
Court system, 14
Coverture, 13
Crook, W. H., 109
Custis, Daniel Parke, 8

Daughters of Liberty, 6
Daughters of the American Revolution
        (DAR), 140, *141,* 208
Davis, Loyal, 261, 262
Declaration of Independence, 17
Declaration of Sentiments, 162
Democratic party, 71, 83, 86, 167, 207, 256

Depression, Great, 175–76, *176,* 178, 197,
        207, 208
De Re Metallica, 196
de Wolfe, Henry, 182
Divorce, 50, 180
Dix, Dorothea, 49
Donelson, Emily, 50
Douglas, Stephen A., 93
Drug abuse, 25
    Betty Ford and, 250, 252
    "Just say NO!" campaign and, 264, *265*

Eagle Forum, 179
Economic opportunities, for women, 5, 6,
        14, 46–47, *48, 104,* 105, 175–78
Education
    of African-Americans, 199, 200, *200*
    of women, 15, 17–18, 27, 46, 52, 103,
        138, 141, 179, 198–200
Eighteenth Amendment, 124
Eisenhower, Dwight, 216–20, *218, 219,* 244
Eisenhower, Mamie, *216,* 216–20, *218, 219,*
        226–27, 238
    family background and upbringing of,
        217–18
    as first lady, 216–17, 219–20
    as military wife, 218
Emma, queen of Hawaii, 109
Epidemics, 23, 24
Equal Rights Amendment (ERA), 178,
        179–80, 250, *251,* 258
Expansionism, 45, *46,* 48–49, 71, 73

Feinstein, Diane, 180
Feminine Mystique The, (Friedan), 178
Ferraro, Geraldine, 180
Field, Cyrus, 129
Fifteenth Amendment, 99
Fillmore, Abigail, *78,* 78–80
    family background and upbringing of, 78–79
    as first lady, 80
Fillmore, Mary Abigail, 80
Fillmore, Millard, 78–80
First Continental Congress, 9

First ladies
    campaigning by, 207, *209, 233,* 234, 235,
        237–39, *238, 251,* 256, 258, 276–77
    first radio broadcast by, *195,* 197
    first to accompany president on overseas
        mission, 172
    first to have graduated from college, 117,
        119
    first to hold job outside home, 78–79
    letters and papers of, 53–54
    origin of term, 33
    pensions for, 62, 97, 129
    photographs and public image of, 153–55
    role of, 1–2, 11, 88
    Smithsonian's collection of belongings of,
        279–80
    term of address for, 11, 33
    White House portrait gallery of, 151, *152*
    woman other than president's wife as, 88
Fish, Mrs. Hamilton, 115
Fisk College, 200
Ford, Betty, 226, *247,* 247–52, *251*
    family background and upbringing of, 248
    as first lady, 250–51
Ford, Gerald, 250–52
Betty Ford Center for Drug and Alcohol
        Rehabilitation, 252
Fourteenth Amendment, 99
Frank Leslie's Illustrated Magazine, 34
Frank Leslie's Illustrated Newspaper, 46
Freedmen's schools, 200
French Revolution, 36–38, *37*
Friedan, Betty, 178
Frontier Nursing Service, 24
"Front porch" campaigns, 237

Galt, Norman, 170
Gardiner, David, 59, 61
Garfield, James, 125–29, 237
    assassination of, 62, 125–26, 129, 130
Garfield, Lucretia, 62, *125,* 125–29
    family background and upbringing of, 126
    as first lady, 125–26, 128–29
Garrison, William Lloyd, 67

General Federation of Women's Clubs, 103
Gilded Age, 120
Girl Scouts, 196
Godey's Lady's Book, 46
Graham, Martha, 248–49
Grant, Julia, *111,* 111–16, *113, 115,* 120
    battlefield visits of, 114
    family background and upbringing of, 111,
        112–13
    as first lady, 2, 111–12, 114–15
Grant, Ulysses S., *94–95,* 110, 111–16, *115,*
        120
    Army career of, 113–14, 116
Great Britain
    American colonies ruled by, 3–6
    War of 1812 and, 26–27, 31
Grimké, Angelina, 66–67
Grimké, Charlotte Forten, 65, 66
Guiteau, Charles, 126

Habitat for Humanity, 259
Hale, Sarah Josepha, 46
Hampton College, 200
Harding, Florence, *181,* 181–85, *183,* 237
    family background and upbringing of,
        181–82
    as first lady, 184–85
Harding, Warren, 161, 181–85, *183,* 190,
        237
Harper's Weekly, 5, 33, *48*
Harrison, Anna, 55
Harrison, Benjamin, 55, 135, 138–41, 237
Harrison, Caroline, *137,* 137–41, *141,* 151,
        237
    family background and upbringing of, 138
    as first lady, 137–38, 139–41
    White House remodeled by, 135, 137–38,
        139–40
Harrison, William Henry, 55, 57, 138
Hayes, Lucy, 105, *117,* 117–21
    family background and upbringing of,
        118–19
    as first lady, *89,* 120
Hayes, Rutherford B., *89,* 117–21, 158

Health care
    Clinton's reform effort and, 273, *277,* 278
    infant and maternal death rates and, 23–25
    in urban slums, 24, *25*
Hemings, Sally, 22
Hine, Lewis, *167*
History
    topics typically studied in, 52
    written records and, 52–54
Home economics movement, 103
Hoover, Herbert, 192–97
Hoover, Lou, *192,* 192–97, *195*
    family background and upbringing of,
        192–94
    as first lady, 195–97
    as geologist, 192–96
Hostess role, 11, 88
House of Representatives, U.S., 33
    first woman granted seat in, *31*
    see also Congress, U.S.
Housework, 48, 127–28
    home economics movement and, 103
Howard College, 200
Howe, Julia Ward, 162–63

"I Like Ike" stockings, *239*
Immigrants, 24, 46, 52, *100,* 101–2, 168
Impeachment, 110
Inaugurations, 30, 171–72, *226–27*
Indian Wars, 8, 55
Industrial Revolution, 6, 45
Infant mortality rate, 23–25
Inheritances, women's legal rights and, 13
Irish immigrants, 101
Irving, Washington, 30

Jackson, Andrew, *43,* 50, 69, 70, 82
Jackson, Helen Hunt, 100
Jackson, Rachel, 50
Jackson, Sarah Yorke, 50
James, Cassie Myers, 279
Jay, John, 19
Jefferson, Maria, 22
Jefferson, Martha (daughter), 22

Jefferson, Martha Wayles (mother), 22
Jefferson, Thomas, 22, 30
Johns Hopkins University Medical School,
    141
Johnson, Andrew, 96, 106–10
Johnson, Eliza, *106,* 106–10
    family background and upbringing of, 107
    as first lady, 106–7, 108–10
Johnson, Lady Bird, *226–27, 230,* 230–36,
    233, 236, 239
    beautification projects of, 235, *236*
    campaigning by, 234, 235
    family background and upbringing of,
        230–32
    as first lady, 235
Johnson, Lyndon B., 228, 230, 232–36
Johnston, Frances Benjamin, *133, 153, 154,*
    154–55
Johnston, Henry Elliott, 86–87
"Just say NO!" campaign, 264, *265*

Keller, Helen, *188*
Kelley, Abby, 49
Kennedy, Jacqueline, *221,* 221–29, *224,*
    226–27, 263, 264
    family background and upbringing of,
        222–23
    as first lady, 221–22, 225–28, 234–35, 245
    after president's assassination, 228–29
Kennedy, John F., 174, 210, 221–28, 234, 244
    assassination of, 228, 235
    inauguration of, *226–27*
Kennedy, Robert, 234
King, Dr. Martin Luther, Jr., 178
Kling, Amos, 181, 182
Knickerbocker, Cholly, 223

Labor reform, 101–2, 123
Lafayette, Madame de, 36–38, *37*
Lane, Harriet, 33, *72, 84,* 84–87
    family background and upbringing of, 85
    as first lady, 84–85, 86
    marriage of, 86–87
League of Nations, 172

League of Women Voters, 206
Lee, Robert E., 114
Liberator, 65
Library of Congress, 54, 129
Life, 152
Lincoln, Abraham, 62, 86, 91, 92–96, *94–95,*
    107–8
  assassination of, 96, 148
Lincoln, Mary, *ii–iii,* 62, *90,* 90–98, *94–95, 97*
  erratic behavior of, 90–91, 93, 96–97, 98
  family background and upbringing of,
    91–92
  as first lady, 33, 93–96
  after president's assassination, 96–98, 108,
    129
Literacy, 46, *269,* 271
Lockwood, Belva, 103
Lyon, Mary, 199

McCarthy, Joseph, 220
McElroy, Mary Arthur, 130
McKee, Benjamin Harrison, 140
McKinley, Ida, *142,* 142–46
  family background and upbringing of, 143
  as first lady, 142–43, 146
McKinley, William, 143–46, 150–51
  assassination of, 146, 150–51
Madison, Dolley, 22, *26,* 26–32, *31,* 35, *72*
  family background and upbringing of,
    27–28
  as first lady, 2, 26–27, 30–31, 33
  Washington portrait saved by, 26–27, *29*
Madison, James, 28, 30–32, 38, 43
Manifest Destiny, 71
March on Washington (1963), *179*
Marion Star, 183
Maternal mortality rate, 23–25
Means, Abby, 83
Mercer, Lucy, 205
Methodist Woman's Home Missionary Soci-
    ety, 121
Mexican War (1846–1848), 48, 71, 76, 80,
    83, 113
Mitchell, Maria, 103

Monroe, Elizabeth, *35,* 35–38
  family background and upbringing of, 36
  as first lady, 38
  in release of Madame de Lafayette, 36–38
Monroe, James, 35–38
Mott, Lucretia, 65, 67, 162
Mount Holyoke College, 199
Mourning rituals, 24, *24, 97*

Napoleonic Wars, 42
Napoleon III, emperor of France, 92
Nation, Carry, *124*
National American Woman Suffrage Associa-
    tion (NAWSA), 104, 163–64
National Anti-Slavery Standard, 65
National Association of Colored Women's
    Clubs, 103, 200
National Council of Jewish Women, 103
National Health Care Reform Task Force,
    273, *277, 278*
National Museum of American Art, 87
National Museum of American History,
    279–80
National Organization for Women (NOW),
    178
National Security League, 136
National Woman's Party, 164
National Women's Political Caucus, 179
Native Americans, 4, 48, 52, 100–101
Needlework Guild, 136
New York City, as first capital, 11, 36
New York Herald, 33, 61
New York Journal-American, 223
New York Times, 215
Nineteenth Amendment, 104, 164
Nixon, Pat, *219, 226–27,* 238, *240,* 240–46,
    243, 245
  family background and upbringing of, 240,
    241–42
  as first lady, 244–46
Nixon, Richard, 241–46, *245,* 250, 251,
    276
Novelists, women as, 46–47
Nursing, 24, *25,* 49, 101, 139, *189*

Oberlin School, 199
Office of Public Buildings and Grounds, 139–40
Onassis, Aristotle, 225, 228–29
Oral history, 52, 54

Pan American Exposition (1901), 146
Patterson, David T., 108
Patterson, Martha Johnson, 108, 109, *109*
Paul, Alice, 164
Peace movements, 47, 123
Peale, Rembrandt, 7
Perkins, Frances, 176
Persian Gulf War (1990), *271*
Philadelphia, as second capital, 20, 28
Philadelphia Female Anti-Slavery Society, 64
Phillips, Wendell, 67
Photography, 153–55
"Photo ops," 140, *183*
Pierce, Franklin, 80, 82–83
Pierce, Jane, *81*, 81–83
    family background and upbringing of, 81–82
    as first lady, 83
Plantations, 45, 62
Polk, James K., 32, 68–73, *72*
Polk, Sarah, 62, *68*, 68–73, *70, 72*
    family background and upbringing of, 69
    as first lady, 68–69, 71–73
    as husband's political partner, 68–70, 71–72
Presidential libraries, 53–54
Presidents
    assassinations of, 62, 96, 125–26, 129, 130, 146, 148, 150–51, 228, 235, 264
    campaigning of. *See* campaigns
    first bachelor to serve as, 84
    preservation of papers of, 53–54
    term of address for, 33
President's Commission on Mental Health, 257–58, *258*
Press secretaries, 61
Preston, Thomas Jex, 136
Prohibition, 123
Property rights, 8, 13

Quakers, 27, 28, 30

Radcliffe College, 199
Rayburn, Sam, 235
Reagan, Nancy, *260*, 260–66, *263, 265,* 270
    acting career of, 261–62
    family background and upbringing of, 261
    as first lady, 260, 263–66
Reagan, Ronald, 180, 258, 260–66, *263*
Reconstruction, 99, 110
Red Cross, 205
Red Record, A (Wells-Barnett), 100
Reform movements, 47, 48, 49, 122–23
    opposition to slavery and, 6, 21, 44, 47, 49, 64–67, *67,* 104, 162
    temperance and, 47, 103, 117–18, 122–24, 162
    urban poverty and, 167–68
    woman suffrage and, 104, 120, 122, 124, 162–64, 175
    working-class problems and, 101–4
Regan, Donald, 264–65
"Republican motherhood," 15
Republican party, 86, 93, 108, 110, 130, 149, 152, 161, 180, 188, 218, 228
Rest rooms, for working women, 168
Revolutionary War, 4–6, *5,* 7, 9–10, 17, 18–19, 27, 36, 40, 75, 162
    women's legal and political status and, 13–15
    women's roles in, 5–6
Roosevelt, Alice (daughter), 149, *150,* 151, 155
Roosevelt, Alice Lee (mother), 149
Roosevelt, Edith, *147,* 147–52, *150, 152*
    family background and upbringing of, 147–48
    as first lady, 151
    as public speaker, 152
Roosevelt, Eleanor, *201,* 201–10, *204, 209,* 215, 226, 254
    campaigning by, 207, *209,* 235, 237–38, *238*
    as delegate to UN, 209–10

Roosevelt, Eleanor (*cont'd*)
    family background and upbringing of,
       202–3
    as first lady, 2, 176, 201–2, 207–9
    husband's infidelity and, 205–6
    press conferences of, 176, *206*
Roosevelt, Franklin Delano, 151, 176, 203–9,
       214, 237–38
    stricken with polio, 206–7
Roosevelt, Sara Delano, 204–5, 207
Roosevelt, Theodore, 148–52, *150*, 156, 202,
       203, 205

Sacramento Union, 33
Safer, Morley, 252
Schlafly, Phyllis, 179
Schwarzkopf, Norman, *271*
Segregation, 99–100
Senate, U.S., 161, 180
    future presidents' service in, 41, 139,
       183–84, 213, 223–24, 234
    Johnson's impeachment and, 110
    see also Congress, U.S.
Seneca Falls, N.Y., women's convention in
    (1848), 49, 162
Settlement houses, 101–2, 203–4, 205
Sharecroppers, *176*
Sheppard-Towner Act, 25
60 Minutes, 252
Slater, Samuel, 6
Slavery, 3–6, 21, 27, 45, *47,* 61, 62, 86, 93
    opposition to, 6, 21, 44, 47, 49, 64–67, *67,*
       104, 162
Smith College, 199
Smithsonian Institution, 87, 279–80
Social work, 101–2
Spanish-American War (1898–1900), 150
Stanton, Elizabeth Cady, 67, 162
State dinners, *89*
    china for, *121,* 137, 151, 263–64
Stereo cards, 154
Stevenson, Adlai, 210, 239
Stone, Lucy, 65, 162–63
Stowe, Harriet Beecher, 46–47, 64

Stuart, Gilbert, 26, *26, 29*
Suffrage movement, 104, 120, 122, 124, 127,
    162–64, 175
Sumner, Charles, 71
Supreme Court, U.S., 103, 161

Taft, Helen, 105, *156,* 156–61, *159*
    family background and upbringing of,
       157–58
    as first lady, 159–61
Taft, Robert, 158, 161
Taft, William Howard, 156–61, *159*
Taylor, Margaret, *74,* 74–77
    family background and upbringing of, 75
    as first lady, 76–77
Taylor, Zachary, 33, 74–77, 80
Television, 155
Temperance movement, 47, 103, 117–18,
    122–24, 162
Thirteenth Amendment, 67, 99
Todd, John Payne, 28
Troy Female Seminary, 198–99
Truman, Bess, *211,* 211–15, *214,* 226
    family background and upbringing of,
       212–13
    as first lady, 214–15
Truman, Harry, 177, 209, 210, 211–15, *214*
Truth, Sojourner, 65, *65*
Tubman, Harriet, 65, *66*
Tuskeegee College, 200
Twenty-third Amendment, 124
Tyler, Elizabeth, 57
Tyler, John, 56–58, 60–63, 134
Tyler, Julia, *58,* 58–63, *60, 63*
    family background and upbringing of,
       56
    as first lady, 58, 61–62
    after husband's death, 62–63
Tyler, Letitia, *56,* 56–57
Tyler, Patricia Cooper, 57

Uncle Tom's Cabin (Stowe), 46–47
Underground Railroad, *66*
United Nations (UN), 209, 270

Universal Declaration of Human Rights
(1948), 209
Urbanization, 45
public health and, 24, *25*
settlement houses and, 101–2

Van Buren, Angelica Singleton, 51
Van Buren, Hannah, 51
Van Buren, Martin, 51
Vassar College, 103, 199, 223
Victoria, queen of England, 85, 116, 126
Vietnam War, 178, 274
Visiting Nurse Association, 24, *25, 190*
Volunteer work, 139, 172, 203–4, 205
Voting rights
for African-Americans, 99, 110, 178
for women, 1, 13–14, 49, 104, 120, 122,
124, 127, 162–64, 175
Voting Rights Act (1965), 178

Wales, prince of (future King Edward VII),
85–86
War of 1812, 26–27, *29*, 31, 38, 42
Warren, Bill, 249
Washington, D.C.
attacked in War of 1812, 26–27, 38
cherry blossoms in, 161
Washington, George, 7–12, 36, 40, 53, 114
Stuart's portrait of, 26, *29*
Washington, Martha, *xiii*, 5, *7*, 7–12, *33*, 53
battlefield visits of, 9–10, *10*
family background and upbringing of, 8
as first lady, 11–12, 19, 20
wedding of, 8–9
Watergate scandal, 246, 251, 276
WAVES (Women Accepted for Volunteer
Emergency Service), *178*
Wedgewood, Josiah, 67
Wellesley College, 199, 268, 274–75
Wells-Barnett, Ida, 100
Wheatley, Phyllis, *4*
Whig party, 76, 80
"Whistle-stop" campaigns, *233*, 237, *238*,
239

White House, 164
atmosphere of royal courts emulated at, *33*,
61
china services at, *121*, 137, 151, 263–64
herd of sheep at, 172
last family cow at, *160*, 161
library at, 80
living in, *21*, 43
pets at, 191
portrait gallery of first ladies at, 151, *152*
renovations and refurbishments of, 61, 135,
137–38, 139–40, 151, 225–28, 245, 279
War of 1812 and, 26–27, *29*, 38
weddings in, 38, 57, 116, 131, 134
working women's visits to, 135
Willard, Emma, 198–99, *199*
Willard, Frances, 103, 122–23, *123*, 124
Wills, women's legal rights and, 13
Wilson, Edith, 105, *169*, 169–74, *173*,
226–27
family background and upbringing of,
169–70
as first lady, 171–74
as husband's political partner, 171, 172–74
Wilson, Ellen, *165*, 165–68, 171
family background and upbringing of,
165–66
as first lady, 167–68
reform agenda of, 167–68
Wilson, Woodrow, 164, 166–68, 171–74,
173
stroke suffered by, 172–74
Woman's Christian Temperance Union
(WCTU), *117*, 122
Women
in antebellum period, 45–49
from Civil War to World War II, 99–105
in colonial period, 3–6
dearth of information about lives of, 52–54
domestic role of, 6, *14*, 19, 46
economic opportunities for, 5, 6, 14,
46–47, *48, 104*, 105, 175–78
educational opportunities for, 15, 17–18,
27, 46, 52, 103, 138, 141, 179, 198–200

Women (*cont'd*)
   enslaved, 3–4, *4,* 6, 49
   legal and political rights of, 8, 13–14, 17,
      21, 49, 64, 66–67
   maternal mortality rate and, 23–25
   in modern times, 175–80
   moral concerns of, 6, *14,* 47, 122. *See also*
      Reform movements
   "republican motherhood" role of, 15
   voting rights for, 1, 13–14, 49, 104, 120,
      122, 124, 127, 162–64, 175
   working, 6, 45–46, *48,* 99, 101–2, *104,*
      105, 123
Women's clubs, 103, 124
Women's colleges, 199
Women's Equity Action League, 179
Women's history, 54
Women's Legal Defense Fund, 179

Women's McKinley Club, *145*
Women's movement
   anti-slavery movement and, 49, 66–67
   in modern era, 178–80, 254
   Seneca Falls convention and, 49, 162
   suffrage and, 104, 120, 122, 124, 127,
      162–64, 175
Women's Trade Union League, 206
Women's War Work, 105
Woodhull, Victoria, 103
Working women, 6, 45–46, *48,* 99, 101–2,
   104, 105, 123, 135, 168
World's Anti-Slavery Convention (1840), 67,
   162
World War I, *104,* 105, 136, 168, 171, 172,
   196, 205, 213, 218
World War II, 175, 176–77, *177, 178,* 208,
   219, 270